Social Sciences as Sorcery

Books by the same author

Military Organisation and Society
  (ROUTLEDGE & KEGAN PAUL, 1954)

The Uses of Comparative Sociology
  (WEIDENFELD & NICOLSON, 1964)

Parasitism and Subversion: The Case of Latin America
  (WEIDENFELD & NICOLSON, 1966)

The African Predicament
  (MICHAEL JOSEPH, 1968)

Herbert Spencer – Principles of Sociology, *ed.*
  (MACMILLAN, 1969)

Herbert Spencer – Structure, Function and Evolution, *ed.*
  (MICHAEL JOSEPH, 1971)

Prospects of a Revolution in the U.S.A.
  (TOM STACEY, 1972)

Social Sciences as Sorcery

Stanislav Andreski

 ANDRE DEUTSCH

First published 1972 by
André Deutsch Limited
105 Great Russell Street London WC1

Printed in Great Britain by
Ebenezer Baylis and Son Ltd
The Trinity Press, Worcester, and London

ISBN 0 233 96226 3

Contents

Acknowledgments

As with my previous book, a large share in whatever merit resides in the present work belongs to my wife, whose forthcoming books on the conflict between the sexes and the mother child relationship contain criticism of the current literature on these subjects which point to somewhat similar conclusions.

I am grateful to Mrs Audrey Yates for her work on the typescript and to my past and present colleagues of all ranks in the sociology department at Reading for their good will, initiative and smooth co-operation which have permitted me to remain a thinker and writer while discharging an administrative function.

I am grateful to the following for permission to publish extracts from their books:

Talcott Parsons, *Societies: Evolutionary and Comparative Perspectives*, Prentice-Hall, Englewood Cliffs, New Jersey, USA, 1966.

Claude Lévi-Strauss, *The Savage Mind*, George Weidenfeld and Nicolson, London, 1966.

Norbent Wiener, *I am a Mathematician*, Victor Gollancz, London, 1956.

Bertrand Russell, *ABC of Relativity*, George Allen and Unwin, London, 1969.

J. P. Nettl and Roland Robertson, *International Systems and the Modernisation of Societies*, Faber and Faber, London, 1968.

F. Zweig, *The Quest for Fellowship*, Heinemann Educational Books, London, 1965.

There are four chief obstacles to grasping truth, which hinder every man, however learned, and scarcely allow anyone to win a clear title to knowledge; namely, submission to faulty and unworthy authority, influence of custom, popular prejudice, and concealment of our own ignorance accompanied by the ostentatious display of our knowledge.

ROGER BACON

Foreword

To forestall any possible misunderstanding, I must state emphatically at the outset that I neither accuse nor even suspect anyone mentioned by name in this book of deliberately concocting a stunt, disseminating falsehoods knowingly, or of being prompted by a desire for dishonest gain or an advancement obtained through corruption. A renowned author would have to have a most extraordinary character (indeed, he would have to be in a way superhuman) to be able to write prolifically in the full knowledge that his works are worthless and that he is a charlatan whose fame is entirely undeserved and based solely on the stupidity and gullibility of his admirers. Even if he had some doubts about the correctness of his approach at some stage of his career, success and adulation would soon persuade him of his own genius and the epoch-making value of his concoctions. When, in consequence of acquiring a controlling position in the distribution of funds, appointments and promotions, he becomes surrounded by sycophants courting his favours, he is most unlikely to see through their motivation; and, like wealthy and powerful people in other walks of life, will tend to take flattery at its face value, accepting it as a sincere appreciation (and therefore confirmation).

Rather than among noted writers, cynical charlatans can be found among manipulators who write little or nothing, and whose egos are consequently not invested in any particular notion or approach, and who do not care, therefore, which gimmick they use to milk fund-dispensing bodies. Although I know one or two individuals of this kind, none of them is mentioned by name – which would not only entail unprovable imputations of motive, but also be beside the point, as my task here is to combat wrong ideas . . . not to compile a list of shady academics. Even individuals of this type, moreover, find

1*

hard-boiled cynicism difficult to sustain and normally end by persuading themselves of the value of whatever they are doing, because nobody likes to admit to himself that he is making a living by unworthy means. In any case, the most deadly agents of cultural infections are not the brazen cynics, but the sectarians prone to self-delusion and the timorous organization men anxious not to miss the band-waggon, who unquestioningly equate popularity and worldly success with intrinsic merit.

As the present book deals with the phenomena which must be judged as undesirable from the standpoint of intellectual progress, the references to the literature are as a rule derogatory. This does not mean that I believe that nothing of value has been produced; but one cannot write about everything at once, and this is a tract rather than a treatise. Numerous positive contributions to knowledge are cited in my previous publications, and many more will be mentioned in other books which are in preparation, particularly if I live long enough to write a general treatise. I argue on the pages which follow that much of what passes as scientific study of human behaviour boils down to an equivalent of sorcery, but fortunately there are other things as well.

Chapter 1

Why Foul One's Nest?

To judge by quantity, the social sciences are going through a period of unprecedented progress: with congresses and conferences mushrooming, printed matter piling up, and the number of professionals increasing at such a rate that, unless arrested, it would overtake the population of the globe within a few hundred years. Most of the practitioners wax enthusiastic about this proliferation, and add to the flood by writing exultant surveys of their crafts 'to-day', readily affixing the label of 'revolution' to all kinds of most insignificant steps forward . . . or even backwards; and sometimes even claiming to have crossed the threshold separating their fields from the exact sciences.

What is particularly dismaying is that not only does the flood of publications reveal an abundance of pompous bluff and a paucity of new ideas, but even the old and valuable insights which we have inherited from our illustrious ancestors are being drowned in a torrent of meaningless verbiage and useless technicalities. Pretentious and nebulous verbosity, interminable repetition of platitudes and disguised propaganda are the order of the day, while at least 95% of research is indeed re-search for things that have been found long ago and many times since. In comparison with half a century ago, the average quality of the publications (apart from those which deal with techniques rather than the substance) has declined in a number of fields.

Such a far-reaching verdict naturally calls for evidence, and much of the present book is devoted to supplying it. But perhaps even more interesting than to prove is to explain; and this is the second task of this book, the third being to offer a few hints on how this sorry state can be, if not remedied, at least alleviated. I shall, among other things, try to show how the bent towards sterility and deception in the study of human affairs stems from widespread cultural, political and economic trends of our time; so that the present work can be put under the vague heading of sociology of knowledge, although 'sociology of non-knowledge' more correctly describes the bulk of its contents.

As such an attempt ineluctably leads to the question of vested interests, and entails imputation of unworthy motives, I hasten to say that I know very well that logically an *argumentum ad hominem* proves nothing. Nevertheless, in matters where uncertainty prevails and information is mostly accepted on trust, one is justified in trying to rouse the reading public to a more critical watchfulness by showing that in the study of human affairs evasion and deception are as a rule much more profitable than telling the truth.

To repeat what has been said in the foreword, I do not think that the *argumentum ad hominem* in terms of vested interests applies to the motives of the inventors of fads, who are much more likely to be doctrinaires and visionaries so wrapped up in the cocoon of their imagination that they cannot see the world as it is. After all, in every society with widespread literacy there are people writing all conceivable kinds of nonsense. Many of them never get as far as the printer, and among those who pass this hurdle, many remain unread, neglected, or quickly forgotten, while others are boosted, acclaimed and idolized. It is at the level of the process of social selection, which governs the dissemination of ideas, that the question of their subservience to vested interests is more germane.

The general problem of the relationship between ideas and interests is one of the most difficult and fundamental. Marx based all his political analyses on the assumption that social classes uphold ideologies which serve their interests, a theory which seemed to be contradicted by the fact that no believer will admit that he has chosen his tenets for their value as instruments in the struggle for wealth and power. Freud's concept of the unconscious, however, implies what might be described as the unconscious cunning – the idea which has been developed in a form especially applicable to politics by Alfred Adler. If such mechanisms of the mind can produce unconscious subterfuges and strategies in individuals' behaviour, there is no reason why they should not operate on a mass level. But by what kind of evidence can we back imputations of this kind? What makes the problem even more difficult is Pareto's convincing point that the ruling classes often espouse doctrines which usher them along the road to a collective demise. The mechanisms of selection (emphasized by Spencer), which weed out 'unfit' patterns of organization, normally insure that only those social aggregates endure which cherish beliefs which bolster up their structure and mode of existence. But, since disintegration and destruction of collectivities of all kinds and sizes are just as conspicuous as their continuing survival, Pareto's view (or model, if you like) is as applicable as Marx's. A satisfactory theory will have to synthesize these valid partial insights and transcend them, but this is not the place for such an attempt. In the present essay I cannot go beyond imputations, resting upon circumstantial evidence of congruence between systems of ideas and collective interests, of roughly the same degree of plausibility (or vulnerability) as the usual marxist assertions about the connections between the contents of an ideology and the class interests. The chief intellectual shortcoming of the marxists on this score is, firstly that they restrict unduly the applicability of their master's key concept only to groupings (i.e., social classes) which he himself has singled out; and secondly that (naturally enough) they will not apply this scheme of interpretation to themselves and their own beliefs.

Every craft, every occupation – no matter whether shady or even downright criminal – gravitates towards the principle that 'dog does not eat dog'. The ancient and exclusive professions – such as law and medicine – emphasize this rule to the point of endowing it with the halo of a fundamental canon of ethics. The teachers, too, ostracize those who openly criticize their colleagues and undermine their standing in the eyes of the pupils.

As with all other human arrangements, this custom has good and bad sides. Without something of this kind, it would be difficult to maintain the friendly relations required for fruitful co-operation, be it in a workshop, an operating theatre or a boardroom. By consistent tripping one another up and indulging in mutual recriminations people can not only make their lives a misery but also condemn their work to failure. Since a patient's peace of mind and the chances of recovery depend to a considerable extent on his faith in the physician – which in turn depends on the latter's personal reputation as well as on the status of the profession – the effectiveness of medical care would be gravely impaired if practitioners fell into the habit of denigrating one another. Likewise the teachers who undermine each other's standing in the eyes of the pupils will end by being unable to teach at all; given that the adolescents are normally prone to disorder and the number of those with a spontaneous desire to learn always remains small.

On the other side of the balance, however, there can be little doubt that the appeal of the 'dog does not eat dog' principle derives its strength less from an altruistic concern for fruitfulness of the work – except in so far as this makes life easier – than from the quest for collective advantage, be it pecuniary or honorific. By strictly enforcing occupational solidarity, the medical profession has not only attained affluence which in most countries is grossly out of proportion to its relative level of skill – not to speak of the extremely advantageous immunity from punishment for incompetence and negligence – but has also been able to procure for its members a substantial psychic income by putting them in a position where they can play God, regardless of frequent shortcomings of knowledge and intelligence. True, members of the medical profession enjoy an especially favourable position because they handle people at their weakest: when they are afraid and in need of a solace; reduced to the condition of patients – a very revealing word which goes far to explain why in so many public hospitals (at least in Britain) the front entrance is reserved for suppliers of the services, while the customers have to sneak in through the back door. The lawyers too manage to boost up their prestige and income by couching documents in needlessly abstruse language, designed to impede a layman's understanding, and to compel him to resort to costly legal advice.

Among the suppliers of services of immediate utility to the consumers, the custom of refraining from mutual criticism merely serves as a shield against responsibility for negligence and a prop for monopolistic gains; but when it comes to an occupation which justifies its existence by claiming that it is dedicated to the pursuit of general truths, an adherence to the 'dog does not eat dog' principle usually amounts to a collusion in parasitism and fraud.

Businessmen who do not feel squeamish about admitting that their main goal is to make money, and whose occupational ethics consist of few moral prohibitions have less use for dissimulation than those who earn their living in an occupation ostensibly devoted to the furtherance of higher ideals; and the higher these are, the harder it is to live up to them, and the greater the temptation of (and the scope for) hypocrisy. Honesty is the best policy for the purveyor when the customer knows what he wants, is able to judge the quality of what he gets, and pays out of his own pocket. Most people can judge the quality of shoes or scissors, and hence nobody has made a fortune by producing shoes which immediately fall apart or scissors which do not cut. In building houses, on the other hand, the defects of the work or the materials can remain concealed for much longer, and consequently shoddiness often brings profit in this line of business. The merits of a therapy, to take another example, cannot easily be assessed, and for this reason medical practice has been for centuries entangled with a charlatanry from which it is not entirely free even to-day. Nonetheless, no matter how difficult it may be to evaluate a physician's or a lawyer's services, they clearly minister to concrete needs. But what kind of services does a philosopher or a student of society render, and to whom? Who cares whether they are worth anything or not? Can those who care judge their merit? And, if so, do they decide on the rewards or bear the cost?

Doubts about the worth of their services are seldom entertained by the practitioners; and if ever raised, are promptly warded off with invocations of professional standards with their presumptive power to ensure integrity and progress. Looking at this matter realistically, however, one can find few grounds for assuming that all the professions inherently gravitate towards honest service rather than monopolistic exploitation or parasitism. In reality it all depends on what kind of behaviour leads to wealth and status (or, to put it another way, on the link between true merit and reward). To analyse various types of work from this standpoint would provide a useful programme for the sociology of occupations, which might lift it above its present level of uninspired cataloguing. Seen from this angle, the social sciences appear as an activity without any intrinsic mechanisms of retribution: where anybody can get away with anything.

Criticizing the prevailing trends and the top people may be profitable if done with the backing of a powerful pressure group – perhaps a fifth column subsidized from abroad. But unfortunately, the contours of truth never coincide with the frontiers between embattled parties and cliques. So, a free thinker can consider himself lucky if he lives in a setting where he merely gets cold-shouldered rather than imprisoned and called 'a pig who fouls his nest' – to use the felicitous expression which the Soviet police chief, Semichastny, applied to Boris Pasternak.

Whether exhortation helps much may seriously be doubted, for despite centuries of inveighing against stealing and cheating, these misdemeanours do not appear to be less common nowadays than at the time of Jesus Christ. On the other hand, however, it is difficult to envisage how any standards whatsoever can continue to exist without some people taking upon themselves the task of affirming them and preaching against vice.

As one could spend a whole life and fill an encyclopaedia trying to expose all the foolish antics which pass for a scientific study of human conduct, I have limited myself to a few influential examples. In any case, demolishing the idols of pseudo-science is relatively easy, and the more interesting and important task is to explain why they have found and are finding such a wide acceptance.

I do not envisage that this blast of my trumpet will bring down the walls of pseudo-science, which are manned by too many stout defenders: the slaves of routine who (to use Bertrand Russell's expression) 'would rather die than think', mercenary go-getters, docile educational employees who judge ideas by the status of their propounders, or the woolly minded lost souls yearning for gurus. Nevertheless, despite the

advanced stage of cretinization which our civilization has
reached under the impact of the mass media, there are still
some people about who like to use their brains without the lure
of material gain; and it is for them that this book is intended.
But if they are in a minority, then how can the truth prevail?
The answer (which gives some ground for hope) is that people
interested in ideas, and prepared to think them through and
express them regardless of personal disadvantage, have always
been few; and if knowledge could not advance without a
majority on the right side, there would never have been any
progress at all – because it has always been easier to get into the
limelight, as well as to make money, by charlatanry, doctrinairism, sycophancy and soothing or stirring oratory than by
logical and fearless thinking. No, the reason why human
understanding has been able to advance in the past, and may
do so in the future, is that true insights are cumulative and
retain their value regardless of what happens to their discoverers; while fads and stunts may bring an immediate profit
to the impresarios, but lead nowhere in the long run, cancel
each other out, and are dropped as soon as their promoters are
no longer there (or have lost the power) to direct the show.
Anyway, let us not despair.

Chapter 2
The Witch Doctor's Dilemma

Most of the intellectual difficulties besetting the study of society (which we must distinguish from the obstacles created by passions and vested interests) stem from the disparity in size, longevity and power between the object and the investigator. True, geologists and astronomers study objects which are vaster, more enduring and even less accessible for the purpose of experimentation; but at least they are simpler, as there is nothing in the known cosmos that equals the complexity of a human brain. Understanding is sometimes described as the building of models of external reality in one's brain. This should not, perhaps, be taken too literally; but if we accept the view that conceptual understanding has some physiological counterpart, and bear in mind that the number of configurations of neurons and synapses is finite, though astronomically large, then it follows that whereas the mind might be able to make a perfect model of things simpler than itself, its ability to work out models of objects which are equally or more complex must be subject to severe limitations. It seems impossible therefore that our understanding of other minds and their aggregates could ever reach the degree of adequacy of physics and chemistry, made possible by the simplicity and invariance of their objects.

Reasoning along these lines, we might also infer that it is logically impossible that anyone could ever acquire an understanding of his own mind which would enable him to make exact predictions about its future states; because, even apart from the question of the knowledge of the future impacts of the environment, the mind would have to contain a model as complex as itself as well as an agency which would draw inferences. In other words, such a faculty would require a part to be as large as the whole and still remain only a part.

Another source of tremendous difficulty in making generalizations about the networks of human relations (known as groups, societies, states, economies, etc.) is their ubiquitous fluidity. In his *ABC of Relativity* Bertrand Russell discusses the relationship between the constancy of the phenomena and the possibility of scientific theorizing:

Circumstances on the surface of the earth, for various more or less accidental reasons, suggest conceptions which turn out to be inaccurate, although they have come to seem like necessities of thought. The most important of these circumstances is that most objects on the earth's surface are fairly persistent and nearly stationary from a terrestrial point of view. If this were not the case, the idea of going on a journey would not seem so definite as it does. If you want to travel from King's Cross to Edinburgh, you know that you will find King's Cross where it has always been, that the railway line will take the course that it did when you last made the journey, and that Waverley Station in Edinburgh will not have walked up to the Castle. You therefore say and think that you have travelled to Edinburgh, not that Edinburgh has travelled to you, though the latter statement would be just as accurate. The success of this common-sense point of view depends on a number of things which are really of the nature of luck. Suppose all the houses in London were perpetually moving about, like a swarm of bees; suppose railways moved and changed their shapes like avalanches; and finally suppose that material objects were perpetually being formed and dissolved like clouds. There is nothing impossible in these suppositions. But obviously what we call a journey to Edinburgh would have no meaning in such a world. You would begin, no doubt, by asking the taxi-driver: 'Where is King's Cross this morning?' At the station you would have to ask a similar question about Edinburgh, but the booking-office clerk would reply: 'What part of Edinburgh do you mean, sir? Prince's Street has gone to Glasgow, the Castle has moved up into the Highlands, and Waverley Station is under water in the middle of the Firth of Forth'. And on the journey the stations would not be staying quiet, but some would be travelling north, some south, some east, some west, perhaps much faster than the train. Under these conditions you could not say where you were at any moment. Indeed the whole notion that one is always in some definite 'place' is due to the fortunate immobility of most of the large objects on the earth's surface. The idea of 'place' is only a rough practical approximation:

there is nothing logically necessary about it, and it cannot be made precise.

If we were not much larger than an electron, we should not have this impression of stability, which is only due to the grossness of our senses. King's Cross, which to us looks solid, would be too vast to be conceived except by a few eccentric mathematicians. The bits of it that we could see would consist of little tiny points of matter, never coming into contact with each other, but perpetually whizzing round each other in an inconceivably rapid ballet-dance. The world of our experience would be quite as mad as the one in which the different parts of Edinburgh go for walks in different directions. If – to take the opposite extreme – you were as large as the sun and lived as long, with a corresponding slowness of perception, you would again find a higgledy-piggledy universe without permanence – stars and planets would come and go like morning mists, and nothing would remain in a fixed position relatively to anything else. The notion of comparative stability which forms part of our ordinary outlook is thus due to the fact that we are about the size we are, and live on a planet of which the surface is not very hot. If this were not the case, we should not find prerelativity physics intellectually satisfying. Indeed we should never have invented such theories. We should have had to arrive at relativity physics at one bound, or remain ignorant of scientific laws. It is fortunate for us that we were not faced with this alternative, since it is almost inconceivable that one man could have done the work of Euclid, Galileo, Newton and Einstein. Yet without such an incredible genius physics could hardly have been discovered in a world where the universal flux was obvious to non-scientific observation.

The foregoing passage fits very well what we have to deal with in the study of society and culture, indicates its purely intellectual difficulties, and shows how much easier are physics, chemistry or even biology. Even this, however, is not the whole story: for imagine how sorry would be the plight of the natural scientist if the objects of his inquiry were in a habit of reacting to what he says about them: if the substances could read or hear what the chemist writes or says about them, and were likely to jump out of their containers and burn him if they did not like what they saw on the blackboard or in his notebook. And imagine the difficulty of testing the validity of chemical formulae if, by repeating them long enough or persuasively enough, the chemist could induce the substances to behave in accordance with them – with the danger, however, that they might decide to spite him by doing exactly the opposite. Under such circumstances our chemist would not only have a hard time trying to discover firm regularities in his objects' behaviour but would have to be very guarded in what he said lest the substances take offence and attack him. His task would be even more hopeless if the chemicals could see through his tactics, organize themselves to guard their secrets, and devise countermeasures to his maneouvres – which would be parallel to what the student of human affairs has to face.

On the other hand, we need not make our task unduly difficult by making it dependent upon the doctrine of universal determinism, and in particular upon the assumption that human behaviour can be studied scientifically (i.e., with a view to discovering regularities) only if there is no such thing as free will.[1]

There is no reason to deny the existence of phenomena known to us only through introspection; and a number of philosophers have pointed out the impossibility of carrying out Carnap's programme (accepted as a dogma by the behaviourists) of translating all statements about mental states into what he calls the physicalist language. I would go even further and argue that physics itself cannot be expressed in the physicalist language alone because it is an empirical science only insofar as it includes an assertion that its theories are corroborated by the evidence of the senses; and we can assign no meaning to the latter term without entailing a concept of the self. If you ask a physicist to tell you how he tested a hypothesis he will say: 'I did this, I did that; I saw this and that . . . '. If you disbelieve him and he invites you to take part in experimenting you will say: 'Ah, now I see . . . this moves here and that moves there . . . now I see such a colour or line or what have you'. Thus you cannot give an account of the evidential foundations of physics without hearing and uttering 'I'. And what kind of meaning can you attach to this word without using the knowledge obtained through introspection; and without postulating

1. In addition to what follows see the arguments on the Uncertainty Principle, determinism and teleology in *The Uses of Comparative Sociology*, Ch. 2 and 3.

the existence of other minds within which processes are taking place which are similar to those which you alone can observe?

In order to further the understanding of society it is not even necessary to accept the arguments in favour of a residual indeterminacy of human actions. Indeed, it is perfectly legitimate to suspend judgment on this issue because neither determinism nor indeterminism can be verified as ontological principles, and must remain therefore articles of metaphysical faith. Determinism could be proved only when the last cause of the last hitherto unexplained event has been ascertained; while indeterminism could be proved only if it could be demonstrated beyond all doubt that this will never happen. In other words, to prove determinism we would have to show that one day knowledge will ineluctably become total; and although it is impossible to demonstrate that this has not occurred or will not occur in the mind of God, it seems rather implausible that mortals will ever attain it. It can be argued, moreover, that perfect predictability is intrinsically impossible with regard to a system of which the observer-predictor forms a part, so that his actions (including his predictions) affect the other events. As in such a case his predictions would form part of the causal sequences occurring within the system, he could make predictions only if he could predict his predictions as well, which would only be possible if he could predict his predictions of his predictions . . . and so on in infinite regression.

Luckily, to pursue our studies we do not need to accept the doctrine of universal determinism. It suffices if we assume that many phenomena can be causally explained, that not all possible causal explanations are known, and that it is possible to discover new ones. This is enough to justify the scientific endeavour but, as a tenable metaphysical view, indeterminism can be restated as the belief (which I personally hold) that mortals will never reach a stage when their knowledge will be complete and there will be nothing left to discover.

At this point let me say a few words about the often debated question whether any of the social sciences is a 'real' science. As often happens with such debates the arguments for as well as against omit the obvious truth that the answer to this question will depend on what we mean by science. If we mean exact science like physics or chemistry, then neither economics nor psychology nor sociology nor any other kind of research into human conduct is a science. But if we agree to affix this honorific label to any kind of systematic study which aims at providing careful descriptions, substantiated explanations and factually supported generalizations, then we can say that the above mentioned branches of learning are sciences – although the propriety of this appellation will depend on whether we decide on the basis of aspirations or actual performance, and whether we look at the average or at the highest achievements. Anyway, the verbal nature of this dispute can be demonstrated by translating it into another language, as it vanishes when stated in German, Russian or Polish and is much weakened in French or Spanish. It has generated so much heat in Britain because of the peculiarly rigid division between 'arts' and 'sciences' in English schools; and because it provides good openings in the game of status-seeking versus status-refusing.

If we do not regard universal determinism as an indispensable basis for the study of human behaviour we need not object to the idea of personal responsibility. Many psychologists criticize administration of justice based on the idea of free will and responsibility without realizing that, if valid, determinism applies to everybody: if a criminal cannot avoid committing a crime, then neither can the judge avoid sentencing him, nor can the executioner avoid quartering him. Unless we assume that individuals can make decisions, and are responsible for at least some of their deeds, there is no reason why we should regard any action as good or bad, or try to refrain from doing harm to our fellow beings; and moral exhortation is meaningless.[1]

Taken as proof of non-existence of responsibility, the doctrine of psychological determinism exculpates the supporters of apartheid and the police torturers in Brazil just as much as the mixed-up young delinquents, but in practice this argument is used very selectively in accordance with the 'scientist's' likes and dislikes, often applied only to those who provide him with vicarious gratification of his pet hatreds and suppressed proclivities. To a large extent it all boils down to the game of

1. In *The Uses of Comparative Sociology*, I have tried to show how this ties up with the problem of teleological explanation.

playing God by psychologists, sociologists and above all psychiatrists who borrow the prestige of science to foist their often very crude moral notions upon the public. As I shall argue at length in a forthcoming book, the denigration of the concept of responsibility, based on the unwarranted dogma of psychological determinism, has contributed significantly to the undermining of our civilization.

Though formidable enough, the methodological difficulties appear trivial in comparison with the fundamental obstacles to the development of an exact science of society which puts it on an entirely different plane from the natural sciences: namely the fact that human beings react to what is said about them. More than that of his colleagues in the natural sciences, the position of an 'expert' in the study of human behaviour resembles that of a sorcerer who can make the crops come up or the rain fall by uttering an incantation. And because the facts with which he deals are seldom verifiable, his customers are able to demand to be told what they like to hear, and will punish the unco-operative soothsayer who insists on saying what they would rather not know – as the princes used to punish the court physicians for failing to cure them. Moreover, as people want to achieve their ends by influencing others, they will always try to cajole, bully or bribe the witch-doctor into using his powers for their benefit and uttering the needed incantation . . . or at least telling them something pleasing. And why should he resist threats or temptations when in his speciality it is so difficult to prove or disprove anything, that he can with impunity indulge his fancy, pander to his listeners' loves and hates or even peddle conscious lies. His dilemma, however, stems from the difficulty of retracing his steps; because very soon he passes the point of no return after which it becomes too painful to admit that he has wasted years pursuing chimeras, let alone to confess that he has been taking advantage of the public's gullibility. So, to allay his gnawing doubts, anxieties and guilt, he is compelled to take the line of least resistance by spinning more and more intricate webs of fiction and falsehood, while paying ever more ardent lip-service to the ideals of objectivity and the pursuit of truth.

If we look at the practical results of the proliferation of social scientists we find more analogies to the role of witch-doctors in a primitive tribe than to the part played by the natural scientists and technologists in an industrial society. Later we shall examine the vagaries of political scientists and sociological system builders, but in a way they largely escape the pragmatic test because it is difficult to find examples of big policy decisions based on their advice. The breed which has probably had the most profound influence on human behaviour is the psychologists and family sociologists who (especially in America) have largely succeeded in foisting upon the public their views on human nature, thus profoundly influencing customary behaviour.

Unevasively interpreted, psychology is perhaps the most difficult of all the sciences – whether natural or social – wherein man tries to lift himself by his bootstraps, using the mind to understand the mind; and where, consequently, significant discoveries are rare, and must remain exceedingly approximate and tentative. Most of the practitioners, however, do not like to admit this and prefer to pretend that they speak with the authority of an exact science, which is not merely theoretical but also applied. To examine the validity of these claims I should like to propose a simple, rough and ready criterion.

When a profession supplies services based on well-founded knowledge we should find a perceptible positive connection between the number of practitioners in relation to the population and the results achieved. Thus, in a country which has an abundance of telecommunication engineers, the provision of telephonic facilities will normally be better than in a country which has only a few specialists of this kind. The levels of mortality will be lower in countries or regions where there are many doctors and nurses than in places where they are few and far between. Accounts will be more generally and efficiently kept in countries with many trained accountants than where they are scarce. We could go on multiplying examples, but the foregoing suffice to establish the point.

And now, what are the benefits produced by sociology and psychology? True, it could be maintained that they are purely speculative branches of learning without as yet any practical uses, which is a tenable viewpoint, though rather unpopular, as it would raise the question of whether so many people of modest intelligence ought to be engaging in abstruse cogitation. So to examine the validity of the claim that these are highly useful branches of knowledge, let us ask what their contribution to mankind's welfare is supposed to be. To judge by the cues from training courses and textbooks, the practical usefulness of psychology consists of helping people to find their niche in society, to adapt themselves to it painlessly, and to dwell therein contentedly and in harmony with their companions. So, we should find that in countries, regions, institutions or sectors where the services of psychologists are widely used, families are more enduring, bonds between the spouses, siblings, parents and children stronger and warmer, relations between colleagues more harmonious, the treatment of recipients of aid better, vandals, criminals and drug addicts fewer, than in places or groups which do not avail themselves of the psychologists' skills. On this basis we could infer that the blessed country of harmony and peace is of course the United States; and that it ought to have been becoming more and more so during the last quarter of the century in step with the growth in numbers of sociologists, psychologists and political scientists.

It may be objected that this is no argument, that the causation went the other way round, with the increases in drug addiction, crime, divorce, race riots and other social ills creating the demand for more healers. Maybe; but even accepting this view, it would still appear that the flood of therapists has produced no improvement. What, however, suggests that they may be stimulating rather than curing the sickness is that the acceleration in the growth of their numbers began before the upturn in the curves of crime and drug addiction. And there are other little pointers in the same direction.

Let me ask the following questions: Which field of activity in America is the least efficient? And which employs the largest number of psychologists and sociologists? The plain answer is, Education. And in which field has the quality of the product been declining most rapidly? And where has the number of psychologists and sociologists been increasing fastest? Again: in education. Or, if instead of comparing it with other sectors within the society, we compare the American educational situation with that of other nations, we get a similar result. For where do the schools employ a proportionately larger number of psychologists and sociologists and all kinds of hybrids between them? In America, almost needless to say. Nonetheless, if we judge by the amount of knowledge imparted (rather than the number of diplomas issued) in relation to the expenditure incurred, then there can be no doubt that the American schools are the least efficient in the world, not excluding the poorest countries of Africa or Latin America. I do not think that anywhere else in the world can you find students who have been going to school for at least twelve years but who can read only with difficulty, such as you can meet quite frequently in American universities. What is more, the schools have been getting worse as the number of personnel trained in sociology, psychology and education has been increasing.[1] Perhaps it is all a coincidence. But in no other country can you become a professor at a top university without having first to learn how to write competently. And this doesn't include people of foreign origin or those brought up in a different language, but men and women who know no other language but American English, and yet contravene the rules stated in American grammar books and use words with scant regard to what it says in Webster's dictionary. And in which subjects do they congregate? Inevitably in sociology, psychology and education; and now increasingly in anthropology, political science and even history, as these subjects become more 'scientific'. It may not be, then, very far-fetched to conclude that the decline in the quality of education may have had something to do with the expansion of the social sciences – to be sure, not because of any logical necessity, but owing to the character which these subjects have acquired.

These trends are not confined to the USA, and in other countries too a decline in the standards of literary expression has gone in step with the expansion of the social sciences. It may be to the point to mention that a vocabulary test administered to students in England has revealed that the students of the social sciences have a more limited vocabulary than any

1. A brief discussion of the educational disaster can be found in my forthcoming book *The Prospects of a Revolution in the USA*. (Harper & Row, N.Y.)

others, including engineers and physicists who operate with mathematical symbols rather than words in the course of their work. So we find individuals who expatiate on the great problems of collective life arising from the march of our civilization without having learned how to write properly in their own language.

Even big business has been getting less efficient at the same time as the number of sociologists and psychologists employed has been increasing, which, of course, does not prove that they are the cause of the deterioration but which casts some doubt on their utility. There is, however, one special use to which a psychologist (especially of a psychoanalytic persuasion) can be put: in some places, when a worker becomes too demanding, they send him to see the psychologist who starts unearthing in him all kinds of incestual or homosexual desires and gets the fellow so worried that he forgets about his claims for more money.

In France the recent collapse of the educational system has been preceded by a rapid increase in the number of sociologists and psychologists; while in a number of other countries there seems to be a positive though rough parallel between the rise in the number of family counsellors and child psychologists and in the rates of divorce and drug addiction. True, apart from the possibility that all this might be mere coincidence, the connection may be that the aggravation of the social evils has stimulated the demand for the services of experts, thus fostering a growth in their number. One conclusion, however, is inescapable: that these experts have not been able to help; and that it cannot be ruled out that they may be making things even worse by misguided therapies. If we saw that whenever a fire brigade comes the flames become even fiercer, we might well begin to wonder what it is that they are squirting, and whether they are not by any chance pouring oil on to the fire.

In matters concerning education, personal relations, bringing up children, attitudes to marriage or friendship, the influence of psychology and of the psychologistic sociology has been very great – especially in America which seems to be as much dominated by freudism as Russia is by marxism . . . which does not mean that the founders themselves would approve what is done in their name in either country, particularly as it is a matter of historical fact that Marx detested Russia while Freud despised America. On the major questions of policy it is doubtful whether even Marx was heeded by his devotees once they were installed in power, while in the capitalist countries political scientists or anthropologists might be consulted as possessors of local knowledge of distant places, but I know of no cases of important decisions being crucially influenced by inferences from sociological or politological theories . . . which may have been just as well. So we can hardly blame the political scientists or macro-sociologists for having played an active part in bringing about the world's present ills; and to assess their value to mankind we have to look at what they have tried to do. They deserve some credit if we can find examples of counsels or forecasts which might have been disregarded by the decision-makers but which commanded a wide support within the profession, and which in the light of hindsight can be seen to have been correct or at least more nearly so than the lay opinion. Personally, I do not think that such examples exist, and if anybody knows of any I should be happy to hear about them.

There are, to be sure, instances of individual thinkers making astonishingly perspicacious predictions. As can be seen from recently printed books containing their articles, Pareto and Mosca (independently, it seems) predicted around 1900 in great detail the nature of the system which would arise from an implementation of the marxist programme, although neither said that such a system would in fact come into existence. These were, then, very far-reaching statements which, though not strictly deduced, nonetheless clearly tied up with their authors' theories. About the same time Max Weber committed himself to a less conditional, though also a less detailed, prediction when he forecast a victory of bureaucracy over capitalism in the western world. Being a prophet as well as a scientist, Marx had many visions which did not come true, but he was certainly right about the movement towards the concentration of control over production. Not at all inclined to messianic fugues, de Tocqueville was much more guarded about making prophecies, but he has done better than anyone else, and has hardly made a forecast which has turned out to be totally wrong. However, all these instances, to which a number of other examples could be added, remain individual feats of imaginative foresight, made possible – it is true – by a profound understanding of the nature of human society, but not based on any established and generally accepted corpus of knowledge.

If we look at the beliefs widely shared among social scientists, we see that they contain little if anything that could be attributed to a superior professional understanding; and that, apart from little bits of factual information here and there, they have followed and continue to follow the intellectual fashions of the day: hurrah-patriotic in 1914, pacifist in the twenties, leftist in the thirties, celebrating the end of ideology in the fifties, youth-cultured and new leftist at the end of the sixties. True, in many situations the opinions among social scientists on the great issues of the day were divided, but most commonly along the same lines as among grocers or ledger clerks . . . which does not suggest that supposedly professional knowledge made all that much difference. On the whole their specialist knowledge prompts little divergence from the prevalent opinion of their class – which is not, of course, the bourgeoisie but the class of salaried diploma holders.

The very fact that professional students of society, economy and politics continue to pigeon-hole themselves and their colleagues as being on the left or on the right shows that their categories are not more sophisticated than those of any man on the street. Imagine what kind of science of zoology or crystallography we would have where everything were brought down to one dimension classifying all the objects only by their size or according to whether they were light or dark or smooth or rough. Actually, even that would be better, because at least these qualities do exist and do form a continuum, whereas nobody has succeeded in fixing the meaning of Left and Right and people are continually quarrelling about who is on the Left or Right of whom. Like uniforms and flags, simplistic labels of this kind (whether it is Blues versus Greens as in Byzantium, or Roundheads versus Cavaliers) are needed for organizing crowds so that they know who should fight whom; but what kind of science is it that uses an assumption that all the attitudes on all issues can be arranged in one dimension . . . and then cannot decide where to place them on this scale?

When there is something approaching unanimity it is more in the nature of a cohesion of a pressure group than a consensus based on practically irrefutable verification. The celebrations of the end of ideology, for instance, were prompted by the manna which began to fall upon the American intellectuals and their vassals from the foundations rather than by any reasons which could be described as scientific. The easiest way out is always not to worry unduly about the truth, and to tell people what they want to hear, while the secret of success is to be able to guess what it is that they want to hear at the given time and place. Possessing only a very approximate and tentative knowledge, mostly of the rule-of-thumb kind, and yet able to exert much influence through his utterances, a practitioner of the social sciences often resembles a witch-doctor who speaks with a view to the effects his words may have rather than to their factual correctness; and then invents fables to support what he has said, and to justify his position in the society.

Chapter 3

Manipulation Through Description

The self-fulfilling prophecy constitutes only one (and fairly narrow) manifestation of the much more general disposition of human beings to be influenced by what is said about them and their environment. On the individual plane everybody knows that one can make a person discontented by deploring the circumstances under which he lives, encourage his endeavour by praise, or discourage it by sarcasm; that a physician's reassurance may aid recovery, and that an anxious parent can make the child timid. True, the powers of persuasion are not boundless, and there are many conditions – whether disease or destitution or some other scourge – which no amount of reassurance can alleviate; but in innumerable cases a few authoritatively spoken words can turn the scales.

The impact of the word on the formation of character has been recognized by the earliest writers on education, as well as by the latest psychoanalysts, and is enshrined in all kinds of popular sayings and proverbs. Barring congenital deformities, people can be made self-reliant and bold by being repeatedly told that they are strong and capable, are doing well and could easily tackle even bigger tasks. Or they may lose self-confidence and hope by hearing often enough that they are awkward, brainless or unlucky. If we convince somebody that he lacks the ability needed for learning a language or mathematics, or even learning to drive, he will never acquire these skills, regardless of how groundless our diagnosis might have been when he accepted it. If somebody is led to believe that he can ensure the success of his endeavour by hiring a magician or a psycho-analyst or a computer man, he will do so, regardless of whether any causal link between the activities of these specialists and the desired goals does in fact exist.

The same is true on the collective plane. In a country where no one believes that he can make a success in business, commerce and industry will fall into the hands of foreigners unless put under state control. Or, to take another example, if we show that the idea that 'honesty is the best policy' is groundless, we remove an important incentive to honesty. If we convince the subjects that their ruler's power is irresistible, they will abandon all thoughts of rebellion, while by spreading the view that a revolution is imminent and sure to win, we might be creating one of the conditions necessary for its outbreak. The politicians, generals and managers have, of course, always known about this connection, encouraged the spread of exaggerated notions about their power, and tried to impress them upon the populace with the aid of pomp surrounding high office.

A belief that the enemy is stronger may weaken the resolve to fight and bring about a defeat. True, faith may not be enough for victory, but it is usually a necessary condition of it. For this reason, all governments waging war have censored discouraging information, punished the 'defeatists', propagated optimism among their people, and disseminated depressing news among the enemy ranks. A war situation, however, is only the most extreme exemplification of the general dependence of the outcome on the expectations on the part of those who are trying to bring it about or to prevent it.

As can be seen in every election campaign, the well-known human inclination to jump on the victorious band-waggon provides an incentive to manipulate beliefs about the prospects of contending factions and to exert pressure on the commentators. The power to influence behaviour by making descriptive statements about it is not, of course, limited to politics; and it has been argued that the Kinsey Report fostered indulgence in adultery, promiscuity and perversion by making it known to those who might otherwise try to resist the temptation that, if they succumb to it, they will be in a much larger company than they had thought, and so will have no reason to feel they are freaks or outcasts. Similarly, a criminologist who tells the public how many crimes remain undetected may be encouraging potential lawbreakers.

Even such purely academic theories as the interpretations of

2

human nature have profound practical consequences if disseminated widely enough. If we impress upon people that
science has discovered that human beings are motivated only
by the desire for material advantage, they will tend to live up
to this expectation, and we shall have undermined their
readiness to be moved by impersonal ideals. By propagating
the opposite view we might succeed in producing a larger
number of idealists, but might also help cynical exploiters to
find easy victims. This specific issue, incidentally, is of immense
actual importance, because it seems that the moral dis-
orientation and fanatic nihilism which afflict modern youth
have been stimulated by the popular brands of sociology and
psychology with their bias for overlooking the more inspiring
achievements and focusing on the dismal average or even the
subnormal.[1] When, fraudulently basking in the glory of the
exact sciences, the psychologists refuse to study anything but
the most mechanical forms of behaviour – often so mechanical
that even rats have no chance to show their higher faculties –
and then present their mostly trivial findings as the true picture
of the human mind, they prompt people to regard themselves
and others as automata, devoid of responsibility or worth,
which can hardly remain without effect upon the tenor of social
life. By interpreting every manifestation of warm feelings
between persons of the same sex as latent homosexuality, the
psychoanalysts (to give another example) have debased and
well-nigh destroyed the concept of friendship, and have greatly
contributed to the painful isolation of modern man. Later I
shall say more about the fads and foibles of psychology, but
what concerns us at the moment is not the heuristic merits of
the different approaches, but the fact that apparently pure
methodological conceptions can mould the reality: that up to a
point they can make themselves true by changing the reality
which they are merely supposed to describe and analyse. Thus,
every description of human behaviour becomes to some extent a
persuasive description as soon as its objects get to know of it.

As every thoughtful reader of the newspapers knows, governments always try to facilitate the success of their policies or

1. This point is further discussed in my forthcoming book on Antisocialisation.

moves by organizing the so-called public opinion. What is less widely known is that, despite their professions of objectivity, very many (if not most) social scientists are only too eager to make themselves useful for this purpose. We must remember, however, that this kind of service can be rendered not only to the 'establishments' but also to all kinds of oppositionist and revolutionary movements.

Abstrusiveness need not impair a doctrine's aptness for inducing or fortifying certain attitudes, as it may in fact help to inspire awe and obedience by 'blinding people with science'. The divergent political impacts of the classic economic theory on the one side, and of marxism on the other, provide a good illustration of how it happens.

Marx's theory of surplus value is quite useless for explaining or predicting the movements of prices, and boils down to an obscure and indirect formulation of a strictly ethical judgment on the merits of the capitalist system's distribution of wealth, which gives a pseudo-scientific backing to the workers' feeling (perfectly justifiable often enough) that they are being robbed of the fruits of their labours. To be sure, many people before Marx (such as Simonde de Simondi, Robert Owen, Fourier and Proudhon) have deplored the ill-treatment of the workers and the exploitation of the poor by the rich; but they did so in moral terms without a 'scientific' proof, and consequently could cut no ice against the classical economists' 'scientific' arguments about the price of labour having to be determined by the laws of supply and demand – where the crucial but unstated premiss was that it was just that people should get neither more nor less than what they could obtain through bargaining on the market. Furthermore, by purporting to have proved that the worker's wages can never be raised above the subsistence minimum, Ricardo's iron Law of Wages helped to soothe the consciences of the rich, disinclined to share their profits, and to persuade the workers that their fate was inevitable, and therefore that there was no point in struggling against it. The message of Marx, as everybody knows, was exactly the opposite: namely a 'scientific' proof that the hated system would collapse. The essential ethical point about whether people are treated justly was replaced by two pseudo-scientific proofs: while Ricardo's conceptual system ruled out exploitation by definition, Marx proved its ubiquity by a long chain of obscure and muddled arguments, employing the classical economists' labour theory of value to show that profit and rent were stolen fruits of labour.

Among the many examples of how the interpretations of social reality affect actual behaviour, let us consider the formation of opinions about the character of groups and institutions. If the rank and file come to be convinced that their leaders are crooks, cowards or fools, their actions will differ radically from what they would be, were they convinced that the leaders are dedicated men of great courage and intelligence. Conversely, the leaders' behaviour will to some extent depend on the popular image of their office, which will determine whether the latter carries with it the dignity which they are expected to live up to, or whether they will have no reputation to preserve. Concrete illustrations of this point can be found in *Parasitism and Subversion*, where I have tried to analyse the impact of such notions on Latin American politics. The attitudes of the majority to a minority, and the other way round, will also be largely determined by the reciprocal 'images' which can be influenced by revelations or concealments of truths as well as by exaggerations and lies. Consequently every comment on such matters invites interference from the contestants in the political arena.

Or here is another example of how views on the relative efficacy of causal factors can be of considerable practical importance: think of the so-called conspiracy theory of history. Clearly, if you look for conspirators under every bed, your interpretation of past and present events will be very different from what you would imagine if you regarded every suspicion that there might be a conspiracy at work as an indubitable evidence of acute paranoia. In principle the role of conspiracies in politics appears to be a purely empirical question which could be solved by an examination of evidence, without having to pass judgment on whether conspiracy is a good thing. Nonetheless, almost every discussion of this seemingly theoretical problem generates a lost of heat, because different answers usually lead to divergent stands on the political issues of the day; particularly as an affirmative answer on the point of general importance of conspiracies poses the particular question of where to find them at a given moment. The conspirators, moreover, if they exist, will have an easier task if the public has been persuaded by naive or disingenuous psychologists that to suspect a conspiracy constitutes a proof of insanity; while the organs of state 'security' have a vested interest in exaggerating the dangers of infiltration and subversion.

Even when no vested interests are affected, factual findings may be enthusiastically welcomed or vehemently criticized simply because they pander to, or offend, current preconceptions, even if these are cherished for no other reason than sheer mental inertia, since most people hate to hear what might compel them to think again. The fashionable craving for novelty makes no basic difference because it only leads to a chase after superficial innovations which demand no mental effort. As we shall see later, this is the reason why purely verbal innovations easily gain popularity.

Mental inertia, of course, is by no means confined to the students of human affairs; and most natural scientists and technologists also resent having to re-think their views, and would like to suppress innovations which devalue their painfully acquired knowledge. As the history of science amply shows, many of its practitioners succeeded very well in doing precisely that, but nowadays the demand from industry and the armed forces makes it more difficult (though by no means impossible) to suppress a useful technical innovation. The advantages obtainable through misinformation are fewer in this field because command over nature can be gained only through acquisition of true knowledge, whereas people can be manipulated through incantations, brain-washing and the dissemination of false beliefs. Our attitudes towards other people, moreover, carry a much greater emotional loading than our attitudes towards things; and consequently we get much more upset when we find out that a person (or a group) about whom we have strong feelings is not what we thought he was, than when we have to revise our beliefs about the nature of some material objects. Even when it is a question of valued personal property, a man is unlikely to react with equal vehemence to somebody picking faults in his house or car or even horse or dog, as he would to a similar exercise in respect of his wife, child, parent, occupation or nation.

The difficulty of verifying assertions about human relations gives a wide scope to ulterior motives, and provides immunity for the purveyors of false information. A political scientist or an economist can hardly ever be brought to admit that his opinion or advice was wrong, because he can always find some argument which explains away his error. After all, even if what happened to people who acted upon his diagnosis or recommendation was pretty disastrous, it can never be conclusively proved that things would not have turned out even worse, had a different policy been adopted. Nor can it ever be shown beyond all doubt that the advice was correctly implemented and not misunderstood or mis-applied. For example: practically all the historians blame Neville Chamberlain and Daladier for the Munich agreement with Hitler, but who can prove that the outcome would have been better had they refused to make this agreement? We can only guess. Furthermore, the impossibility of verification exposes everybody who voices an opinion on matters of policy to accusations of ignorance, negligence or ill-will which he cannot easily refute. When, during the McCarthy era, the State Department's China experts lost their jobs for having advised Truman against sending troops to Chiang Kai Chek's aid, they had no means of proving that their advice was good; which could only have been done by demonstrating that the consequences of the alternative course of action would have been even worse – a perfectly arguable conclusion in the light of the hindsight provided by the war in Vietnam and the split between China and Russia. Given the impossibility of proving anything, the advisers could not even exonerate themselves from the accusations of having acted in bad faith which (to make matters even more complicated) might have been justified in some cases. Small wonder, then, that on such issues people prefer to be evasive.

The preceding example may not be representative of the difficulties facing the social scientists, only a minority of whom concern themselves with equally intractable and portentous issues of high policy. Nonetheless, even the politically non-engaged students of society invariably get into trouble with dictatorial governments. In freer countries the powers that be use the carrot rather than the stick – applying the method well described by the Zulu proverb that 'a dog with a bone in his mouth cannot bark'. However, even without pressures from the politicians, capitalists or bureaucrats, the desire for popularity can undermine independence of thought and induce anxious conformity. The orthodoxy thus obeyed need not, however, be the one imposed by the 'establishment' and may equally well consist of the line decreed by a subversive party. Anyway, from whichever direction the pressures come, a student of society who does not go in for beating about the bush and mealy-mouthed pussy-footing has little chance of being left alone like his colleagues in the natural sciences. And, as not everybody has a stomach for a never-ending fight for intellectual integrity, most social scientists gravitate towards problems, methods and conclusions which, no matter how sterile, are least likely to incur the displeasure of the potentates or of the populace. Prompted by the desire to play safe they often go even further than necessary in trimming their sails to the prevailing winds.

If you listen to the practitioners of social and economic research talking informally, you will easily find that not only are they very well aware of the aforementioned pressures, but also that they fully take them into account in making plans and arrangements about what to study, to write, or to say. This, however, happens on the everyday bread-and-butter level, while neither their pronouncements *ex cathedra* nor their publications ever mention that these pressures might make a difference to the trustworthiness of the results of social research, and to the prospects of its ever attaining the level of objectivity and reliability of the natural sciences.

To summarize: the propensity of human objects of inquiry to react to what is said about them creates three kinds of obstacles to the development of the social sciences. The first is of a methodological nature and consists of the difficulties surrounding the task of verifying propositions which can influence the happenings which they purport merely to describe or analyse. The second kind of impediment stems from the pressures upon the direction of the inquiry and the dissemination of its results, motivated firstly by the awareness that what is said might influence what will happen; and secondly by the desire (whether on the part of the potentates or the masses) to hear what pleases them. The disarray wrought by the operation of the two aforementioned factors produces the third kind of impairment in the shape of ample opportunities for getting away with falsehoods and crypto-propaganda.

The following chapters attempt to disentangle the workings of these three kinds of impediment, but before going further I should like to offer a few methodological suggestions on how the self-fulfilling or self-negating effects might be taken into account in assessing the validity of hypotheses. The first point is that the inability of the dead to respond to what is said about them enhances the value of retrodiction in comparison with prediction as a test of validity of hypotheses. Furthermore, by not having to consider the reactions of their objects, historians enjoy a greater freedom to be guided by mainly cognitive criteria – which explains, I think, why (especially during the last two decades) historical writings have greatly surpassed in quality the most applauded publications in sociology and political science. As S. R. Elton says in *The Practice of History*:

The future is dark, the present burdensome; only the past, dead and finished, bears contemplation. Those who look upon it have survived it: they are its product and its victors. No wonder, therefore, that men concern themselves with history.

Another methodological principle which emerges from the foregoing arguments is that, while examining the empirical evidence for a theory, prediction or diagnosis seemingly borne out by subsequent events, we must take into account the possible effects upon these events of the enunciation and dissemination of the statement in question. This means in the first place that we must try to find out whether those involved in bringing about these events knew about and believed in the validity of that statement. If we take, for instance, Marx's best prediction – namely, the so-called Law of Industrial Concentration – we can confidently assert that its corroboration had nothing to do with self-fulfilment: that the well-attested historical trend which this theory describes, and which is continuing till this very day, could not have been set in motion or maintained by the enunciation and dissemination of the theory; because few, if any, builders of industrial empires took any notice of what Marx said (if they had heard about him at all), and in any case they were not the kind of people who would let themselves be governed by abstract doctrines. On the other hand, the intellectuals and proletarians who believed in Marx had no part in making decisions which cumulatively produced the trend towards concentration which made this particular prophecy come true.

In contrast to the preceding example, Marx's forecasts about class struggles did contain an element of self-fulfilment (although in fact they have turned out to be only very partially true) because here many of the people whose actions played a part in bringing about the events did believe in the theory which these events have partially corroborated. Actually, the maze of causal relations was even more complicated than that, because it is arguable that other groups and individuals, who knew about the theory but did not regard it as pre-destined to come true, deliberately set out to make it false by embarking upon reforms and propaganda campaigns designed to remove the conditions of its fulfilment. So it seems that the dissemination of this theory has had a self-negating as well as self-fulfilling effect; and it is impossible to be sure which outweighed which.

A property of being self-negating can be found also in much simpler situations: for instance, if I told you that I would stab you tomorrow night when you were asleep, my prediction would lose all its likelihood as soon as it was communicated to you. In view of their self-fulfilling and self-negating effects, the only way to test predictions in the social sciences as fully as predictions in the natural sciences are tested is to make sure that nobody takes any notice of them. Best of all, write them out, put in a sealed envelope, tell nobody what it says . . . and wait for the day of fulfilment or make a provision in your last will for the envelope to be opened. Lucky astronomers . . . they do not have to resort to such tricks in order to find out whether their predictions were justified.

Problems of this kind have not only a theoretical but also a
2*

practical significance. For example: in the discussion of the efficacy of the anti-inflationary policies, inspired by keynesian economics, it has been argued that these no longer work because businessmen do not respond to the changes in the bank rate in the way they did in the days of Keynes, because nowadays they know that its rise is no augury of a depression, but a government-sponsored gambit which will be reversed as soon as the slightest sign of a real depression appears on the horizon. The self-fulfilling and self-negating effects had also been discussed in connection with the problems of strategy; and especially the question whether the atomic deterrent deters, and if so, then whom, how, when and from what. As to the methodology of the social sciences, it seems certain that without taking this factor into consideration, it must remain on the level of unrealistic pontification, no matter how refined its statistical techniques might be.

Chapter 4
Censorship Through Mass Production

Once an activity becomes a profession – that is, a way of making a living – the dedicated amateurs tend to fall into second place, greatly outnumbered by the practitioners guided primarily (if not solely) by the normal motives of the market place – which commonly boil down to the desire to get the most at the least cost to themselves. In other words, as soon as it becomes apparent that there is money in it, the saleability of goods rather than their intrinsic excellence becomes the dominant criterion. Hence the quality of the goods is attended to only in so far as the buyers are interested in it, able to judge and willing to pay for it. Only under such circumstances is honesty the best policy, and the efficiency of advertising campaigns shows how far we are from this ideal situation even as far as ordinary commodities are concerned. Nonetheless, with products of obvious and easily ascertainable utility, the consumers' resistance does prevent an indefinite deterioration of quality. Though easily deceived on finer points, people will not go on buying soap which does not remove dirt at all, or knives and forks which break as soon as they are used; whereas with products which do not serve as instruments for a clear and obvious purpose there is no natural limit to shoddiness, particularly when the canons of taste can be manipulated by vested interests.

The techniques of mass production have an intrinsic tendency to bring everything down (though also up) to the average – which may not matter (or may even bring benefits) when it affects commonplace utilitarian objects like umbrellas, shopping bags or even motor-cars, but which wreaks havoc in the realms of higher culture, as only a small minority are able to appreciate the merits of the more complex works of intellect or art, while few people fall short of the capacity to judge the quality of the various brands of washing machines or motor-cars. Owing to the distribution of the innate potential along the statistically normal distribution curve, most people cannot be brought to understand (let alone create) the true contributions to knowledge; and consequently the market for publications embodying them can never become the most alluring from a commercial viewpoint.

An increase in the number of people who read books has often in the past stimulated intellectual progress because, other things being equal, a larger reading public will contain a larger number of individuals especially gifted in any given direction; and might, consequently, offer a market for books with a rarified appeal, which could not be published if the total market were much smaller. It is easier, for instance, to publish without a subsidy a book on Byzantine musical notation in English than in Finnish. Thus a larger market permits, other things being equal, a greater variety of products. Unfortunately, however, among the factors which are not equal are the economies of scale in the publishing business which (as in other industries) foster a trend towards standardization. As the big profits lie in the best sellers the publishers have an obvious interest in the mediocre; for what would be the advantage of spending large sums on advertising an author who is too difficult for the average (or even slightly above the average) mind? And the larger the sums involved the stronger is the incentive to appeal to the lowest common denominator.

At the price of deviating from the question of the social sciences I must say a few words about the film industry which provides perhaps the best illustration of the inverse relationship between the cost and the quality, with the result that all the very expensive films are trashy . . . which, of course, does not mean that the cheap ones cannot be trashy too. Furthermore, although one can think of a few actors whose financial rewards might be attributed to an inimitable gift, the vast majority of film stars could be replaced by hundreds if not thousands of runners-up able to play the parts just as well, if not better. The stars' lavish remuneration in no way reflects the scarcity of their skills, but forms part of sales promotion. They are paid so much money in order to build up their aura in the eyes of a gullible public, who readily assume that anybody who gets so much money must be worth watching. Which among thousands of equally eligible aspirants gets catapulted into stardom might be a matter of luck, or skill in sycophancy and intrigue, or of efficiency in supplying heterosexual or homosexual gratification to directors and managers; but as soon as a big sum of money has been invested in an actor's image he acquires an independent bargaining power, as the owner of a name which can attract sheepish oglers. Many of these resemble Pavlov's dogs so closely that, once they are persuaded that somebody is funny, they will laugh as soon as he says anything, no matter how flat. This kind of conditioning of television viewers has lately been facilitated by a trick of reproducing tape-recorded laughter at the moments deemed appropriate by the stage managers, so that the gullible telly-gapers are stimulated to laugh by being deluded that thousands of people are highly amused. The downward pull of large-scale production accounts for the fact that the best films have been made by small teams, and in recent years mostly in countries like Italy, Japan and Poland, whose language limits the market; while Hollywood, the largest centre, has produced no real masterpiece and very few films of even moderately high quality. The need to appeal to the most commonplace proclivities, dictated by the scale of operations, also explains the harmful influence of television on intellectual and aesthetic standards.

The same is true of books; and one of the more reliable methods of finding out what is not worth reading is to look through the lists of instant best sellers, whose quality deteriorates as the amounts of money involved increase and the advertising techniques improve. The advertisers have a vested interest in stupidity because it pays them to focus on the least critical section of the populace who can be hoodwinked with the greatest ease. Furthermore, since gullible people are likely to bring the most immediate returns on advertising expenditure, it is in the interest of the advertising business to promote gullibility, and to propagate the idea that a refusal to follow slavishly the latest fashion must stem from neurotic or anti-social tendencies. Those who reason too much are depicted by the mass media as crazy egg-heads, because the most desirable customer is an acquisitive, conformist and semi-educated snob who can never tire of buying standardized goods. The inherent tendencies of large scale publishing and sales promotion exert a strong downward pull on the quality of the products of scholarship as well, unless (as in the exact sciences connected with technology) the practical needs enforce rigorous standards.

Especially in the United States, the techniques employed for putting into the limelight sensation-mongering novelists or exhibitionist journalists have come to be applied for boosting up all kinds of mediocre writers on the social sciences. Here too we get hyperbolic advertisements hailing platitudes as epoch-making discoveries, pressure upon, and cajolery of, editors responsible for deciding what will be reviewed and by whom, softening-up of reviewers by wining and dining (with darkly hinted possibilities of retaliation), leaks about the fabulous earnings of the genius in question (designed to impress readers accustomed to judging everything by money), and revelations about his connections with the charmed circles of power and wealth. The most stultifying effects of this state of affairs stem from the commercial preference for publications which neither demand much mental effort nor offend any widespread prejudices, and yet have a sensationalist appeal – the stuff of which instant best sellers are made.

Some American salesmen go even to the lengths of tempting teachers with promises of an influential author's recommendation for a job, or a grant in exchange for prescribing the latter's textbook for their students. Conversely, by recommending a book which criticizes the academic potentates of the day, a teacher incurs the risk of being cold-shouldered when he seeks an appointment, a promotion or research funds . . . or at least he did so until the academic establishment came under fire from the 'revolutionary' students and junior academics. Although, owing to their inclination to unreason and intolerance, the latter are no improvement on the old manipulators, the clash of the opposing orthodoxies might give more room to free thought than when one of them reigned unchallenged.

Progress requires, especially in a branch of learning which

readily lends itself to propagandist uses, an unfettered circulation of ideas among scholars genuinely dedicated to the pursuit of truth. And these, even in the academic profession, constitute a minority. Consequently, any form of concentration of control over the production and dissemination of knowledge must impede the progress of understanding – regardless of whether this control rests in the hands of public authorities or commercial interests.

The concentration of the publishing business imposes conformity, not only because it reduces the number of openings for an author and the amount of competition between them, but also because increased size entails bureaucratization with its well-known tendency to discourage unorthodox opinions. A small independent publisher may try out anything that takes his fancy so long as it does not lead him into bankruptcy, whereas in a large house the decision will be made by a committee or a series of committees with concurrence of the *established* experts, all normally tending to give preference to the 'sound' rather than the original, let alone the iconoclastic. This is especially true of the publishing houses owned by other commercial interests, whose sole criterion is profit, where there is no room for flights of inspiration or fancy or counter-suggestibility. It is not surprising, therefore, that (at least in the field of the social sciences) the lists of the biggest publishers exhibit a depressing monotony; and that one can usually see a decline in quality as the firm expands. The academics interested in freedom of thought ought to try to counteract the trend towards concentration in the publishing business, by favouring (within the bounds of fairness) smaller publishers when choosing textbooks for their students. Another useful rule would be never to buy or recommend anything lavishly advertised.

Lest some readers jump to the conclusion that everything would be well if we could only eliminate the profit motive, I hasten to add that the market (provided it is not under a monopolistic control) often constitutes the chief (or even only) bulwark against an orthodoxy imposed by a bureaucratic machine; because in a large mass of readers there will always be some who (if only out of sheer boredom) would like to read something a little different, so that a smallish publisher can make a reasonable profit by satisfying this desire. When profit does not matter, and the decisions about what to publish depend solely on clique politics, nobody has an incentive to risk the displeasure of the powers that be by printing controversial (let alone iconoclastic) works. To see this it is enough to look at government publications in even the most liberal countries, or at the publications of the various agencies of UNO – which may be worth consulting for innocuous statistical data but cover up every important problem with public relations verbiage. Or look at the university presses: many of them perform a useful service by publishing scholarly works which are too esoteric to be profitable; but has any of them ever published an iconoclastic book on current affairs? They may be right in not regarding this as their task, but somebody must do it if free thinking is to survive; and since the very big firms, with their overriding interest in massive editions, invariably tend towards the lowest common denominator, the small commercial publishers are left as the sole bastion of liberty.

That a freedom from commercial pressures may be a doubtful blessing can also be seen in the example of many of the so-called learned journals, which can subsist on automatically renewed subscriptions from the libraries even when nobody reads them. The absence of the need to arouse interest has removed all restraints on the lengths to which vacuity and tedium can be pushed on their pages. True, depth and originality may be an obstacle in attracting a wide readership, and they certainly help less than slickness and loquacity; but even the latter qualities require some brains and rule out plain dullness, which is a help rather than impediment in writing 'scientific' papers on social research. If somebody writes something which the coterie dominating the subject dislikes, but which is sufficiently readable to be bought by at least two-thousand readers, a publisher, who is not directly involved in academic politics, may take it to make a little bit of money, whereas an editor of a journal will more often than not be guided solely by the consideration of clique mechanics.

It might be appropriate at this juncture to insert a few words about reviewing in order to help students and other beginners to avoid certain pitfalls. The first thing to remember is that one must never assume without good evidence that the reviewer knows better than the author. Admittedly, in a field without firm standards the odds are that the book is in fact pretty awful, but it is equally likely that the reviewer is either too ill-informed to understand what it is all about, or too lazy to read the text on which he is passing a verdict, or too timorous to produce anything himself and consequently eager to assuage his envy by denigration, if he is not simply playing clique politics. There are innumerable gambits in the latter game, the simplest being straight discrimination against an outsider: always needed in defence of the established insiders, since fame and influence are ineradicably scarce while the aspirants thereto are legion. Thus even without attacking established names, a new writer is likely to attract ill will merely by excelling in something, and will for this reason be attacked by the established men's retainers. On the other hand, regardless of their merit, books by prominent personalities always stand a good chance of getting fulsome praise, which, again, might be deserved but which can not be taken at its face value unless we know that the reviewer is not courting favours. Hostile reviews written by rivals who have written – or who are about to write – on the same subject must be treated with caution; but equally suspect (though for the opposite reason) are opinions of near colleagues and individuals belonging to the same circle, because one of the most common ploys is a tacit exchange of praise. Almost needless to say, mutual praise may stem from a genuine harmony of views, but in a field infested by charlatans it more commonly occurs as an unprincipled collusion which enables the partners to circumvent the customary taboo on boasting. Such manoeuvres often have the aim of bringing control over money taps into the hands of the clique. It would be an interesting topic for research (though hardly likely to attract large funds) to apply to the machinations inside academic institutions and foundations the method which Lewis Namier used to study eighteenth-century English politics. The methodological lesson which emerges from all this is that the trustworthiness of the publications in this field (no matter

how scientific they claim to be) can be assessed only by applying
to them the criteria which the historian uses in evaluating his
sources, which include an enquiry into the author's passions
and vested interests.

Chapter 5

In the Footsteps of Monsieur Pangloss and Dr Bowdler

Rediscovering America is one of the most popular occupations among practitioners of the social sciences, and it requires that the original discoverer should be consigned to oblivion. Thus, for example, Herbert Spencer has been recently kept in oblivion largely because he said more clearly, as well as somewhat earlier, what some of the influential theorists of today claim as their discoveries. For Spencer not only introduced the concepts of what is now called 'structural-functionalism', but also laid foundations for a cybernetic analysis of social phenomena, in addition to developing the ideas which, in an inarticulate (and therefore bastardized) form, underlie most of contemporary thinking about such matters as 'development' and 'resistance to change'.

Spencer's key concept was 'evolution', by which he meant the process of increasing differentiation (that is to say, specialization of functions) and integration, by which he meant mutual inter-dependence of the structurally differentiated parts and co-ordination of their functions. In *Principles of Sociology*,[1] Spencer tried to demonstrate three main points: firstly, that societies can be classified in terms of increasing differentiation and integration; secondly, that there is a necessary filiation of the types of total social structure as well as of the types of partial structures such as industrial, political or ecclesiastic; and thirdly, that a general trend towards growing complexity can be discerned in the long run. In addition to making evolution into the dominant approach to the study of society during his lifetime, Herbert Spencer begat a more remote offspring: namely, functionalism, which was developed when the step of applying Spencer's concepts to an analysis of concrete situations was taken by Malinowski and Radcliffe-Brown.

1. See the abridged edition, Macmillan, London, 1968.

These were the first to gather and order ethnographic data with an explicit purpose of disentangling the relationships of mutual dependence between various customs and beliefs. This sounds simple enough but it was neither an easy nor an unimportant step, as can be seen by confronting their works with older ethnography (or later but unaffected by their influence) where one finds each institution or custom described in isolation without any attempt to view society as a system. To avoid unwarranted pretentions, functionalism can be interpreted as a directive to search for the relation of mutual dependence between customs and institutions; but functional *explanations* seldom amount to more than descriptions of effects, as can be seen from the examples examined in Chapter 4 of *The Uses of Comparative Sociology*. There can be no objections so long as by 'functionalism' we mean the programme of searching for relations of mutual dependence, the result of which will constitute a 'functional analysis' which demonstrates how a trait or institution A could not operate or 'function' without a trait or institution B – in other words, how and why B is a necessary condition of A. This alone is normally quite a tall order, but the entire argument becomes in most instances very tenuous, if not entirely gratuitous, when a statement to this effect is offered to explain why B has come into existence and continues to exist; as this raises the question (commonly not only left unanswered but even unrecognized) of why should A itself or, indeed, the entire system to which it belongs, exist at all. It is the little word 'to' that is the source of the difficulties, as when we say that the function of B is *to* produce A. Such a statement acquires validity only when we can specify a causal chain in the form of a regulatory mechanism which is set in motion by an absence of A (due to the previous disappearance of B) in such a way as to bring about a reappearance of first B and then A. The complexity of this specification of what is minimally required suffices to show that to satisfy it cannot be an easy matter. Indeed, I doubt whether in the entire literature produced by the 'functionalists' there is a single piece of analysis which satisfies this requirement – which, of course, should not be taken as implying that the 'functionalist' approach has produced no worthwhile insights of an intuitive and approximate kind – at least in anthropology where the wholes, within which the functional relations are supposed to operate, are more isolated and not so often subject to radical changes which cast doubt on whether these entities are still in existence or have given way to something new.

In contrast to the modern functionalists, Spencer cannot be accused of propounding a theoretical framework which excludes change. On the contrary: his transformist orientation (derived from Lamarck and re-inforced by Darwin) explains social change very well: societies and institutions are struggling for living space, and only those survive which are able to adapt themselves to the changing environment.[1] The extension of the notion of natural selection to the competition between polities and institutions positively entails change, rather than merely allowing for it. What is equally important, the selectionist viewpoint provides a justification for the otherwise gratuitous functionalist assumption that every enduring institution must have a function – in the sense of Radcliffe-Brown's definition of 'making a contribution to the continued existence of the whole'. We must reject the view of the so-called diffusionists that a culture is an accidental assemblage of customs and beliefs if we accept Spencer's theory of the survival of the fittest; for the latter posits that a system consisting of structural parts whose functions are not adjusted to each other or to the demands of the environment will be destroyed by its competitors.

In addition to providing a justification for the fundamental assumption of functionalism, the notion of the natural selection of social systems and institutions constitutes the cornerstone of evolutionism, because it accounts for the secular evolution of social systems towards greater complexity, provided we accept the additional assumption (more than plausible in sociology though debatable in biology) that an increase in differentiation and integration – or to use Spencer's favourite expression 'an advance in organization' – more often than not bestows a superiority of power in the struggle for survival. No doubt it was these associations with the idea of the struggle for survival

1. See Herbert Spencer: *Structure, Function and Evolution*, Michael Joseph, 1971.

between states and other human aggregates that led to the supplanting of 'evolution' by 'development' and 'change' – words employed in a much more crassly unilinear sense than 'evolution' ever was; because in the days when everybody professes to love peace such brutal facts of life are eagerly swept under the carpet.

From a logical point of view, Spencer's organicism should be welcomed by the rulers of authoritarian collectivist states, but ideological affinities derive not from logic but from expressions of sentiments; and here the determining fact is that Spencer's explicit pronouncements favoured the ideals and interests of the free enterprise, anti-statist, bourgeoisie (that is to say, independent, small and middling businessmen, farmers and artisans) who have since been thoroughly demoted. Whereas Marx thundered against this now defeated class, Spencer fulminated against bureaucracy which has turned out to be the winner. So the managerial society has justly punished him for his anticipatory blasphemies by giving a free rein to the expropriators of his theories, who have expurgated his hankerings after free enterprise and free-thinking individualism, and converted his organicist ideas into an ideology buttressing the reign of bureaucratic and big business manipulators, and inculcating a belief in the existence of a perfect harmony under which discord can only stem from a lack of communication.

Functionalism's sudden rise to predominance in American sociology after the Second World War appears strange in view of the American anthropologists' long-standing rejection of Malinowski's and Radcliffe-Brown's brand of functionalism. The difference in this respect between anthropology in the United States and in the British cultural sphere can be explained by the environment. It is no accident that the Americans concentrated on traits of culture (tracing their origins, diffusion and clustering, and calling their discipline 'cultural anthropology') while the British focused on a holistic analysis of social systems under the flag of *social* anthropology: American Indian tribes no longer functioned as coherent entities, and only disjointed remnants of their culture could be seen in the reserves or the musea, while in the British colonies large populations continued to follow their traditional ways of life, scarcely disturbed by the remote administration and the coastal trade. These could be studied fruitfully as living wholes from a functionalist viewpoint. Nonetheless, even in this field functionalism imposed not only the methodological limitations mentioned earlier, but also quite serious distortions of ideological origin. Indeed one could say that (although invented by a Pole) 'functionalism' has found a well-nigh universal acceptance among British anthropologists, not only because of its purely intellectual merits, but also because it fitted well with the concept of indirect rule, the aim of which was to govern with the least disturbance of native traditions.

By showing how neatly dovetailed were the traditional ways, the functionalists were supplying a justification for not pressing too hard with modernization, so suicidal for colonial rule. Seeing what havoc the rash neo-colonialist modernization is playing in Africa, one can feel a great deal of sympathy with this quietistic hidden message; but what interests us here is not whether this ideological message was right or wrong but that there was one . . . as a matter of fact, more than one.

The second ingredient in the anthropologist's ideology was a reaction against the racialist haughtiness of the British settlers and administrators which, though very often accompanied by a genuine good will towards the subjects, was incompatible with the ideals of equality and democracy professed in the metropolitan country, to which the intellectuals were particularly attracted. By showing that the native beliefs and customs were much subtler and more rational than appeared to a foreigner at first sight, the anthropologists hoped to defend the Africans and Asiatics against unjustified imputations of racial inferiority. This was a laudable task, because among the uneducated Europeans racialist contempt often went so far that many of them imagined that the rich and highly complex African languages had no grammar and contained only a few simian sounds.

Though on the whole kinder to the common people than their native successors, the British colonial officials retained until the end a condescending attitude to their subjects; and by a movement of a dialectical pendulum the anthropologists, like most of the intellectuals, have fallen into the opposite and equally irrational habit of idolizing everything exotic. Under the influence of this revised version of Rousseau's old myth of the 'noble savage', unsullied by the depravities of civilization, everything African had to be whitewashed, the importance of warfare played down, every cruel custom explained away (if mentioned at all), every evidence of fraud, extortion or terror swept under the carpet unless perpetrated by the Europeans. The anthropologists' well-intentioned and starry-eyed covering up of the social warts has afforded a preview of the potentialities of functionalism as an instrument of apologetics.

Since after decolonization the Africans could no longer be ordered about, but advantages could be obtained by hood-winking them with the aid of flattery, much of anthropology, historiography and other branches of African studies became essential tools of business and diplomacy. Far from being unique, this is only an unusually gross manifestation of the common tendency to foster international studies not for the sake of finding the truth but for the purpose of cultivating the foreigners' good-will by writing nice things about them.[1]

Despite its aforementioned methodological weaknesses functionalism remained within reason so long as it presided over the study of fairly self-contained and static tribes and primitive kingdoms. But when applied to the rapidly changing American society, full of glaring contrasts, deviations and conflicts, it lost all its value as an instrument for advancing understanding, and acquired the character of pseudo-scientific crypto-propaganda, widely acclaimed in the American universities and their dependencies overseas, when the public-relations-minded academics were winning friends in high places by proclaiming the end of ideology.

The degradation of functionalism from a useful, though somewhat one-sided, programme for anthropological studies into a method of stultifying real inquiry by diverting attention to mere labels, took place largely under the influence of R. K. Merton, whose disservice to sociology has been more insidious than that of Talcott Parsons because, free from the latter's monumental muddle-headedness, he was able to

---

1. A frank analysis of the present situation, which has caused a lot of indignation and tut-tuttings, can be found in *The African Predicament*. (Michael Joseph, London, 1968, Atherton Press, New York, 1969.)

sterilize the subject without falling into absurdity. I do not, of course, maintain that he did it on purpose, as there is no reason to doubt that he, as well as his many disciples, believed that they were making great contributions to science. Nonetheless, despite a few minor real contributions to knowledge here and there, the unintended effect of their approach (its latent function, to use Merton's own term) on the balance amounted to a thoroughgoing bowdlerization of the subject. Very well written in comparison with the style which became dominant later, his articles (reprinted in the famous volume, *Social Theory and Social Structure*) nonetheless boil down to an impressive sounding re-labelling devoid of any explanatory or predictive power (such as substituting 'functional' for useful or good; 'dysfunctional' for detrimental; 'manifest' and 'latent function' for proclaimed and real purpose or reason), or to restatements of the obvious such as the dictum (ritually reprinted as obeisance to the king-maker in all kinds of publications) that theorizing depends on empirical research, and vice-versa, or that deviance consists of pursuing legitimate ends (e.g., money) by illegitimate means (e.g. theft). Another example is the advice (quoted *ad nauseam*) that we should concentrate on the 'theories of the middle range', accompanied by no indication about how to find out where that blessed middle lies, which alone could make this advice worthwhile.

If everything is wonderfully dovetailed and adjusted, then we should leave things alone. More insidiously than nineteenth century organicism, functionalism propagates a conservative ideology in the name of science; while, for those things its practitioners do not like, they have the aforementioned epithet 'dysfunctional', which enables them to insinuate a condemnation without openly saying so, and to enlist the authority of science for their ideologies or personal preferences. For if somebody says that something is good or bad, he might be asked: for what?, or for whom?, or why?. So he might be obliged to take off the mask of objective omniscience and to reveal, firstly, his values and, secondly, the reasons for his assumptions about the likely consequences of various arrangements or courses of action; whereas by using 'functional' and 'dysfunctional' instead of 'good' and 'bad', a functionalist can hide behind a façade of objectivity and invoke the magic of science to back his crypto-propagandist insinuations.

In comparison with what came later, Merton's essays (as well as the publications of his early followers) appear as wonderfully clear, which weakness led to the supplanting of this variant of Panglossian sociology by a more potent medicine. For if you reiterate the same few notions in a language which (though open to serious criticism) is at least comprehensible, people will eventually notice the repetition, whereas if you wrap them up in incomprehensible mumbo-jumbo, you can go on and on safely without anybody knowing what you are saying anyway. And if you are a famous man in a top position and with a lot of influence, few people will dare to say, or even think, that it is all nonsense, lest they be accused of ignorance and lack of intelligence, and forfeit their chances of obtaining appointments, invitations or grants. So the panglossian functionalism came to be replaced by a super-panglossian structural-functionalism shrouded in heavy clouds of opaque verbiage.

Chapter 6

The Smoke Screen of Jargon

The human mind is scarcely provided with the means of grappling with a reality which is not only staggeringly complex but also fluid, elusive and opaque – a reality which can be apprehended only with the aid of abstractions, which are themselves so indirectly based on sense perceptions that they are always slipping into the realm of pure fancy completely out of touch with reality. As the terminological confusion is just one aspect of the general lack of understanding, the definitions given in dictionaries of sociological or political terms can inform merely about how people use these terms, without providing much guidance on how they ought to be used, because in the present state of the social sciences current usage always leaves much to be desired. On the whole, apart from the economists, the anthropologists have sinned much less on this score than their colleagues in other social sciences; because, describing strange customs and beliefs, they had less need to wrap up their findings in an impressive-sounding opaque jargon than have the sociologists or psychologists, writing about situations familiar to their readers and about which, consequently, it is much more difficult to say something original. If you are a mentally alert black-coated worker, you might learn a thing or two from a book about your class, but you are unlikely to find any startling news there. But, if you are a European or an American and have not studied Moroccan ethnography, you could not guess what goes on in the mountains of the Atlas.

What is at least equally important, during the great days of anthropology the objects of the inquiry were unlikely to learn what the anthropologist had said about them; and even if they did, and did not like it, they would not normally be in a position to cause the author any great annoyance. The shrinking of the world, combined with decolonization, has radically altered the situation, with the consequence that the anthropologists are now just as cagey as anybody else – if not more so – owing to the touchiness of the objects of their enquiries. Actually, many had to rename themselves as sociologists in order to get a visa to some of the new states.

Although the value of conceptual analysis unaccompanied by constructive theorizing must remain limited, it does not follow that such analysis must be entirely useless. On the contrary, constant attention to the meaning of terms is indispensable in the study of human affairs, because in this field powerful social forces operate which continuously create verbal confusion, much greater than what is inevitable in view of the rudimentary state of this branch of learning.

The prime example of obscurity is, of course, Talcott Parsons, as can well be seen even in a book which is less burdened by this vice than his other works: namely, *Societies: Evolutionary and Comparative Perspectives*. The great merit of this book (as well as of its author's other works) is that it has higher aspirations than the popular image of the sociologist as an unreflecting fact-finder rushing around with questionnaires, not in the least interested in such impractical questions as the evolution of mankind or the nature of the social bond. Unfortunately, however, and despite the author's good intentions, what he says is sadly lacking in clarity. Indeed, he can make the simplest truth appear unfathomably obscure. As every schoolboy knows, a developed brain and acquired skills and knowledge are necessary for attaining specifically human goals, but our author feels that he must tell us this, and this is how he puts it.

Skills constitute the manipulative techniques of human goal attainment and control in relation to the physical world, so far as artifacts or machines especially designed as tools do not yet supplement them. Truly human skills are guided by organised and codified *knowledge* of both the things to be manipulated and the human capacities that are used to manipulate them. Such knowledge is an aspect of cultural-level symbolic processes, and, like other aspects to be discussed presently, requires the capacities of the human central nervous system, particularly the brain. This organic system is clearly essential to all of the symbolical processes; as we well know, the human brain is far superior to the brain of any other species.

The author's addiction to nebulous verbosity shows itself especially in the first chapter, where he offers us some glimpses of his famous general theory of action which in reality consists of incredibly ponderous restatements of the obvious. On page 7, for instance, we read:

Within the limits imposed by the genetic species-type on the one hand and the patterning of the culture on the other, lies the opportunity for given individuals and groups to develop independently structured behavioral systems. Because an actor is genetically human, and because his learning occurs in the context of a particular cultural system, his learned behavioral system (which I shall call his personality) shares certain broad features with other personalities – e.g., the language he habitually speaks. At the same time, his organism and its environment – physical, social, and cultural – are always in certain respects unique. Hence, his own behavioral system will be a *unique variant* of the culture and its particular patterns of action. It is therefore essential to consider the personality system as not reducible to either the organism or the culture – *what* is learned is part of neither the 'structure' of the organism in the usual sense nor a feature of the cultural system. It comprises an *analytically independent system*.

The idea which the author is trying to express is that although every individual is in many ways similar to other human beings, he is also unique in a way which is predetermined neither by the properties of his organism nor by the state of the culture. Again . . . hardly a revelation. Sometimes the author's insensitivity to the meanings of words and his lack of feeling for logic prompt him to make statements which are not merely platitudinous but plainly silly, as when he writes on page 30, 'In the realm of action, the gene has been replaced by the symbol as the basic structural element'. As if we could be here at all if our genes had been replaced by symbols, or as if our capacity to use symbols did not depend on the nature of our genes. After all, worms cannot speak and crocodiles cannot write.

After the first chapter the book becomes slightly better, as the author leaves his system alone and proceeds to tell us about the societies of the Australian aborigines and the Shilluk, and later about social structures in ancient Egypt, Mesopotamia,

India, Israel, Greece and Rome, and the Islamic empires. Though hardly novel, the account might be of use to new-comers to comparative historical studies, were it provided in a succinct and clear manner instead of being wrapped up in pompous and nebulous phraseology; as, for instance, on page 56, where (to find out that in ancient Egypt the common people were liable to be conscripted for work) we have to read the following passage:

For those whose roles primarily involved the performance of services, as distinguished from assumption of leadership responsi-bility, the main pattern seems to have been a response to the leadership's invoking obligations that were concomitants of the status of membership in the societal community and various of its segmental units. The closest modern analogy is the military service performed by an ordinary citizen, except that the leader of the Egyptian bureaucracy did not need a special emergency to invoke legitimate obligations.

Herbert Spencer – who, as we saw earlier, introduced the concept of evolution in the study of society as well as coined the term 'comparative sociology' – gets a mention in the conclusion, where the author says:

The present analysis differs significantly from most evolutionary theories in that the developmental dimension I have used is fully compatible with the idea that there is considerable variability and branching among lines of evolution. The evidence we have reviewed indicates that, in the earlier stages of evolution, there have been *multiple* and *variable* origins of the *basic* societal types. Thus, we need not postulate one primitive origin of all intermediate societies, even though we consider such factors as independent cultural legitimation and stratification *necessary* conditions of all intermediate societies. At all stages, the importance of such variability can be adequately treated, we argue, only by an analytic theory of variable factors and components. The impressive development of such theory since Spencer's time enables us to construct a much more sophisticated evolutionary scheme than his.

In reality, however, the scheme offered is an inferior version of Spencer who, with much greater clarity, formulated the idea of evolution as the tendency towards increasing differentiation and integration. Such a trend can indubitably be discerned in the history of human society, whereas Parsons' own addition – 'the enhancement of adaptive capacity' – is untenable, and reflects a demoded popular biology. Is the adaptive capacity of the elephant greater than that of the fly? Or of man greater than that of a virus? Is the adaptive capacity of the Americans greater than that of the Eskimos? What about adapting to living without iron or petrol or paper? The real difference is, as Spencer has pointed out, which social entity can absorb or destroy which.

Nor can Parsons' classificatory scheme – dividing societies into the primitive, intermediate and modern – be regarded as a step forward, as it is much cruder than the taxonomies of much older writers, beginning with Morgan, Marx and Spencer, or even Adam Ferguson and John Millar. Later, Leonard Hobhouse, Rudolf Steinmenz and Richard Thurnwald proposed much more sophisticated classifications.

Sometimes the verbal substitutions masquerading as contributions to knowledge are so inept and gross that it is difficult to believe that the authors really think that they are revealing new truths (which must be the case), and that they are not laughing up their sleeves at the gullibility of their audience. One of the crassest examples of such delusions is the recent vogue for the letter 'n', chosen to deputize for the common word 'need' because of its status-bestowing properties stemming from its frequent appearances in mathematical formulae. So by scribbling the letter 'n' all over their pages some people have succeeded in surrounding their platitudes with the aura of the exact sciences in their own eyes, as well as those of their readers who might have seen some books on mathematics without being able to understand them. As an example of the consequences of the belief in the occult powers of this magic letter, we can take a book by a Harvard professor, Everett E. Hagen, with a presumptuous title, *On the Theory of Social Change*. As Heraclitus said, everything changes all the time; and, therefore, a work offering a theory of social change without specifying any restrictions should in strict logic amount to a comprehensive treatise on general sociology. However, in Hagen's book, 'social change' means only one of its possible variants: namely, technical innovation; and, in trying to find the sources of this the author shifts the viewpoint without warning, employs the term 'innovation' in the widest possible meaning, and proceeds to discuss the psychological determinants of innovation in general. An economist by profession, Hagen has become disenchanted with economic theory on the justifiable grounds that it fails to account for economic backwardness, and has set out to supplement, or rather supplant, it by a partly sociological but mainly psychoanalytic explanation.

Laudably looking further than the usual mental horizon of his fellow economists, Hagen contends that the factors which decide whether an industrial take-off will take place or not are of a psychological nature. This is possible, but to prove it (let alone to prove that the specific psychological factors which he mentions are really crucial) he should have compared societies on a roughly similar cultural, economic and technical level which differed in respect of the psychological traits of their members, instead of confronting psychological characteristics of peoples living under circumstances so contrasting that all other conceivably relevant factors are different too. We might inquire into the role which differences in so-called national character may have played in determining the relative rates of industrial development in France and Germany, but it is ludicrous to attempt to account for the slow speed of technical innovation among the Sioux Indians or the ancient Celts as compared with the United States of today by pointing out the differences in the methods of bringing up children and toilet training. Suppose the Sioux Indians, or even the Burmese peasants, of today were mad on technical innovation, would they then be able to make nuclear reactors or supersonic aeroplanes?

The picture of the 'traditional mentality' painted by the author (on the basis of various studies of American specialists who never bothered to learn the language and who mechanically applied to the inhabitants of the Arabian desert or Burmese jungles the ready-made questionnaires prepared for students in Milwaukee) is on the level of travellers' tales translated into obscure psychoanalytic jargon. Notwithstanding the statement on page 426 that 'with the fibers of their nervous system, not merely with their minds, many individuals in underdeveloped countries must fear Americans . . . ', nobody who has had even a brief contact with peasants and tribesmen will believe that they are all anxiety-ridden obsessionals, or that they are less capable of reasoning than ordinary dwellers in modern cities. A hunter or a herdsman has more opportunities of making decisions and taking risks (and is less likely to be anxiety-ridden) than an average employee of General Motors or Unilever. The author's low opinion of the mental state of the inhabitants of unindustrialized countries is supported by the evidence of their inability to give satisfactory answers to questions which he regards, in all seriousness, as appropriate for illiterate peasants. On page 253 he quotes the following passage from the book of his worthy colleague, Daniel Lerner, *The Passing of the Traditional Society*:

Two of the questions are: 'If you were made editor of a newspaper, what kind of a paper would you run?' and 'Suppose that you were made head of the government, what are some of the things you would do?' As I have suggested in Chapter 5 in discussing world cognition, many peasants are simply unable to answer some such questions.

Surprising, is it not? Why not test the level of 'world cognition' (that is general knowledge) of the President of the United States or the editor of Foreign Affairs by asking him which is the best way of milking a camel.

Though clearly insufficient to account for the differences between societies in respect of the rate of technical progress, psychological considerations should help to explain why certain individuals make innovations while the others do not. Hypotheses about the connection between infant training and inventiveness could be tested by drawing upon biographical material about inventors and confronting it with the data on the general history of customs; but this the author does not attempt. Had he done so, he would have seen that instead of resembling the out-going, novelty-seeking American 'kids', many, if not most, of the giants of scientific discovery were timid and anxious recluses like Newton, or had a very severe and authoritarian upbringing like Gauss. In any case, Hagen would have been prevented from discovering any significant

3

psychological connection by his employment of the blanket term 'innovator', which covers among others Ghengis Khan, Jesus Christ, Al Capone, Dior and his models, Albert Einstein, the Beatles and the Prince of Wales, who inadvertently introduced the fashion of having turn-ups on trousers. What can be their psychological common denominator? If it is some special kind of toilet training, it remains to be proved.

Hagen's framework of psychological analysis is based on the idea of 'needs' which he regards as an innovation, notwithstanding the fact that it occurs in the Bible. It must be noted, however, that unlike the ultra scientific psychologists, the Bible does not confuse need as an objective requirement necessary for survival with mere desire. There is, however, one real innovation which the author makes or adopts from a psychologist named Henry A. Murray: namely a contravention of one of the basic rules of English (including American English) grammar, which stipulates that if a noun is used in an adjectival sense it must precede the noun which it qualifies – not the other way round. Hagen employs, for instance, the expression 'need aggression' – not, mark, aggression need – to designate the inclination to commit aggression. Since the dawn of philosophy innumerable writers have discussed this proclivity – calling it pugnacity or combative instinct or aggressive drive or what not – but none has invented a term equally well designed to make speech unintelligible. Self-reliance is called according to this dictionary 'need autonomy'; ambition – 'need achievement'; sociability – 'need affiliation'. In Hagen's own words (page 107): 'need understanding is the need to understand . . . to make thought correspond to fact'. Obviously 'need for understanding' or 'wish to understand' would not be scientific enough. On page 106 we read: 'Need order is the need to put things in order'.

The historical material is handled with the same acumen. For example, on page 346 we are told about Colombia: 'The proximate answer to the question why growth began is: Because of the enterprise of the Antioquenos'. Antioquia, however, was inhabited long before this 'take-off', but we are not told why its inhabitants waited so long or did not wait longer; although we are informed that their pre-eminence in

Colombian business was due to the fact that 'they manifested high need autonomy, need achievement and need order' – which means that they were self-reliant, ambitious and orderly.

Actually, a bird's-eye survey of the agrarian relations in Colombia readily suggests an explanation of the Antioquenos' competitive advantage. In contrast to the rest of Colombia – divided into large estates where the peasants had no chance of improving their lot through work, while the landowners had no need to exert themselves – much of the land in Antioquia was in the hands of peasant proprietors who were neither exploited nor in a position to exploit others, and for this reason more frequently developed the habits of self-reliance, foresight and hard work needed for success in business. Why the spurt in industrial development took place at this particular time rather than another cannot, of course, be explained without taking into account the sequence of political and economic circumstances not only in Colombia but in its leading commercial partners as well. The explanations of business enterprise or scientific creativity in terms of toilet training remain wildly implausible, but such a factor might have something to do with the desire to deface the language with distasteful excrescences.

No doubt many critics of sociology are prompted by an obscurantist prejudice against systematic study of human affairs. Moreover, there is sometimes a need for a new term (and in my *Uses of Comparative Sociology* I have tried to specify the conditions which make a neologism justifiable); but it is quite clear that the fashionable sociological jargon consists almost entirely of distasteful and confusing verbal innovations which represent no new ideas whatsoever.

On the other hand, there are some good terminological innovations. Reisman's 'inner-directed' and 'other-directed man', for instance, are very good terms because they point to an important phenomenon, cannot be replaced by any previously existing word and (though vaguely self-explanatory) need a fairly long statement to explain their meaning exactly.

To prove to myself that I too can make such discoveries, and that my opposition to this kind of thing is not motivated by impotent envy, I have written the following report which was published in one of the sociological periodicals. To make this piece comprehensible I must explain that in addition to our old friend 'n Ach', the equally ungrammatical 'n Aff' stands for 'need affiliation' or, more grammatically, the need to affiliate – that is to belong to a group – the human characteristic known since time immemorial as sociability. 'N. Bam' is my own addition, the meaning of which you are invited to guess.

In connection with David McClelland's article it might be relevant to report that the preliminary results of our research project into the encoding processes in communication flow indicate that (owing to their multiplex permutations) it is difficult to ascertain direct correlates of 'n Aff'. On the other hand, when on the encephalogram 'dy' divided by 'dx' is less than 'O', 'n Ach' attains a significantly high positive correlation with 'n Bam', notwithstanding the partially stochastic nature of the connection between these two variables.

After the publication of this letter I was approached by some industrial research organisations who offered co-operation. Perhaps you would like to try to decipher what my letter says: then you can compare it with my own translation into plain English, printed upside-down below:

Owing to the waywardness of human nature, it is difficult to find out why people join a given group, but observation of how people speak and write clearly suggests that, when the brain is slowing down, a desire to achieve often gives rise to a need to bamboozle.

The article to which I referred in my letter supplied one or more of the innumerable instances of that ever-popular kind of explanation which consists of a tautological rephrasing which tells us nothing that we did not understand before. An explanation which Molière ridiculed three hundred years ago in one of his plays, where one of the characters answers the question about why opium makes people sleep by saying that it is because of its soporific power. In historiography and the social sciences this kind of explanation crops up again and again. Thus, to take an example of a great scholar who luckily did not confine himself to this, Werner Sombart attributed the development of capitalism to the spread of 'the spirit of capitalism', without telling us how we could find out that this spirit was spreading except by observing activities which add up to the process known as the development of capitalism.

The 'n Ach' business is in the same vein, except that it is not accompanied by the wealth of other interesting ideas and data which we can find in Sombart's tomes. It has a long genealogy in all kinds of writings purporting to explain the differences in economic and scientific progress between the East and the West by attributing to the Westerners a gift or an inclination in these directions and the lack of it to the Orientals. However, even the racialist Gobineau did not go to the length of imagining that the benighted Orientals did not want to achieve anything at all. In reality no tribe, nation, creed or race has been seen so far about whom we could say that they generally lack the desire to achieve. The Negro truant whom the test-obsessed American educational psychologists find lacking in the 'need to achieve' may care nothing about scholastic achievement, but will make great efforts to attain a respected position in his gang through achievements (such as gambling, womanizing or robbery) which rule out good scholastic performance. Far removed from the spirit of capitalist enterprise, the monks and hermits of old tried to achieve holiness and salvation: goals which often led to bitter rivalries about who was the humblest. The American Indian warriors had no knowledge of money, but had a great desire for achievement as measured by the number of scalps; while the hidalgo depicted by Cervantes had neither skill nor taste for accumulating capital, but strove madly to maintain his dignity and to achieve fame.

The crucial question always is not the presence or absence of the desire to achieve, but the problem of why, in a given society, this desire is canalized towards one goal rather than another. To explain India's poverty by attributing to the Hindus a lack of the desire to achieve reveals ethnocentric blinkers, firstly because (as I have tried to show in *African Predicament* and *Parasitism and Subversion*) under certain circumstances 'the spirit of enterprise' may call forth behaviour which impedes economic progress; and secondly because, even if the entire population of India consisted of fakirs, this would prove not that they lack the desire to achieve but merely that they are pursuing goals which do not appeal to an ordinary American or European. If Murray, McClelland, Hagen or any of their followers doubt this, I challenge them to have a try at one of the fakir's lesser achievements such as lying on a bed of nails.

The constant recourse to the letter 'n' helps to *cash in* on the prestige of mathematics, which seems to be the only ground for replacing 'desire' by 'need', which lends itself to this impressive abbreviation. As anybody with a mind undamaged by negative education knows, people often desire what they do not need, and what may even do them harm (such as an excessive accumulation of wealth or excessive consumption of food), while needing what they do not desire: for instance, unpolluted air or fair criticism. The grammatically more correct but equally obtuse expression 'need reduction', so beloved by the psychologists of late, means the same thing as 'satisfying the desire'; and though there is little danger of grave ambiguity when we are experimenting on a rat's reaction to the withholding of food, the term acts as a vision-distorting piece of mumbo-jumbo when we talk about (often unquenchable) human propensities such as ambition. Here we have another example of pseudo-scientific jargon being much less discerning than the literary language in which 'reducing a need' does not mean the same as 'satisfying it'. When we say that so-and-so has reduced his need for sleeping pills (e.g. by changing his habits or diet, or moving to a quieter place) we imply that he can now satisfy his need with fewer pills. A need thus reduced may remain unsatisfied if he can obtain no pills, while an 'un-reduced' one may be perfectly satisfied if he can get enough of them.

Equal lack of discernment underlies the use of the term 'reinforcement', which in the psychological jargon has replaced the word 'incentive' in the wide sense of the word, which covers positive incentives (that is, rewards) and negative incentives (that is, punishments). As is always the case with jargon, this substitution confuses the issues instead of clarifying them because, whereas 'incentive', 'reward', 'punishment', and 'deterrent' refer only to the manipulation of motivation of some human beings by others, or of higher animals by men, the word 'reinforcement' is much vaguer, as it can be applied to military operations, building techniques or the manner of advancing arguments in a debate. Moreover, this usage in psychology does violence to the meaning of the prefix 're-', which obliges us to restrict the connotation of 'reinforcement' to the acts of making stronger something that already has some force, rather than use it to cover situations where incentives are instituted in order to induce certain individuals to act in a way for which they had no antecedent inclination. When, for example, I set up a business and induce people to enter my employment by offers of wages, I am not reinforcing their tendency to work for me, but creating it. The same is true even of animals: when by an ingenious application of rewards and punishments Skinner taught pigeons to play ball, he could only reinforce their inclination in that direction after he had instilled it into them. What he was doing at the beginning when he was furnishing or withholding food might be called applying incentives but not reinforcements.

The problem of how to control the behaviour of men and animals through punishments and rewards has been treated in innumerable treatises on penology, legislation, education, management and animal training, beginning with the works of Aristotle and Confucius, not to speak of countless proverbs and adages. To say something important and new on this subject is always possible but very difficult. But one piece of pseudo-scientific terminology can confuse and intimidate people into accepting as a significant discovery an over-simplified (and therefore less valid) version of old folk wisdom.

Although it originated in America, the disease of jargon has spread far and wide, aided by the European academics' desire to make friends with rich Americans. Anyway, owing to the strength of the human tendency to imitate, even quite intelligent people will accept the crassest nonsense once a collective folly sets in – particularly if they are anxious to be 'with it'.

In the halls of the schools of swordsmanship in old Japan, they used to have inscriptions 'Do not think. Thinking makes cowards'. Although they would not go so far as to write it out, the motto of today's academic sheep seems likewise to be: 'Do not think. Thinking will make you unpopular at the next annual meeting of your Pseudological Society'.

To forestall the impression that I am picking on American writers for some ulterior political reason, I must emphasize that Europeans are quite capable of emulating (and surpassing) the worst American examples. Inspired by the founding masters,

Merleau-Ponty in philosophy and Gurvitch in sociology, a proliferating breed of literary contortionists has sprung up in France, who, by fusing a pot-pourri marxism with the worst excrescences of the Germano-American jargon, have broken the Boston supremacy and have made Paris into the most productive centre of mumbo-jumbo, often packaged under the labels of existentialism and structuralism. Even without enquiring into the nature of the contents, these labels alone should arouse suspicion because they are so meaningless. Obviously we exist; things exist, and everything that exists must have a structure. It has hitherto been regarded as too obvious to call for elaborate comment that all the sciences have been, and are, studying the structures of the objects of their interest; and the sole innovation of 'structuralism' is a tireless persistence in repeating this word, which can be regarded either as a gimmick or a compulsive neurosis. However, to avoid the difficult task of translating passages which resemble writings by schizophrenics, I shall forego an attempt to give you a sample of what passes for philosophy, sociology, psychology, linguistics and even historiography in the homeland of Descartes and Voltaire. Instead, let me give you a milder example made in Britain: the book by J. P. Nettl and Roland Robertson, called *International Systems and the Modernization of Societies*. It consists of three essays: 'Modernization, Industrialization or Development', 'The Inheritance Situation', and 'Modernization and International Systems'. According to the authors . . . 'They are neither the product of any specific research, nor are they individual think-pieces. Instead they result from a great deal of informal discussion between two authors who were for some time colleagues in the Department of Social Studies at the University of Leeds'. (p. 7.) A Columbia professor, Amitai Etzioni, who has provided an introduction, adds pompously that . . . 'The authors of the present book make several significant contributions toward a theory of societal guidance' (p. 15) and . . . 'the discussion of industrialization and modernization – which occupies much of the following pages – extends the foundations for a theory of societal guidance as these two are central societal processes through which efforts at guidance are largely channelled.' (p. 16.) 'Societal guidance', incidentally, is a euphemism for 'planning' – which word excites the ire of American business-men except when applied to their own activities.

The purpose of the work is to clarify some basic concepts, but the tortuous style produces an exactly opposite result. It would be difficult to find a more muddled piece of writing than the following passages in which the authors indicate the scope of their book:

... Our major concern is to deal with the relationship between concept and referent. In other words our discussion of concepts having to do with processes and patterns of social, especially societal, change hinges largely on the motivation to analyse in an *ostensive* and *real*, as opposed to a *nominal*, manner. We want to point up the pressing need for a greater interest in the phenomenal variables to which the three major as well as other associated concepts refer. (p. 17.)

and

A scheme for the analytical breakdown of individual societies into functional sub-systems has been evolved by Parsons, Smelser and others. This basically consists in the categorization of aspects of social interaction in terms of the four functional exigencies with which, it is postulated, all viable social systems must cope. We propose to utilize the notion of functionally specific sub-systems, including the idea that one of the four will tend to manifest primacy and greater situational relevance at particular times. ... We are here concerned primarily with the implications of the phase model for so-called twentieth centuries. The evidence of primacy or emphasis or relevance is of course rather sketchy and inconclusive: especially in respect of the actual societal, as opposed to the merely social-scientific, preoccupations. In emphasizing the link between primacy or interest or attention in the writings of social scientists or philosophers, and the paramountcy of functional emphasis in the societies about which they wrote, we believe that indications of any such focus among the former at least partially reflect evidence of corresponding paramountcy in the latter – allowing, of course, for the previously mentioned possibility of professional-scientific autonomy sustaining an academic style beyond the terminal point of its 'real' relevance. This quite basic postulate, which in itself makes no assumptions about cause and effect, but only about correlation, probably applies more accurately to the past than to the present – *when the sheer quantity of social research makes the identification* of primacy of concern with functional paramountcy more difficult. (p. 21)

3*

Even the more coherent pages exhibit a scholastic mentality in comparison with which the Hindu theologians appear as paragons of matter-of-fact rationalism. Thus, for instance, one would think that the word 'modernization', being a common-sense rather than a scientific label for the process of adopting recently invented methods and gadgets, calls for no lengthy exegesis. Nonetheless the authors devote fifteen pages to contemplating its meaning, and at the end come up with the following definition: ('Atimic status' or 'atimia', incidentally, is a scientific term for being behind the times)

Thus our conceptualization of modernization runs as follows: Modernization is the process whereby national elites seek successfully to reduce their *atimic* status and move towards equivalence with other 'well-placed' nations. The goal of equivalence is not a fixed but a moving 'target'; and the perception of it will depend both on the values and exigencies in the international system and on the values, dispositions and capabilities of the nation in question, as experienced particularly by national elites. Although the international system is the focal point of our analysis, we do not wish to impose a teleology on the international system. Rather, we have viewed the international system as one 'where (nearly) everybody's values and objectives are (usually) formulated in relation to somebody else's', and where the choice of technological objects for acquisition and use is also based on a widely diffused 'pool' of knowledge, and a high degree of selectivity in relation to varying definitions of modernity.

(pp. 56–57)

Having been initiated into these semantic mysteries we come to Part II, called *The Inheritance Situation: A Model of the Formation of Actor Orientations in the Third World* where, taking a common-place metaphor literally, the authors search for equivalents between inheritance of wealth from one individual to another and the transition from colonial rule to independence. The most curious feature of this disquisition is that, despite their claim to have incorporated Marx into their system, the authors refer to the former rulers as 'the benefactors' and to the new states as 'the beneficiaries'.

At the end of the book we get a summing-up. If you wish to find an explanation of what is happening in the Congo or

Venezuela or whatever the place might be, you must behold the mandala below, bearing in mind that 'from being embedded in pattern-maintenance and tension-management structures (L) other more specialized structural forms become separated out relative to integrative functions (I) then political functions (G) and finally adaptive (principally economic) functions (A) as the social system "develops"' (p. 146). If you are mystified, try a freudian interpretation of its meaning.

Structure of International G-System
(Goal-Commitment; Goal Attainment)

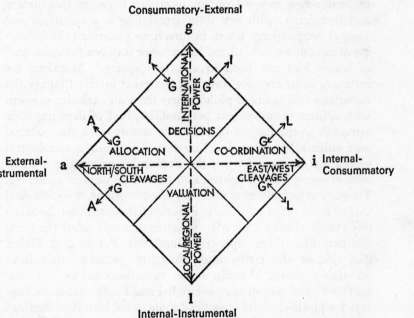

With a further 'categorization of international objects of orientation' and 'a reduction of atimia', this scheme could become almost as helpful for 'societal guidance' as the prophecies of Nostradamus.

To insure an international coverage for our little sample of the inexhaustible flora of pseudo-scientific phraseology let us look at an example which comes from the pen of an author of unimpeachable Third World origin, and who is a programme director at the United Nations Research Institute for Social Development: *Subversion and Social Change in Colombia*, by Orlando Fals Borda (Columbia University Press, 1969). Though one would hardly guess it from the title, the book is a kind of history of Colombia from the precolonial until our times. As the author is a professor of sociology, the book raises the problem of whether an acquaintance with the dominant currents of today's sociological theory helps to understand the past.

As in other fields, all the significant advances in historical understanding depend on an interplay between fact-finding and theorizing: with new data stimulating new questions and general propositions, which in turn have prompted the gathering of data of a new kind, the importance (or even the existence) of which had not been previously suspected. Marxism, for instance, in its creative days had the great merit of jolting the historians and political philosophers from an exclusive concern with actions of prominent personalities, and of drawing their attention to the impact of economic factors upon the political and cultural phenomena. Likewise, Durkheim's sociological school has impressed upon the French historians the need to look at every item of culture as a part of an organic structure. To open genuinely new vistas for the historians, a sociological theory must point to hitherto unsuspected connections between observable classes of events – which is precisely what the great theorists like Marx, Spencer, Durkheim, Pareto and Weber did, despite the errors into which, as pioneers, they have inevitably fallen. Among other contributions to full employment, the output of new-fangled and flashy verbal packagings for platitudes and inanities has included historical writings which pretend to shed a new light on the past by couching well-known information in incomprehensible jargon.

Fals Borda's book contains no data which cannot be found better presented in standard works on Colombian or general Latin American history; its only distinction consisting of a pretentious and obfuscating terminology. For example, it is no news that the conquest and conversion of the Indians produced a new social order; which piece of information is dressed up by labelling this change as a 'dialectical refraction', its agents as 'disorgans' and 'conditioners', the new faith as 'prescriptively rigid countervalues', the new moral code as 'acritical counter-norms', the old tribal structure as 'topia nr 1', and the succeeding seignorial society as 'topia nr 2'. 'Topia', incidentally, means a social system which has existed or exists, as opposed to a utopia. Since, in Fals Borda's vocabulary, 'subversion' means bringing about a change in society, the title of the book is pleonastic; and the word 'subversion' merely rouses in vain the reader's expectations of gleaning inside information about some sinister machinations.

Pleonasm, however, is a very minor offence in comparison with the mental fog exuded by the mixture of watered-down marxism with a patchy parsonianism. It should, however, have a soothing effect in the high circles of the international 'cultural' bureaucracy, where one must be diplomatic and show good will towards both superpowers. What capitalist will not be cheered when he hears that, instead of a bloody revolution, he will only experience an instrumentalization of counter-values and counter-norms of topia nr 5 by counter-élite reference groups?

One of the most effective sales campaigns of recent times was set in motion around the works of Marshall MacLuhan, 'hired' (as the Americans say) at the time by the Jesuit-run Fordham University in New York, at a fabulous and duly publicized salary. A well-concerted chorus of critics greeted MacLuhan's volumes as the greatest revelation of recent times, some comparing him to Freud, others (more modestly) to Arnold J. Toynbee. Even the latter, however, could not have read *The Study of History*, or they would not be putting it into the same category with Marshall MacLuhan's flights of fancy. Analysed from the viewpoint of logic and scientific method, Toynbee's theories can be shown to be vague, unsubstantiated and tautological, but his books are full of recondite factual information, and merit respect as products of serious scholarship. They embody an immense amount of work, and bear no resemblance to the linguistic contortions of an author who openly proclaims his rejection of logic and declares his contempt not only for orderly argument but even grammar. Answering one of his critics on the pages of *The Listener*, MacLuhan says: 'Miller's confusion begins with his assumption that I have "notions" and theories, concepts rather than percepts.' Toynbee's comparisons and confrontations may not prove his general points, and may appear superficial in comparison with the analytical and comparative sociologists such as Herbert Spencer and Max Weber, but they are seldom without interest, are often suggestive and sometimes illuminating. In contrast, MacLuhan's thesis (not to speak of subsidiary foibles) that under the influence of television human beings are becoming less 'visual' and more 'audio-tactile' is completely gratuitous, to put it mildly. When people look at television instead of reading books they certainly do not become less visual – they are still using their eyes just as much. In fact one could say that their perceptions become less symbolic and more visual. Nor is there a shred of evidence that before television, transistors and piped music, people were using their ears less than they are now – only they were listening to their companions or live music or natural sounds instead of the box. The final absurdity is the claim that the telly gapers' tactile impressions are more intense than those of the previous generations. How and where? Certainly neither in their hands nor feet. The only possible place is the buttocks. Nonetheless, MacLuhan does manage to insert into his flood of free association a few snappy phrases which hit the nail on the head (such as that the medium is the message or the massage of the brain, or that more important than the question of whether there is life after death is nowadays the question whether there is life before death), which is more than his more 'scientific' compeers manage to do. On the other hand, statements (which are meant to be more serious) such that television has turned the world into a 'global village' are slick but hyperbolic and nonsensical metaphors.

One of the most common examples of a boring fad is the predilection for the word 'feedback', which (outside its proper technical context) usually merely replaces more precise words like 'report' or 'reaction'. Equally laughable – and illogical too – are the nouns 'in-group' and 'out-group'; because the words 'in' and 'out' have no meaning without a specification (which may be left tacit if sufficiently self-evident) of the entity to which they are supposed to refer. There is no point in speaking about 'in-pencils' and 'out-pencils', unless these prefixes refer to a position in relation to some bounded space such as a drawer. Colloquially (and, as always, metaphorically) we speak of 'insiders' and 'outsiders'; and if this is all that the expressions 'in-group' and 'out-group' mean, then they are completely superfluous. The latter, moreover, is in that case grossly misleading because there is no reason to assume that the outsiders must form one group, as they might have no connections with one another at all, or only through the insiders. The customers of a football pool agency form a logical category, but not a group in a sociological sense because they do not interact with one another. For the same reason it would be equally misleading to call the non-members of a given group the 'out-group'. If we followed this convention we would have to count Mr Chou En Lai and the Emperor Haile Selassie as members of the Pangbourne College Chess Club's out-group, which would contravene all the definitions of the word 'group'.

If 'in-group' is supposed to connote the members of a given group, then it is utterly superfluous as well as confusing. If it is supposed to mean a group which has members as distinct from one which has not, then the expression is silly because we can only have an empty set in logic but there can be no human group without members. Only in the adjectival sense can these expressions be used with some justification, as when we speak of 'in-group attitudes' (meaning the attitudes towards the co-members) as opposed to 'out-group attitudes', that is attitudes towards non-members. Like the fad for replacing 'individual' or 'somebody' by 'actor', which we shall look at in a moment, the habit of adorning the noun 'group' with meaningless prefixes must be treated as a pseudo-scientific false pretence.

There are many other examples of verbal fads of this kind. No doubt owing to the militarization of science, the word 'strategy' came into fashion and replaced 'method' without any gain in discernment. On the contrary, as with most fads, this substitution has led to an impoverishment of the language because, instead of two words with distinct though overlapping meanings, only one is used indiscriminately – so indiscriminately indeed that people talk pleonastically about 'strategy of conflict', as if there could be a strategy which does not refer to a conflict.

One of the most futile fads centres round the word 'role' whose metaphorically sociological usage dates from the eighteenth century at the latest. Although this metaphor has by now become utterly commonplace, the suddenly developed addiction to repeating it interminably has been baptized as 'role theory'. This 'theory' consists of pompous, nebulous and incredibly lengthy re-statements of what has been common knowledge for a very long time; namely, that in every group the members play different roles which sometimes are complementary and sometimes contradictory; that sometimes individuals change or exchange their roles; that often one person acts in several roles which may be mutually reinforcing, but also may be incompatible; that a group can act effectively only if the roles of its members are in harmony. These platitudes can be equally well expressed without ever using the word 'role', which proves that this fad in no way leads to an improved understanding.

Perhaps the saying that 'every portrait is a self-portrait' might help to understand why, in the company of sociologists and psychologists, one hears the words 'role' and 'actor' as incessantly as the well-known four-letter words among soldiers. Why not 'individual' or 'person' or 'doer' rather than 'actor'? Bothered, maybe, by the gnawing doubt that their brand of science is a mere pretence, the addicts may be sub-consciously trying to protect their self-esteem by insinuating through their choice of words that all social life is mere play-acting. The plebeian taste of their verbal somersaults, however, calls for a further rephrasing in the shape of a replacement of the word 'actor' by 'clown'. Just get hold of a text on role theory and you will see that it makes a much better sense with the aid of this substitution.

Not that there is anything wrong with 'role', which is a perfectly useful word, provided we use it unpretentiously when needed instead of treating it as a magic incantation which opens up the Sesame of otherwise inaccessible knowledge. As a rule a good test of whether we are offered a new idea or merely a new way of talking is to see what happens when we use different words. In this case it is perfectly clear that, though quite convenient, 'role' can be replaced without any loss of meaning by other words such as 'position' or 'place'. There is no difference in meaning between 'his role in the group' and 'his place in the group', or 'his position in the group', all three terms being in fact metaphorical designations for the recurrent elements of human interaction. It would, of course, be possible to define these terms so as to give them slightly different connotations; but, instead of doing this, what the 'role theorists' have done is merely to provide eager aspirants to authorship with an opportunity for rephrasing the old commonsense knowledge in accordance with the new fashion.

Actually the only writer who made a good use of the concept of role, and has succeeded in saying something beyond the obvious, is Ervin Goffman, who takes it in the least metaphoric sense, most closely adhering to the theatrical use, and looks at social relations as repeated encounters in which each person 'shoots a line' or 'plays up', attempting (deliberately or automatically) to foist upon his interlocutors the desired image of himself, thus paralleling an actor's efforts to convey to the audience the picture of the character he is playing. Although this approach has brought forth no great revelations so far, it has enabled Goffman to make useful contributions to knowledge and to write a number of books which contrast very favourably with the arid scholasticism of 'role theory'.

The tendency to seize upon and labour *ad nauseam* the most trivial points, covering up banality by obscure and pompous jargon, is well exemplified by the famous theory of social action. Weber's muddled classification of social actions into types such as *Wertrational* and *Zweckrational* played no part whatsoever in his substantive explanatory theories; nevertheless, it was adopted by Talcott Parsons as the foundation stone of his own system, in preference to Weber's more substantial comparative studies. In *Structure of Social Action*, Parsons devotes about six hundred pages to showing that the chief merit of Alfred Marshall, Weber, Pareto and Durkheim was that they pointed the way towards 'the voluntaristic theory of action' finally formulated by him. Translated from the tenebrous language in which it is couched, this theory amounts to saying that in order to understand why people act as they do, we must take into account their wishes and decisions, the means at their disposal, and their beliefs about how the desired effects can be produced.

The emergence of this piece of knowledge amounted, no doubt, to an important step in the mental development of mankind, but it must have occurred some time during the Paleolithic Age, as Homer and the Biblical prophets knew all about it. True, none of the writers treated in Parsons' book has made any explicit statements to this effect, but this was not because they did not know about it but because they took it for granted that no sane reader needed to be told about such an obvious thing. Nor did they specify other equally important pre-requisites of social action, such that people can remember, communicate, reason and move – which does not mean that the world must wait for another Harvard professor to discover this.

The attraction of jargon and obfuscating convolutions can be fully explained by the normal striving of humans for emoluments and prestige at the least cost to themselves, the cost in question consisting of the mental effort and the danger of 'sticking one's neck out' or 'putting one's foot in it'. In addition to eliminating such risks, as well as the need to learn much, nebulous verbosity opens a road to the most prestigious academic posts to people of small intelligence whose limitations would stand naked if they had to state what they have to say clearly and succinctly. Actually, the relationship between the character of a jargon-mongerer and the amount of his verbiage can be expressed in the formula below, which I propose to call The Equation of Jargon-Mongering, which can be applied in the following manner. The first step is to assign intuitively estimated scores for an author's ambition, designated by A, and to knowledge, designated by K (which must always be greater than O, as nobody knows exactly nothing). A must also be positive because, if somebody's literary ambition is nil, then he writes nothing, and there is nothing to apply our equation to. V stands for verbose jargon. Our equation then is

$$\frac{A}{K} - 1 = V$$

Why −1? Because when the knowledge matches the ambition, there is no verbiage. When knowledge exceeds the ambition V becomes negative; and negative verbiage amounts to conciseness. However, since there is a limit to conciseness, V can never become less than −1; whereas there is no limit to verbiage, and so V increases indefinitely as ambition grows, while knowledge vanishes.

Our formula cannot, of course, be treated as exact until measurable indices are devised for the variables, and then checked against empirical data. I do believe, however, that it is approximately true, and I invite readers to try it on the authors they read as well as on their colleagues, teachers or students. Its predictive and explanatory power is roughly the same as that of most theorems of mathematical economics. The advantage of our formula is that it explains the behaviour of many different kinds of people, ranging from an undergraduate who is trying to scrape through a dissertation without having learned anything, to a scholar with a fairly extensive knowledge but devoured by a craving for greatness.

Leaving aside the economists, the only European who can compete with the top American pundits in influence and fame is Claude Lévi-Strauss – a man of impressive knowledge and brain power whose first major work – *Les Structures Elémentaires de la Parenté*, published in 1949 – constituted a valiant attempt to provide a unified explanation of the workings of a large number of variegated kinship systems, based on an extensive survey of data and a highly ingenious theoretical scheme. This volume was to be followed by another where the remaining kinship systems of the world would be analysed with the aid of a similar circulatory model. Unfortunately, however, certain awkward factual data were shown to contradict his theory – which incidentally proves that it was no mere tautology but a truly inductive generalization. Lévi-Strauss could perhaps have saved his thesis by examining possible limiting factors, and by restricting the applicability of his model to a subclass of systems which the existing version encompasses. Had he tried that and succeeded he would have converted his valuable but tentative interpretation into a solid contribution to knowledge, but he would have had to renounce his claim to having discovered a universal master key. The feat would have been praiseworthy, but insufficiently far-reaching to form a title to true greatness. Maybe he is still trying to do it, but insofar as one can judge from what has appeared in print, he has changed course rather drastically. Abandoning the clarity of his earlier work, he began to spin out speculations sufficiently vague to be safe from the danger of a confrontation with awkward facts, where undigested bits of mathematics and linguistics are juxtaposed with an unordered array of bits of ethnography, seasoned with marxism à la mode and served with that coffeehouse philosophy known as existentialism. Although the product resembles in many of its parts some kind of surrealist poetry, it is linked with the movement known as structuralism which claims to be some kind of super science, or a quintessence of all the sciences, in the sense of having found the most fundamental ingredients of them all – which discovery boils down in fact to nebulous and tirelessly repetitive affirmations of the unsurprising finding that everything has a structure, adorned by constant invocations of this sacred word in its various transsubstantiations ending with 'ed', 'ing', and, of course, 'tion'. As an account of the ways of thinking of pre-literate peoples Lévi-Strauss's *La Pensée Sauvage* is a great deal more defective than Lévi-Bruhl's thesis that primitive people cannot think logically, expounded in several books written at the beginning of the century, one of which was translated into English with the title, *How Natives Think*. Nonetheless, Lévi-Strauss has become a great guru, a status which no-one in the social sciences (not even Keynes) could achieve, along the hard road of clear and realistic reasoning.

When stripped of the embellishing stylistic pyrotechnics, his theories about the primitive (or, as he calls it sensationally, 'savage') thought process boil down to an alchemical synthesis of Lévi-Bruhl's theory of pre-logical mentality, with Bastian's century-old concept of *Elementargedanke* (a kind of universal basic ingredient of all belief systems), and Jung's notion of archetypes, couched in abstruse terminology taken from linguistics. Nevertheless, in keeping with what remains in him of the old gallic 'esprit', and in contrast to the stodgy teutonic emetics of the parsonians, his writings about myths narrate many captivating stories which, together with his clever crossword or pun-like comments, supply a most suitable material for smart table talk. Apart from the advantages accruing from praying ardently to Marx, a facility for startling and often entertaining play upon words, suitable for a salon, accounts no doubt for much of Lévi-Strauss's celebrity, although (as we shall see later) equally effective in this respect must be his highly original technique of persuasion (reminiscent of a sorcerer's spell-casting) based on threatening people with mathematics: muttering darkly about algebraic matrices and transformations without revealing their exact nature.

The usage of mumbo-jumbo makes it very difficult for a beginner to find his way; because if he reads or hears famous professors from the most prestigious universities in the world without being able to understand them, then how can he know whether this is due to his lack of intelligence or preparation, or to their vacuity? The readiness to assume that everything that one does not understand must be nonsense cannot fail to condemn one to eternal ignorance; and consequently, the last thing I would wish to do is to give encouragement to lazy dim-wits who gravitate towards the humanistic and social studies as a soft option, and who are always on the lookout for an excuse for not working. So it is tragic that the professorial jargon-mongers have provided such loafers with good grounds for indulging in their proclivities. But how can a serious beginner find his way through the verbal smog and be able to assess the trustworthiness of high ranking academics?

Addressing myself to such readers, I would suggest that the only way of going about it is, firstly, to test your brain power on texts falling within a field where there is little room for bluff, and which are intellectually demanding without requiring extensive specialist knowledge: namely the less technical books on the philosophy of the natural sciences, such as P. W. Bridgman's *Logic of Modern Physics*, or Rudolf Carnap's *Philosophical Foundation of Physics*, or Bertrand Russell's *Introduction to Mathematical Philosophy*, or J. H. Woodger's *Biological Principles* – to mention just a few among many eligible titles. Now, if despite a serious effort – and remember that these are not bedside books, and require concentration and persistence – you cannot understand them, then keep away from high-powered theories and do not attempt to produce anything very abstract yourself. Be honest and adjust your aims to your abilities. There are many areas of sociology, anthropology, political science, psychology and economics where useful work can be done without recourse to high-powered abstractions, many areas where common sense coupled with a good range of factual information suffices. However, if you have mastered a number of books such as those just mentioned and despite having made a decent effort, still cannot understand what some sociological or politological or psychological luminary has written or said, then you can legitimately presume that it is his fault rather than yours, and justifiably suspect that it might all be nonsense.

If you happen to be a student, you can apply the same test to your teachers who claim that what they are teaching you rests upon incontrovertible scientific foundations. See what they know about the natural sciences and mathematics and their philosophical foundations. Naturally, you cannot expect them to have a specialist knowledge of these fields; but if they are completely ignorant of these things, do not take seriously grandiloquent claims of the ultra-scientific character of their teachings. Furthermore, do not be impressed unduly by titles or positions. Top universities can usually get the best people in the fields where there are firm criteria of achievement; but at the present stage of development of the social sciences the process of selection resembles, as often as not, a singing competition before a deaf jury who can judge the competitors only by how wide they open their mouths.

For the same reason do not be impressed by the imprint of a famous publishing house or the volume of an author's publications. Bear in mind that Einstein needed only seventeen pages for his contribution which revolutionized physics, while there are graphomaniacs in asylums who use up mounds of paper every day. Remember that the publishers want to keep the printing presses busy and do not object to nonsense if it can be sold. As my grandmother used to say, paper is patient.

Unless restrained by sales resistance, to use an appropriately commercial expression, all sellers can gain by diluting their wares. We have all seen how increasingly flashy packaging usually accompanies a deterioration in the quality of the contents – which is happening not only with foodstuffs but with books as well, especially since the publishing houses began to fall under the control of large trusts whose executives must prove their worth in cash, and cannot let themselves be unduly influenced by ethical or aesthetic considerations. In a mercenary climate of opinion, unpropitious to a pride in craftsmanship, the academics follow those who show them how to spin out words, dilute the content, and wrap it all in an impressive package of pseudo-scientific pomposity; and hound the rate-busters who write too concisely.

In strict logic an *argumentum ad hominem* cannot impugn the value of a statement, but a judge always takes the witnesses' probable motives into account. It may be said that this is irrelevant because a judge has to make a decision as to whom to trust, whereas in science everything is above suspicion. Unfortunately, however, even in the exact sciences cases of fraud have been noted, while in subjects where we cannot check the information by repeating an experiment much has to be taken on trust. A historian assessing the reliability of his sources will try to ascertain the interests and the character of their authors; and the purportedly scientific studies of contemporary situations must be approached with equal caution.

In this connection I should like to suggest that his sense of humour is a fair indicator of a social scientist's value as an observer of human affairs, provided he is not plainly dishonest or lazy and careless. True, the case of Newton and many other examples suggest that in mathematics and the natural sciences this quality may be irrelevant; while even in the study of man such outstanding thinkers as Marx, Schopenhauer and Auguste Comte have lacked it, and were inclined to take themselves very seriously. They combined, however, great originality and profundity with doctrinaire delusions; but, although Max Weber also appears to have been humourless, his judgments on the march of events have been very sober. Nonetheless, I believe that, by and large, there is a connection between a sense of humour and the ability to judge social situations realistically; and I would explain it as follows.

The world never conforms to all our wishes, and nobody can enjoy uninterrupted happiness. Even those who are fairly satisfied with their lot know about the certainty of death and the threats of bereavement, illness and other misfortunes, and are aware of the tragic fate of so many of their fellows, and the sufferings of animals. There is a saying that you can tell a pessimist from an optimist by the fact that when both have drunk half a bottle the pessimist will feel sad that there is only half a bottle left, while the optimist will feel pleased that there is still half a bottle left. The same applies to life in general; and a tendency to dwell upon the pleasant rather than unpleasant aspects of existence is indispensable to happiness or even mental health. However, even those who are not temperamentally inclined to gloomy ruminations have to perceive more unhappiness and evil than they would like to see. They can stave off despondency in two ways: either by deluding themselves that the world is a better place than it is, or by finding its imperfections, as well as their own misfortunes and weaknesses, a bit funny. In other words, laughter is a mental mechanism which enables us to face reality without falling into despondency or delusion. As people who have sunk into apathy seldom bother us by rushing into print, delusion (leaving aside deceit) constitutes the chief obstacle to the progress of our understanding of society, and in this context it usually assumes the form of doctrinairism couched in a mystifying jargon. A sense of humour is the most reliable external indicator of the likelihood of immunity from this folly, and of the ability to appraise social situations realistically.

Chapter 7

The Uses of Absurdity

Even a most cursory survey of human beliefs reveals that man has no innate inclination to seek the truth; and that absurdity and obscurity, far from repelling, have for most people an irresistible attraction. As we shall see in a moment, there are several reasons for this proclivity, but the most general of them is that clarity and logic impose upon our thinking severe constraints which prevent it from wholeheartedly ministering to our desires, hates and whims. To speak in the inexact but evocative freudian terms, logic and clarity are the guardians of the Reality Principle which prevent the flow of our ideas from following the Pleasure Principle, while the latter guides us towards the maximization of mental comfort through believing what we would like to be true, regardless of whether this is in fact the case.

Our pursuit of the Pleasure Principle would have no bounds if we had no need for correct information about the workings of our environment which would enable us to manipulate it in order to satisfy our desires. The extent to which our minds will have to abandon the Pleasure Principle for the sake of the Reality Principle will depend on how hard and immediate are the penalties which reality inflicts upon us for harbouring false notions about it. The immediacy and magnitude of this retribution will depend on whether the success of our practical undertakings depends on the correctness of our views. It will seldom be profitable to hold unwarranted opinions about currents and the rocks when we are sailing, whereas the most absurd views about philosophy can be entertained indefinitely with perfect impunity.

One of the pleasures obtainable through recourse to confusion and absurdity is to be able to feel, and publicly to claim, that one knows when in reality one does not. Closely connected with this advantage is the use of absurdity and confusion as shields for protecting the incumbents of authority, who enjoy no natural superiority of talent or knowledge: for clear and logical thinking is like a game with definite and ascertainable rules, in which any ragged fellow can challenge and may defeat the Master, while in the realm of confusion and absurdity there are no rules of the game which would justify the Master's demotion and a refutal of What He Hath Said.

Confusion and absurdity protect established authority from being disturbed by the effects of its divergence from a natural ranking of talent and skill, just as clothes protect a hierarchy from the subversive effects of nudity; for in a naked crowd nobody can tell who is the Field Marshal or Archbishop.

So long as authority inspires awe, confusion and absurdity enhance conservative tendencies in society. Firstly, because clear and logical thinking leads to a cumulation of knowledge (of which the progress of the natural sciences provides the best example) and the advance of knowledge sooner or later undermines the traditional order. Confused thinking, on the other hand, leads nowhere in particular and can be indulged indefinitely without producing any impact upon the world. In other words, it is intrinsically static; and this characteristic is connected with its ability to act as a cement for social groupings.

We have a tendency to like those who are like us, and to dislike the unlike, unless a difference permits an exchange of some kind (be it of goods, information or sexual gratification). This ubiquitous propensity (which can be found among animals as well as humans) has been called 'consciousness of kind' by Frank Giddings, while Gaston Bouthoil has proposed the term 'heterophobia' for its negative counterpart. We cannot, unfortunately, replace the rather awkward 'consciousness of kind' by its Greek equivalent 'homophilia' because this word has been appropriated for designating homosexuality.

Lest any reader condemn all forms of heterophobia as an irrational atavism, I must stress that a certain amount of it constitutes an indispensable ingredient of social life, which would become impossible if we could make no predictions about our fellows' behaviour, as would be the case without a minimum of conformity. Even more: the very possibility of communication rests upon what we have in common with other people, and without conformity enforced by heterophobia there could be no language. Original thoughts can be understood only in virtue of the unoriginal elements which they contain, and total originality would be useless (were it possible) because it could be communicated to nobody.

Nonetheless, even a small dose of original thinking sets the cogitator apart from most mankind, and makes it more difficult for him to satisfy the gregarious propensity of a normal human being. A prophet remains an outcast until he makes converts, and he may lose them if he persists in the habit of innovation and attempts to recast his doctrine. This seldom happens because (even apart from the difficulty of begetting new ideas), chastened by his sufferings while beyond the pale, the prophet savours the pleasures of having admiring disciples at last, and devotes the remainder of his energies to setting up a School with its new, but not necessarily less rigid, tenets.

Beliefs held in common unite, while controversies divide. And as logical thinking leads to discoveries, which of necessity entail a rejection of previously held (and often deeply cherished) opinions, it tends to disturb the harmony, which can remain perfect only so long as all members of the group continue to hold exactly the same beliefs. However, there is even more to it than that. As logic is a common property of mankind, which anyone can use regardless of where he comes from, it cannot be employed as a barrier which cuts off the insiders from the outsiders. In other words, a category of human beings distinguished by their recourse (and skill in) logical thinking must for ever remain open. An arbitrary dogma, in contrast, can and normally does cut off believers from other people; and the more absurd it is the better can it function as a barrier around a cohesive group. Non-conformity in respect of a belief normally entails a severance of social bonds, and this explains the remarkable longevity of utterly absurd dogmas. This applies not only to ecclesiastical bodies but also to the secular sects such as the freudians or the marxists. So long as they stick to the doctrine they will remain together, whereas once they begin to think independently they will go their separate ways, and an emotionally satisfying solidarity and common way of life will come to an end. If you belong to, say, the New Left where all your friends are, and you begin to suspect that Karl the Father and His Son Vladimir might have been only fallible men, then you must either suppress such blasphemous thoughts or face expulsion from your circle – perhaps without much hope of quickly finding an equally congenial company.

Sacrifice has always been regarded as the most convincing proof of loyalty; and its most common form involves a foregoing of the use of some organic function, as in the case of celibacy or fasting. Of at least equal significance, however, is a sacrifice of the use of reason – *credo quia impossibile* – and the more incredible the assertion, the stronger the proof of the devotion manifested by its acceptance. The Catholic theologians are quite explicit about this, and openly say that by affirming what to the human reason appears absurd, a believer proves his love for God. Although they are never so frank about it, the secular sects make similar demands.

While lending themselves as perfect material for barriers around closed groups, arbitrary and nonsensical beliefs do not discriminate against the majority not blessed with a high intelligence; whereas logic (and its applications, known as science) is available to anyone but only in the measure of his innate ability and hard-won knowledge – which means that it can appeal strongly only to a few.

The natural sciences did not advance in virtue of the universal appeal of rationality. Their theological, classicist and metaphysical opponents were not converted but displaced. All the ancient universities had to be compelled by outside pressure to make room for science; and most nations began to appreciate it only after succumbing to the weapons produced with its aid. To cut a long story short, scientific method has triumphed throughout the world because it bestowed upon those who practised it power over those who did not. Sorcery lost, not because of any waning of its intrinsic appeal to the human mind, but because it failed to match the power created by science. But, though abandoned as a tool for controlling nature, incantations remain more effective for manipulating crowds than logical arguments, so that in the conduct of human affairs sorcery continues to be stronger than science.

You only have to look at the language of politics to see the advantage of vagueness and obscurity in the struggle for popularity, where the secret of success lies in appearing to be on everybody's side, and to leave oneself a way out of any commitment which becomes embarrassing. An especially valuable asset is a doctrine which provides an outlet for wickedness in pursuit of a noble ideal; and all successful and enduring ideologies have to appeal to the base and the noble propensities of mankind at the same time – which can be done only under the cover of doctrinal obscurity. The same tendencies can be discerned in the history of the social sciences; with this addition, that here we also encounter a factor which grows in importance with the advance of professionalization: namely the desire to provide easily executed work for the members of the occupation. Now the easiest kind of work is an endless exegesis of widely known texts; and in this case vagueness and obscurity help to provide such work while clarity and conciseness curtail it. Any author who (like Hegel or Husserl) writes in a tenebrous and ponderous fashion, gives work to a large number of smaller fry who can busy themselves commenting on what he *really* meant; whereas a writer like David Hume or Bertrand Russell, who makes perfectly clear what he means, creates no such opportunities for mediocre intellectuals to make a living by endlessly going round in circles, and so is less likely to become a totem. The creators of mental fog are boosted into fame by the intellectuals to whose parasitic propensities they have ably ministered.

Chapter 8

Evasion in the Guise of Objectivity

The distinction between a judgment in fact and a judgment of value has become one of the corner stones of philosophy ever since Hume wrote his famous statement that 'reason is, and must always remain, the slave of the passions'. (For the sake of readers unacquainted with philosophic usage I must add that a judgment of fact may well be untrue. A confusion on this point may be avoided by couching the above distinction in terms less akin to colloquial language: namely, existential versus normative statements or propositions.) Though beset by the difficulties of application, due above all to the ubiquitous shading-off of concepts into one another, this distinction underlies the ideal of objectivity. In the development of the methodology of the social sciences it was put into the central place by Max Weber, and discussed ever since under the labels of ethical neutrality, non-valuation or *Wertfreiheit*.[1]

The entire discussion, however, refers to the semantic neutrality which is quite a different thing from practical neutrality. Let me make this definition clear.

In the abstract – from the viewpoint of philosophical semantics – what could be more ethically neutral, *wertfrei*, non-hortatory, non-valuative, call it what you will, than the question of how many people fall into which income bracket? Yet the statistics of income distribution can be regarded as highly inflammable material in a system which claims to have abolished inequality of classes. Even in a country where the discrepancy between the official line and reality does not loom so large, data on the distribution of wealth undergo a highly

1. As usual, Weber's point has been misrepresented by theorists unacquainted with logic. See on this point *The Uses of Comparative Sociology*, Chapter 5: 'Ideal Types, the Postulate of non-Valuation and *Die Verstehende Soziologie*'.

partisan vetting. When the Conservatives were ruling Britain the Labour Party writers produced a spate of studies arguing that the distribution of wealth was much more unequal than was generally believed, while the Conservatives were picking holes in this evidence. After the Labour Party's ascent to power, its intellectuals stopped belabouring this point; thus showing that from a practical standpoint such statistics are not quite neutral.

If somebody says that Oswald did not kill John Kennedy, he is making a statement which is perfectly neutral semantically, as there is nothing in the accepted meaning of any of the words composing this sentence which indicates that the speaker is either pleased or appalled by the act, or that he welcomes or regrets that it was not Oswald who did it. From a semantic standpoint you could not have a purer judgment of fact, more neutral ethically. Yet, as everybody knows, this is still one of the hottest issues of American politics; and such an utterance might expose the speaker to the wrath of people who hold an opposed opinion on this seemingly simple matter of fact. Though this could not be inferred from the meaning of the words alone, in the actual context of American politics the utterance in question impugns the honesty of the highest dignitaries of the United States, implies that tremendous power rests in the hands of conspiratorial groups, suggests that American democracy is (at least partly) a sham, and consequently brands the utterer as a subversionist, with all the practical consequences which such a label might entail.

Or take another example: what could be more neutral than population statistics? And yet a dispute about the census returns nearly led to a civil war in Nigeria early in 1964. The reason was that, as the party alignments followed regional lines, their relative strength depended on the size of the population of each region; and so each regional government tried to swell the count of its citizens by all kinds of tricks. At one moment during the dispute the Premier of the Eastern Region offered to accept the census if his region's count were raised by a million. Admittedly this was a rather extreme instance, but there are innumerable less unusual examples to the point.

Many millennia of intellectual progress had to elapse before anybody thought of looking at his society with detachment and an overriding concern for truth – that is to say, objectively. Even to-day, the spontaneous approach of anybody who has made no special effort to accustom himself to viewing his social environment, as it were, from the outside, remains emotional and manipulative; and the overwhelming majority of pronouncements on human affairs are made either for the sake of giving vent to emotions or influencing other people's behaviour. The latter aim can be achieved either by direct command, or by imbuing people with appropriate sentiments, or by instilling into them beliefs about the existing circumstances and causal relations between them which will induce them to behave in the way we want in order to satisfy their desires. Normally, when we speak about human conduct, we condemn or praise, persuade or promise, threaten or cajole; and to be willing and able to discuss social behaviour dispassionately, and without an immediate utilitarian aim in view, remains a hallmark of sophistication uncommon even today, and the first glimmerings of which appeared in the writings of Macchiavelli. The growth of our understanding of society has been inextricably interwoven with the spread of the ability to observe and analyse with detachment.

As might be expected, in view of what has just been said, the oldest disciplines concerned with human affairs – historiography and jurisprudence – supply the earliest examples of the two techniques of influencing human behaviour otherwise than by a direct application of the carrot or the stick: namely, indoctrination with certain attitudes through selective dissemination of information, and the smuggling in of judgments of value disguised as judgments of fact.

It is no discovery, of course, that law is the means of controlling conduct; that it consists of rules prescribing how people ought to behave and what the agents of the state ought to do under various circumstances – which covers civil law as well, as it is backed in the ultimate instance by the power of the state. Nor am I alluding to the obviously manipulative intent which prompts acts of legislation. No; what I have in mind are the methods of influencing behaviour by making people believe in non-existent entities, such as laws which have never been stated and which the judges have to 'find'. If we define law as a set of declarations about permissible, obligatory and prohibited

types of actions, then a moment's reflection suffices to realize
that no law can exist until somebody has enunciated it; and
what the judges are doing when they are engaged in 'finding'
the law is in fact creating it, even if it amounts merely to making
very subsidiary rules within an existing wider network. The
fiction that the law existed before it was declared enhances the
power of its makers by endowing their pronouncements with a
super-human aura. In the United States, for instance, this
kind of fiction has enabled the Supreme Court to produce
substantial changes in the political structure which would not
have been accepted except on the tacit assumption that the
newly-proclaimed rules had been ascertained rather than
created. That the new rules often appeared as inferences from
the pre-existing does not alter the issue because inferences do
not exist until they are made; and in any case legal exegesis
seldom assumes a strictly logical form.

In addition to legislation disguised as law finding, there is,
as already mentioned, the method of influencing behaviour
(apart from that of issuing commands) which consists of
inculcating tacitly a scale of values by propounding definitions
of such abstract concepts as the state, the family, a crime or
freedom. This method has been used as far back as historical
records go; one of the most striking instances being the Reception of the Roman law in early modern Europe, when the
'légistes' smoothed the way for absolutism and capitalism by
changing the prevalent ways of thinking about the law. (An
attempt to assess the causal importance of this phenomenon can
be found in *The Uses of Comparative Sociology*, Chapter 12 – Ideas
as Forces.) The manipulative capability of definitions current
today in the social sciences will be discussed at length in the
chapter on *Ideology Underneath Terminology*; but just to illustrate
how far this kind of thing can go, I shall mention one of the
crassest examples: namely, Hegel's definition of freedom as the
opportunity to obey the state. Treatises on political science or
theory of state were full of such hidden propaganda, though
usually in a slightly less crude form, and it was in order to get
away from this kind of impediment to the development of an
empirical science of society that Max Weber formulated his
canon of *Wertfreiheit*.

4

It was only under the impact of well-advanced physical sciences, as well as of the interest in strange customs awakened by geographical discoveries, that there began to appear historical works, inspired by the desire to understand rather than merely to sing the glory of princes and warriors. As with medicine, philology and physics, the first glimmerings of the scientific (as distinguished from merely eulogistic) historiography appeared first in Greece with Thucydides, and were rekindled in Italy by Macchiavelli, Guiccardini and Sarpi. Later the centre of creativity moved northwards to France and England with Jean Bodin, Hobbes and James Harrington, where it remained throughout the eighteenth century. Despite various excursions into virgin territory by the philosophers of history and politics of the Enlightenment (such as Voltaire, Herder, Kant and Hume) the writing of history remained focused on glorious deeds of great men until the present century. To judge by quantitative preponderance, even today the teaching and writing of history serve mainly the purpose of indoctrination, notwithstanding the shift of interest from great events to institutions, which reflects the trend towards the mass society. We can say nonetheless that, except in totalitarian states, the general trend in historiography during recent decades has been towards a greater objectivity and openness to ideas from economic and sociological theory.

We can also discern a trend towards a more exclusive concern to understand through dispassionate analysis rather than to apportion praise or blame – towards objectivity, if you like – if we compare the early descriptions of primitive cultures, full of indignation about the vicious or silly customs of the benighted savages, with the ethnography written by modern professionals. Nevertheless, from a diagnosis that there has been a trend towards what might be vaguely called objectivity we cannot jump to the conclusion that this goal is fully attainable; although, on the other hand, the impossibility of attaining it perfectly does not mean that the idea is not worth pursuing. The goals of clarity and consistency cannot be attained perfectly either, but without a striving towards them there would be no science at all.

As no writer discussing human affairs can suppress in himself all the favourable or hostile feelings about the deeds and persons which he describes, we ought to welcome any open indication of the nature of his likes and dislikes so that we can discount the biases which we do not share. Indeed, so long as we can easily distinguish the statements apportioning blame or praise from factual information and analysis, we shall have a reason for objecting only if he devotes so much space to vituperation or eulogies that he has little to spare to tell us about the circumstances and the causal relations. Having to discipline one's emotional reactions might conduce to a greater concentration on analysis, but it does not follow that absence of strong feelings about the object provides the best basis for studying it, because an emotional involvement may prompt untiring curiosity; and as a matter of fact some of the most profound insights into the mechanics of social systems have come from people who either hated or admired them. The example of Marx naturally springs to mind.

If the distinction between judgments of fact and judgments of value could be kept clear, mixing them between the covers of a book or during a speech would no more interfere with the communication and cumulation of knowledge than would an insertion of an exclamation about the beauty of the skies in a book on astronomy. In discussions of human affairs, however, only the most extreme forms of judgments of value and judgments of fact appear as entirely distinct. When we are told that somebody's actions or character are admirable or despicable we cannot infer the nature of his deed or the traits of his personality without knowing the scales of values of the speaker. Exclamations like 'bastard' or 'bugger' have lost their informative content referring to an illegitimate birth or specific sexual practices, and have come to be used purely as expressions of hostility and disdain. But epithets like 'liar' or 'coward' do have a factually informative content as well as a hortatory and emotive content; the former would not be applied to someone between whose words and deeds (no matter how abhorrent) no discrepancy could be detected, nor would the latter to someone impervious to fear though addicted to cruelty, duplicity or other repellent vices. To take a further example, the same disposition could be called, according to the speaker's attitude and the scale of values, either 'timidity' or 'prudence', but hardly 'foolhardiness'.

There are two reasons why in describing human conduct we cannot get away from emotively and normatively loaded words. The first is that we do not have enough terms coined for exclusively cognitive purposes to depict the great variety of human interactions. Consequently it would be utterly impossible to give an account of, say, the manoeuvres in a political arena if we had to confine our vocabulary to the terms devised by the psychologists, sociologists and political scientists; not to speak of the question of whether these terms in fact help or impede the understanding. Some people have argued that this is only a matter of time; and that slowly but surely the social sciences will produce terminologies adequate to their tremendous task. Personally, I do not believe this will ever be achieved, because (apart from other obstacles to progress in this field) of the impediment (irremediable to my mind) that, no matter how aseptic and odourless when first coined, psychological and sociological terms very quickly acquire undertones of praise or blame in accordance with whether the reality to which they refer is liked or not. For instance, who likes to be called a 'masochist' or a 'psychotic'? Yet these terms were invented for strictly clinical use, as near to objectivity as anything that we can imagine in the study of man. Or who would like to undergo a public diagnosis as a bearer of an Oedipus or an inferiority complex, a possessor of low intelligence, or an emotionally immature individual? No matter what innocuous sounding substitutes we might invent for 'impotence' or 'onanism', it is hardly likely that, as soon as they have learned what they mean, men would regard them as neutral attributes. So the coining of neologisms for the sole purpose of eliminating evaluative undertones is a fruitless task, particularly as psychological and sociological terms undergo oversimplifying, gross distortions as soon as they gain currency. The only defence against this tendency – very imperfect to be sure – is a genuine sophistication of meaning which renders them inapt for colloquial usage.

Obscurity can be a source of power and income, as can be seen from the example of legal language (mentioned earlier) which is clearly a product of striving to make it incomprehensible to the uninitiated, so as to compel them to rely on the expensive services of lawyers. Politicians and officials often deliberately couch their pronouncements in vague and ambiguous words in order to leave themselves freedom of action or to evade the issue. Even the rules and regulations of various organizations are phrased in the vaguest possible manner so as to permit the wielders of authority to evade responsibility, or even to commit serious abuses. This tendency reveals itself even in such seemingly straightforward matters as the nomenclature of administrative positions. For instance, in order not to offend susceptibilities, an incumbent of a newly instituted position of authority, instead of being called a chief or head or director, will be called a co-ordinator, and the analytically very useful distinction between co-ordination and control becomes blurred in consequence.

The power of words to evoke emotions provides a standing and irresistible temptation to twist their original meanings in order to obtain desired reactions. Prompted by this motive, advertisers, journalists and many other kinds of writers and broadcasters aggravate the confusion by their incessant sensationalism, which has robbed so many words of their meanings. For these reasons terminological discussion remains necessary as a kind of interminable cleaning or weeding, without which our understanding will not only not grow, but will diminish with time; as, indeed, it already has in many ways.

It is no accident that the field where (apart from economic theory) a sophisticated and logically satisfactory terminology has developed is the study of kinship. In addition to the advantage of dealing with structures which can be analysed into fairly constant and isolable elements (such as the relations of being a wife, husband, brother, sister, son, daughter, father, and mother) this branch of social studies has the good fortune of being normally remote from current politics and ideologies. Purely intellectual difficulties, ideological passions, and deliberate efforts to obscure or deceive, all reinforce one another. The stronger the passions, the more difficult becomes the ratiocination, and the greater the effectiveness of propaganda. Conversely, the more difficult it is to find out and prove the truth, the easier it is to fall into 'thinking with the blood' and to succumb to a temptation to appeal to the passions. Finally, the more relevant an issue to the struggle for wealth and power, the more energetic will be the efforts to obfuscate on the part of open or clandestine propagandists, and the more difficult it will be for a genuine seeker after truth to get a hearing.

To realise how difficult it is to separate the informative from the hortative ingredient of the meaning, it suffices to look at a word like 'fascism'. The word was invented as the proper name for the followers of Benito Mussolini, and later began to be affixed to the movements which proclaimed their sympathy with the Italian fascists or resembled them in their programme or organization. The communists have extended the meaning of this label to the point of calling 'fascist' anybody who is not on their side; but the compliment was returned when some people began to call them red fascists. The Russian writer Tarsis even defined communism as a particularly pernicious brand of fascism. So the common denominator of the many uses of this word is purely hortatory or emotive, connoting condemnation. Without knowing the speaker's stance, we can infer nothing about the features of a system or movement when we hear it being called 'fascist'.

In the chapter on *Ideology Underneath Terminology* I shall analyse a number of less obvious examples of hortatory under-tones in ostensibly pure scientific terms. For the moment I should like only to re-emphasize that this kind of smuggling, far from being a recent phenomenon, can be traced throughout the history of the literature on human affairs. The definitions of the State normally contain a persuasive ingredient and often little else. One need not go to great lengths to show that a definition of the State as an emanation of the general will tends to instil a very different attitude from that induced by the conception of the state as an instrument for the protection of the rich against the poor. Opinions on such seemingly theoretical questions as whether the State originated through a conquest or a contract were often dictated by the attitude to the government of the day.

The fundamental difficulty about objectivity stems from the inescapable circumstance that neither the requirement of factual correctness nor the canon of semantic neutrality tell us anything about what to include and what to leave out when we are describing a situation.

I can draw a map of a city which shows the location of musea, schools, theatres and other worthy buildings, as well as one which pinpoints only brothels, dope markets, gambling dens and gaols. Both could be equally true and exact; and there is no reason why one of them should be regarded as less true than the other, or less correct than any other map we might care to draw. Or take a less trivial example: from the standpoint of philosophical semantics a statement that so many schools and hospitals have been built in the USSR is just as neutral or non-hortatory as a sentence about how many millions have died there in the forced labour camps. Nonetheless, a willingness to affirm only the first or only the second or both would provide a good clue to a person's attitude towards that state.

Since the sum total of the traits of any empirical phenomenon is infinite, anybody attempting to describe it must decide (consciously or unconsciously) what to note and what to leave unrecorded, and how much attention and space to give to each mentioned item or aspect. Neither the canons of veracity and exactitude nor the distinctions of philosophical semantics, nor even a recourse to unemotional recondite words, can provide a line of escape from the necessity of making such choices. And as every journalist knows, even a picture of a simple event like an accident or a brawl can be altered out of recognition by picking on one assortment of details rather than another; just as a speech can be utterly distorted by stringing together selected, though literally correct, quotations.

An awareness of these difficulties ought not to lead us to the defeatist conclusion that every account is equally unreliable and that we can never know anything: for this is surely untrue, and common sense, formed by experiences of everyday life, indicates that some witnesses are less biased than others, not to speak of the differences in their reluctance to tell outright lies. What does follow from the foregoing arguments, however, is that the ideal of objectivity is much more complex and elusive than the pedlars of methodological gimmicks would have us believe; and that it requires much more than an adherence to the technical rules of verification, or recourse to recondite unemotive terminology: namely, a moral commitment to justice – the will to be fair to people and institutions, to avoid the temptations of wishful and venomous thinking, and the courage to resist threats and enticement.

Like a judge evaluating witnesses' testimonies, we cannot assess the value of data without passing a tacit judgment on the character of the source; because, like him or the detective, we normally deal with information which we cannot personally check – and neither membership of a professional association nor the observance of methodological technicalities guarantees even an elementary truthfulness, let alone objectivity in the wider sense defined above. Like a judge, moreover, we would never get anywhere if we assumed that every account is equally trustworthy, and that objectivity consists in giving equal weight to all statements, because an impartiality between a truthful witness and a liar amounts to a commitment to half-truths and a connivance at deception.

Every group, every power structure, propagates certain beliefs about its nature, as well as about that of its allies and enemies, which do not correspond to the reality. Consequently, anybody who searches for truth about human affairs and then reveals it cannot avoid treading upon some toes, and can hardly fail to be dubbed as an obnoxious heretic or a dangerous subversive. As there are few issues on which no group holds strong preconceptions, it may be quite impossible to remain absolutely neutral, particularly when (as commonly happens) powerful factions follow the principle that 'he who is not with us is against us'. What is more, a commitment to truthfulness usually entails taking sides because of the enormous variations in self-deception and mendacity among groups and individuals. Thus a resolve to tell the truth commits an inquirer to take a stand against those organizations or schools of thought which delude themselves or resort to deception to a greater extent, and on the side of the opponents less prone to these vices. No honest book on physical anthropology could be neutral in relation to the nazi ideology, with the fiction of the purity of the German race as its cardinal dogma. Likewise, no amount of reluctance to criticize would prevent an honest comparison of the living conditions of manual workers and of top officials from automatically becoming dangerously subversive in a country where the official mythology claims that social inequalities have disappeared while in reality they have not. Nor can the piece of information that the tonnage of bombs dropped on South Vietnam exceeds that which fell on Germany and Japan during the Second World War (though in itself perfectly neutral semantically) remain within the bounds of practical neutrality in the context of the situation, as it casts a serious doubt on the sincerity of the claim that the war is being waged to defend democracy in that part of the world.

The word 'democracy', incidentally, has long ago ceased to have any definite meaning, and in common usage has come to indicate a mere approval of the given system, whatever it might be.

Nobody will be treated as neutral if he reveals what others would like to conceal; and this applies not only to high politics but also to all kinds of other situations, such as an industrial consultant's advice on how to reorganize a business, which entails promotion for some while depriving others of their livelihood. So we must bear in mind the distinction between semantic and practical neutrality. The first, though by no means so simple as the claimants to a scientific status in the social studies would have us believe, is attainable at least in principle; whereas the second is out of the question in this world of ours where secrecy, deception and delusion play such an important part in determining human actions, and especially who gets what and how.

Although there can be no true neutrality in the study of human affairs, pseudo-neutrality is not only possible but eminently profitable, and at the highest levels of skill it brings the benefits of being able to run with the hare while hunting with the hounds.

Leopold Ranke's dictum that the task of the historian is to tell 'how it really happened' has often been criticized for its naivety; and everything that has been said above goes to show that a commitment to simple veracity does not suffice to guarantee impartiality. We can easily see, however, that there is something in Ranke's dictum if we try to affirm its opposite, and say that the task of the historian is not to tell how it really happened. Indeed, we can hardly imagine that historiography or the study of current affairs could remain anything but either a subservient and nefarious propaganda or a purely parasitic occupation if it did not adhere to a sufficient degree to the canon of truthfulness – which is fortunately much easier to attain than objectivity in the fuller sense. Though open to criticism on an epistemological plane, Ranke's famous sentence amounted to an assertion of the primacy of the concern for truth, exactitude and sobriety, as against the adulatory, hyperbolic, and emotional style in writing history, common even today and wellnigh universal at the time.

Despite the elusiveness of its criteria and the impossibility of attaining it fully, objectivity (which includes impartiality as distinct from neutrality) must remain an essential ideal to guide our endeavours. It is not, to repeat, a simple ideal, easily followed by applying a few technical rules, but if we reject it entirely we can only become propagandists or parasites, unless we prefer to become warriors or guerrilleros who, rather than reason, prefer to shoot.

The foregoing arguments point to a conclusion which contradicts the common stereotype that 'facts' are 'hard', while theories are something essentially arbitrary. This does not mean that we are led to some kind of fundamental relativism, because to reason at all we have to postulate the existence of a 'reality' in relation to which statements about 'facts' can be judged as true or false. A complete relativism, consisting of a rejection of the concept of truth, is self-contradictory because its assertion entails a negation of its own truth. It is expressed in the old antinomy: a man says that all Cretans always tell lies. He is a Cretan; therefore whatever he says must be a lie. Nonetheless, even within the normal assumptions of science and common sense that statements about 'facts' can be judged as true or false, even if only approximately, it remains the case that the criterion of truth cannot determine the choice of what to include and what to leave out among the infinite number of true propositions describing 'facts'. Not being constrained by objective criteria, such a choice remains no less arbitrary when it follows conventional manners of listing, and can at best be guided by the vague ideal of justice or an intuitive judgment of relative importance which may be right or wrong. In contrast, well-substantiated propositions about causal relations are limited in number, and cannot be multiplied at will, or modified without making them false, being in fact exceedingly difficult to discover.

Not only general theorems, but also singular propositions about a causal relationship in a given case, are subject to many more constraints than purely descriptive statements. If my task is to indicate the attributes of the entity of A, I can list any true attributes that I may choose. But if I wish to state propositions about causal relations between two attributes of the entity A, explaining the appearance of the attribute x by the existence of the attribute y, then my freedom of choice will be severely limited by my knowledge of causal relationships – often extremely so, if I am able to find any correct propositions of this kind at all.

Interpreting the concept of objectivity as involving some limitations on what we can choose to say, we must conclude that corroborated theories are more objective than true descriptions; and that the latter partake of objectivity in so far as they are based on theoretical propositions about causes and effects, while pure description must always be arbitrary. I must emphasise, however, that this applies only to theories which are clearly phrased, testable and, if not tested, at least supported by factual evidence to a point of high plausibility. Nebulous, untestable, pseudo-theoretical meanderings are, of course, more than arbitrary, being free even from the criterion of elementary correctness.

Chapter 9

Hiding Behind Methodology

More respectable than obfuscating jargon is another stratagem for avoiding the danger of offending powerful groups and individuals, and of staking one's reputation on controversial theses: namely, an insistence on methodological perfection which precludes one from giving an answer to any but the most trivial questions.

In the history of the exact sciences the development of the methods of experimentation and measurement has played a crucial part. It took place, however, in the process of solving substantive problems; and I know of no case of a methodology having been invented in a vacuum, or imported wholesale from another field, and then successfully used to produce important discoveries; although it is true that some branches of mathematics had been invented long before they were first applied, the most notable example being the calculus of so-called imaginary numbers. It must be remembered, moreover, that when people nowadays talk about methodology they usually mean, not the basic principles of inductive inference, but the specific methods of collecting and analysing statistical data.

Methodology is prophylactic in its essence. In the same way as hygiene can help us to avoid some contagions but is powerless to ensure health, methodology can warn us of pitfalls but will not help us to conceive new ideas. The so-called methods of induction are in reality methods of verification: they tell us how to test hypotheses but not how to arrive at them. Indeed, the latter process is just as much a mystery as it was in the days of Socrates: all that is known is that, in order to conceive fruitful original ideas, one must have talent, must immerse oneself in the available knowledge, and think very hard.

The overemphasis on methodology and techniques, as well

as adulation of formulae and scientific-sounding terms, exemplify the common tendency (which also manifests itself in such diverse phenomena as miserliness and barrack room 'spit and polish') to displace value from the end to the means: something originally valued solely as means to an end comes to be valued for its own sake, and the original end is forgotten. A sociologist or psychologist obsessed with frameworks, jargon and techniques resembles a carpenter who becomes so worried about keeping his tools clean that he has no time to cut the wood. These tendencies are reinforced by the feeling of helplessness in the face of an unmanageable complexity of social phenomena, and the fear of dabbling with dangerous issues, which lurk throughout the field of the social sciences. As a result it is forgotten that unfettered thought is the most essential of research methods.

The chief advantage of the mechanical application of routine techniques is that it permits a massive production of printed matter without much mental effort. As we shall see in greater detail in a later chapter, a research boss does not have to bother himself with observation or thinking about what he sees. All he has to do is to raise the money and recruit the staff who will do the work. Another advantage is that no matter how careless or even dishonest the interviewers might have been, the tabulated figures do not tell the story of how they came into existence, and the more massive the tables the more inscrutable they become.

The cooking of interviews is much more common than is generally supposed, although exactly how prevalent it is no one can say. Among cases I have come across there was one of a man employed to carry out interviews in various parts of England who, instead of travelling, composed most of them in his favourite local pub. Previously he assisted another sociologist on a piece of research for which the latter got a professorship at a British university, and did not commit harakiri upon learning about the true habits of his erstwhile principal assistant. An even more amusing example is that of a sociology department in an American university which, having decided to put a stress on exact methodology, appointed as a professor in this field (at top salary) a man who, it was later discovered, had been dismissed from his previous job with a market research organization for 'cooking' the results.

As everybody knows, dereliction of duty and dishonesty occur in every walk of life, and faked discoveries (like those of Lysenko, to mention but the most famous recent example) are by no means unknown in the natural sciences. But the significance of carelessness and fraud depends on how easy it is to get away with it, and in this respect there is a tremendous gap between the experimental sciences where the results can be (and normally are) re-checked innumerable times, and studies dealing with individualized phenomena which cannot be experimentally reproduced. If you do not believe what you have been told about the properties of some metal you can try to find out for yourself, on the reasonable assumption that the piece of metal with which you will experiment will not differ from the pieces used by the sources of your information. But, if you suspect the exactitude, or even the fundamental veracity, of production statistics from China, what can you do except to make an estimate on the basis of indirect evidence? You cannot even check in the full sense of the word what you are told about the number of inhabitants of the city in which you live, and if you disbelieve the figure you are given you can only make an informed guess.

Touchy about being unable to substantiate their claims, the worshippers of methodology turn like a vicious hunting pack upon anybody branded as impressionistic, particularly if he writes well and can make his books interesting. Often enough their motive is sheer envy, as the ability to unearth something really interesting and to present it in a lively style demands a special gift and cannot be acquired by mechanical cramming, whereas anybody who is not a mental defective can learn to churn out the tedious door-to-door surveys which pass for sociology. Furthermore, as the producers of any commodity can enlarge their profits if they can dilute their wares with impunity, the social scientists have a vested interest in padding (since they can get away with it), and regard anybody who can pack a lot of information into a small space as a pernicious norm buster who undermines their livelihood.

No studies have given as lively and rounded a picture of the

British manual workers as Ferdinand Zweig's various books. Yet these have all met with adverse criticisms in the sociological journals on the grounds of being unscientific.

No doubt the kind of sociology represented by Zweig's books is not enough in itself: we certainly need statistical investigations, comparative analyses, historical studies and abstract deductive reasoning as well. But it is a great pity that we do not have more works which, on the basis of careful and protracted observation, depict perceptibly the aspects of social reality which escape the questionnaires and statistics. The reason for this scarcity is the wide acceptance of the dogma that nothing is worth knowing that cannot be counted, and that any information which is tabulated becomes thereby scientific – surely one of the grossest superstitions of our time, whose vogue can only stem from the fact that it enables a large number of people to make a living by indulging in easy pseudo-science.

In comparison with the standard routine of social research, this kind of study involves much more skill and hard work which cannot be abandoned to half-educated research assistants, without falling into the trap of producing assemblages of banalities and boring gossip like many of the so-called anthropological studies of modern communities. Like all human works, Zweig's incisive descriptions must contain faults and errors but, in view of the amount of thought and observation which has gone into working them out, they cannot be called impressionistic – they are purely or mainly qualitative, but they open up vistas which could at least in part be explored with the aid of quantitative methods.

The following extracts from his book of essays *In Quest of Fellowship* give the main points of Zweig's well worth repeating methodological credo:

The act of interviewing does not need to sink to the level of mechanicalness. It can be a graceful and joyful act, enjoyed by the two sides and suffered by neither. What is more, my contention is that unless it becomes such an act, it will only fail in its main function. One cannot conduct an interview by bombarding one's victim with a barrage of questions, which is only tiresome and tiring for both sides. The only way is to make an interview an enjoyable social act, both for the interviewer and the respondent, a two-way traffic, so that the respondent feels not a 'victim' but a true partner, a true conversationalist . . .

Every person is an individual, and must be treated as such . . . the art of interviewing is personal in its character, as the basic tool of the interviewer is in fact his own personality . . . he has to discover his own personal truth in interviewing, how to be friendly with people without embarassing them, how to learn from them without being too inquisitive, how to be interesting without talking too much, how to take great interest in their troubles without patronising them, how to inspire confidence without perplexing them.

An interviewer needs first of all to go deeper into himself and understand himself. Without that understanding of the depth of his own mind, without that self-knowledge, he cannot perfectly understand other human beings. It is my belief that a social scientist must work pretty hard on himself, improving his own understanding of his own mind. And he must not only have a certain understanding of himself but must also have a certain depth of personality. By depth I mean a great range and variety of personal experience, and an understanding of the range of contradictions in himself, which will enable him to understand the ambivalent attitudes which are so frequent in the complex problems of our days.

Sympathy and human warmth . . . are the most valuable resources of any interviewer. And not only is sympathy needed, but also what is called empathy . . . a sort of act of identification, or putting oneself in other people's shoes. But this is only one side of the matter. A successful interviewer needs two contradictory or rather complementary mental techniques. On the one hand he has to identify himself with the people he interviews, to reconstruct in his mind their fears and hopes, their anxieties and frustrations, and on the other hand he has to develop a certain attitude of detachment.

What people say on their own initiative without being asked is, on the whole, more true than what they say in answering questions . . . This is the reason why an interview conceived as a social act is much superior to a questionnaire, because in the former one has a great deal of material supplied by the respondent on his own impulse, which can give one something new to think about and supply the missing links in one's knowledge or experience.

The social investigator must look behind the façade of opinions and views and examine their origin, their background and their genuineness as well as their relation to the past and present situation.

The value of an interview can be very much enhanced by careful observation of the respondent, by studying his face, clothes, gestures, mime, the light in his eyes, the hot blush or puzzlement in his face and so on. The value is still more enhanced if one can interview a person in his own surroundings, at home or place of work, which gives larger scope for observation, as so many of the potential questions are answered immediately and truthfully simply by using one's eyes.

Zweig does not specify that a good sociographer should also have a wide knowledge and literary skill and be highly intelligent as well, but this is subversive talk in the ears of the captains of social research industry.

Several curious distortions underlie the methodological idolatry. The first is a naive inductivism – that is, the belief that if we gather enough 'facts' the explanatory and predictive theories will spontaneously emerge – which continues to find a wide following despite innumerable warnings from all kinds of distinguished thinkers, beginning at the latest with Whewell more than a hundred years ago.

The second grave shortcoming of the prevalent approach to methodology of the social sciences is the exclusive focus on the quantifiable (or supposedly quantifiable) aspects, coupled with the utmost carelessness about the meaning of words. So that we commonly find meticulously worked-out figures accompanying a slip-shod text full of grossly misleading words and phrases, with the results described in the chapter on jargon. Apart from the vested interests involved, the separation of the social sciences from philosophy is largely to blame. Owing to the vagueness of his concepts and theories (with but a very partial exception of economics) a practitioner of the social sciences needs the skills of analytical philosophy to steer clear of logical and semantic pitfalls. For this reason, the present apartheid between the philosophers and the social scientists – with the vast majority in each tribe refusing to take cognisance of the secrets of the other – has fostered the spread of vacuous verbosity. In this respect academics surpass trade unionists in their closed shop mentality and proclivity for demarcation disputes (which goes so far that knowing about A is commonly taken as sufficient evidence that one knows nothing about B), while the contacts between subjects often amount to inter-disciplinary cross-sterilization through symposia by mutually uncomprehending specialists, which resemble choirs of the deaf with each singer emitting piercing sounds in the face of a total obliviousness from the rest.

As much, if not most, of the work in the social sciences outside economics consists of non-quantified description, one would have thought that the question of how to judge their quality would have been dealt with thoroughly, but this is not at all the case. The volumes of methodology which contain elaborate precepts on how to ascertain the 'facts' tell us nothing about how to judge which of them ought to be recorded; which means that they completely leave aside the fundamental question of the criteria for assessing the value of a description.[1]

The quantitative methods of social research, worked out by Paul Lazarsfeld and his followers in America and Europe (such as Blalock, Boudon and Nowak) embody a great deal of sophistication and inventiveness, and constitute an achievement of an entirely different order from the sterile logomachies of the parsonians. Nevertheless, despite the ingenuity of their recipes, the exponents of the over-sophisticated quantitative methods of social research remind me of the old films with Laurel and Hardy or Charlie Chaplin, where you would see boxers flexing their muscles, making energetic knee-bends, fierce faces and menacing gestures, and then waving their arms in the air without ever coming to blows. The proof of the pudding is, after all, in the eating; and the methodological rigorists are like cooks who would show us all their shiny stoves, mixers, liquidizers and what not, without ever making anything worth eating. Actually, in the culinary art as in many branches of social studies, we can detect a general tendency for the product to deteriorate as the gadgets become more elaborate.

Despite many promises about imminent break-throughs, no discoveries in sociology or political science have been made with the aid of the ultra-sophisticated quantitative methods which would add significantly to our ability to explain or predict political events or social transformations – which is not surprising in view of their practitioners' lack of new ideas on the substantive questions of collective behaviour. In nearly all

1. Some criteria have been suggested in *The Uses of Comparative Sociology*, Ch. 1.

instances it is the case of a mountain giving birth to a mouse, as when, after wading through mounds of tables and formulae, we come to the general finding (expressed, of course, in the most abstruse manner possible) that people enjoy being in the centre of attention, or that they are influenced by those with whom they associate ... which I can well believe, as my grandmother told me that many times when I was a child. In their book *Personal Influence*, Lazarsfeld and colleagues have tried to exonerate the mass media from the accusation of exerting undue influence, by showing that people pay more attention to what their friends say than to what they read in the newspapers. The trouble with this contention is that the friends are under the influence of the same media. Naturally, one can say (as Lazarsfeld does) that although no great discoveries have yet been made with the new tools, it is because they have not yet been sufficiently perfected; and that with a bit more effort put into improving them we shall be able to prise open the door to the treasure-house of the exact theoretical science of society. We must admit that nobody can prove that the Messiah will never come, but why should we accept this faith on trust?

Scholars ought to have opportunities to follow their hunches, and nobody has the right to object when others experiment with methods which have not yet yielded any unexpected findings. On the other side of the fence, however, those who are following such hunches ought to be honest and tolerant. They ought to admit that up till now they have discovered next to nothing in substantive matters, and ought to recognize the need to tackle important empirical questions by less rigorous methods. Since they have been at it for several decades by now without achieving very much, they ought to extend forbearance to those who seek tentative answers without waiting for a perfect method of verification; instead of which, unfortunately, they behave like good sectarians; they condemn qualitative studies as unscientific, and often attempt to squeeze their exponents out of teaching or research.

No doubt owing to the desire to cash in on the prestige of the natural sciences, the concern with methodology has become unduly slanted towards quantification at the cost of such essential skills as textual criticism, literary flair and semantic sensitivity, which every social scientist, not excluding the economists, ought to possess. As things are, we get ludicrous incongruities, like a highly placed academic I listened to at a conference in New York, who went on expostulating about some esoteric point of methodology but continued to use 'suspect' for 'suspicious' – declaring himself to be suspect of this and that – not just once or twice through a slip of the tongue but repeatedly throughout his lecture. To judge by the absence of any signs of hilarity, the audience too must have been oblivious of this none too subtle distinction.

As very few important problems can be adequately analysed with the aid of the techniques prescribed by current textbooks, an excessive preoccupation with methodology provides an alibi for timorous quietism. The results can be seen in the contents of the journals. Nobody could ever guess what are the burning issues of the contemporary United States from reading American sociological and politological journals. Worse, even if he knew what the issues were, he could scarcely further his understanding of them by reading such periodicals, and would have to resort to monthlies like *Commentary* or the even much less high-brow *Fortune*. Even a popular weekly like *Time* supplies a much better insight into American society than all the journals of sociology combined; which was certainly not the case before the onset of jargon-mongering and methodological idolatry.

An excessive preoccupation with practical utility can stultify not only the theoretical sciences but the applied branches as well, both of which often benefit most from an indirect approach. But a refusal to have one's mental horizon bounded by a preoccupation with immediate utility is one thing, while a contrived general irrelevance to all practical problems is quite another; and nothing can be said in favour of the second. It is perfectly true that many of the most significant discoveries in physics and chemistry have been prompted solely by the thirst for knowledge, but never have these studies – not even in their embryonic form – been completely irrelevant to technology.

Hiding behind methodology is not, of course, the only way of evading commitment, as it is simply a more technical version of the old everyday stratagem that if you wish to avoid an awkward question you keep on talking about something else. In the social sciences there is an inexhaustible supply of trivial topics well suited to this purpose, ranging from the constant reiteration of expressions like 'role' or 'structure' or 'frame of reference', to highly esoteric neologisms.

By averting the eyes from the explosive issues of the day, methodological purism acts in fact as a prop of the *status quo* whatever it might be; which largely explains the worldly success of its devotees and the wide appeal of their creed. As if this were not enticing enough, this purism has an added attraction as an aid for keeping the study of the social sciences in a watertight compartment so that it does not contaminate cherished dogmas, be they of a revolutionary or conservative nature. For this reason, many marxists take to this purism like ducks to water, thus managing to reconcile their desire for modernity with their devotion to antiquated dogma; because one cannot easily believe that what Marx said a hundred years ago remains the last word of science, if one has absorbed the ideas of other great thinkers with equally wide horizons, particularly as an acquaintance with writers who preceded him cuts Marx down to a human (though still very impressive) figure.

In contrast, by keeping one's nose to the grindstone of statistics and questionnaires, one can escape the need to re-examine the basic assumptions of one's ideological stance and accept any myth which satisfies one's emotional cravings. What is more, methodology can be used as a pure smoke screen; and in Latin America I have seen communist agents who, in their capacity as academic sociologists, taught pure methodology without ever saying a word about substantive issues, while organizing infiltration behind the scenes. Under communist rule, on the other hand (and the same applies to many authoritarian states) methodology constitutes the only aspect of the social sciences which can be cultivated without distorting reticence or servile mendacity and to which, consequently, worthwhile contributions can be made, which accounts for its popularity. The trouble starts only when you try to apply one of the much vaunted methods to any non-trivial question without 'cooking' the data, as a number of social scientists in Poland and Czechoslovakia and elsewhere have found to their cost. We can hardly blame anyone for hiding behind methodology when a few incautious words can make him unemployable for life, or even land him in gaol. But it is an unelevating sight to see people who face no such dangers, and are already making quite a good living, resort to such a subterfuge for the sake of a research grant, a few trips, or a longish holiday in a pleasant place (on full pay and expenses) suitably disguised and enlivened by opportunities for ego-inflating pontification.

Among many other gimmicks the simulation of models of social action deserve a special mention in this context owing to their vogue. Basically, they constitute nothing new because war games – that is simulation of battle situations in miniature as opposed to true to size simulation in manoeuvres – have been known since before Napoleon; and if such methods can be used for training officers, there is no *a priori* reason why they could not be of equal value for business executives, administrators and diplomats. Nonetheless, I have never heard of anybody who has learned to be a good commander or businessman chiefly (let alone entirely) through this method; and I doubt if it ever has or will happen. Not even true-to-size manoeuvres provide a reliable guide to performance on a battlefield; and generals, judged to be promising on the basis of their peace time proficiency, more often than not have to be replaced when a war breaks out.

In spite of its inevitable simplification, a game simulating international diplomacy may perhaps help students of history or politics to appreciate the complexity of the decision-making; provided, however, that it bears a sufficient resemblance to reality, which is by no means always the case. I remember an amusing incident at a conference on the uses of the social sciences in writing history when a devotee of simulation was explaining how they used this method to gain a deeper insight into the causes of the First World War. After his account of how one of the participants played the crucial role of the King of Serbia, a Yugoslav historian got up and said that at the time of the outbreak of the First World War King Peter was mad and took no part in politics.

Even when based on more correct data, simulation games might help to give beginners some idea of the intricacies of a situation quickly, but can hardly supply deeper insights to experts because games of this kind can reproduce neither collective frenzies and delusions, nor individual fear or rage, nor factors such as a steadiness of the nerves which often determine the outcome in a real-life contest. As aids to decision-making, simulation methods suffer (in addition to the afore-mentioned drawbacks) from a fundamental weakness: they tend to focus attention on optimizing something within the initial assumptions rather than examining the latter; and the biggest errors are usually committed through acting upon assumptions which seem so natural that it occurs to nobody to question them. In principle, no doubt, the process could be reversed, and model building could be inverted to analyse the tacit presuppositions of decisions or explanations. In practice, however, simulation models outside relatively simple mechanical situations, like problems of traffic, easily become gimmicks divorced from reality and used for the sole purpose of blinding the public with science.

The United States government is the first in history to possess a large body of advisers skilled in mathematical aids to decision making; and yet its foreign policy has for twenty years persisted (and still continues to do so) in a folly which few rulers and courtiers of old could rival. No profound knowledge of the mathematical theory of games and model-building techniques is required to see that no good can come from treating the biggest nation in the world as a moral leper unworthy of being admitted to the game of backstage arm-twisting at UNO. This sanctimonious ostracism serves no reasonable purpose (such as the preservation of Taiwan's independence) which could not be more effectively furthered by other means. Furthermore, the most elementary canons of military and diplomatic strategy – well known to all the 'pre-scientific' policy makers – is to try to sow discord between one's actual or even potential enemies, in spite of which the American policy towards the two communist powers has always been as if designed to keep them together. That it was possible to foresee a rift between China and Russia, and to offer relevant advice, can be seen from

Chapter XIII of *Military Organization and Society*, written twenty years ago – for which, incidentally, I was criticized at the time by experts in communist affairs as an unworldly theorist.

One reason for the foolish persistence in this clearly erroneous policy seems to be that the Kuo Min Tan regime has put part of the money, which it received from the United States for fighting the communists, into the pockets of influential American politicians; but at least equally important is the simple fear of disagreeing with the prevalent demonology. Playing with computers, game theory and simulation models, far from counteracting these factors, actually makes things worse by providing the 'expert advisers' with an excuse for shirking the duty to speak the truth plainly and to expose the chimeras. When used with circumspection a computer undoubtedly can render many services, but adulation of this wondrous gadget impairs the progress of understanding, and increases the likelihood of disastrous decisions because, to repeat, the worst mistakes most often come not from faulty deductions but from unexamined false premises and proneness to delusion.

The gravest kind of danger stems from the illusion that, because certain kinds of data can be quantified and processed by a computer, therefore they must be more important than those which cannot be measured. It appears that an error of this sort lay at the root of the decision to send the American troops to Vietnam: the quantities of weapons, numbers of soldiers and means of transport were, no doubt, carefully calculated without taking into account the mental factors; although a bit of ability to put oneself into other people's shoes and a wider acquaintance with history could have helped the decision-makers to imagine what might be a popular reaction to a massive influx of tactless, self-indulgent and fabulously paid soldiers of strikingly different physique and with manners extremely repugnant to the natives. Another unstated reason for the disastrous decision to intervene in this particular way was the unexamined underestimation of the character and talent of scantily clad peasants inured to hardships and unperturbed by the sight of death, coupled with an overestimation of the battle-worthiness of the over-fed, pampered and hedonistic American boys – both notions deriving firstly from an unavowed racial conceit, and secondly from a superstitious belief in the strength-giving effects of high consumption. As if this were not enough, yet another superstition clouded the judgment: namely the belief that since communism is bad, therefore it can only be espoused by a wicked minority which then foists it by force upon an unwilling majority – which fits well enough the history of the communist seizures of power in Poland, Hungary, Czechoslovakia and to a lesser extent even Russia – while the possibility of a genuine conversion to communism of the entire nation (or at least of its most active and idealistic elements) does not appear to have been considered; although the Bay of Pigs fiasco should have taught the Pentagon planners that a communist dictator need not be without a large number of devoted followers. This cluster of dangerous fictions includes the baseless notion that communism and nationalism are naturally opposed – which is true enough in Poland, Hungary or Czechoslovakia, but not at all in Vietnam or China where the maoists are far more nationalistic than Chiang-Kai Chek ever was. On the top of all this, and despite the lessons which should have been drawn from what happened in Germany at the end of the last war, foolish tactics of indiscriminate bombing were adopted, based on the belief that the Vietnamese can be easily cowed by fear, but which seems to have produced more converts to communism than any other circumstances, not excluding the brazen venality rampant throughout the Saigon-controlled army and bureaucracy. As it is not my aim here to supply an adequate diagnosis of the situation in Vietnam, I shall desist from adding further items to the foregoing list of elusive factors. For the present purpose it suffices to stress that so long as immensurable forces of this kind continue to affect outcomes of political decisions, neither the computers nor the techniques of model building can provide a sufficient basis for rational choice, and may be positively dangerous if they induce in the decision makers false notions about the adequacy of their knowledge.

Such abuses of methodology have produced its equally obscurantist antithesis in the shape of a rejection of the fundamental principles of logic and scientific method, denigration of science, and a reversion to the old mystic notion that truth can be discovered without a disciplined inquiry by an effortless, sentimental and perhaps psychedelic rumination.

Chapter 10

Quantification as Camouflage

As has often been said, measurement is the beginning of science (if we mean thereby exact science) because our ability to predict the behaviour of a phenomenon must remain very restricted until we can measure it. It does not follow, however, that no knowledge whatsoever is possible without measurement, nor that such knowledge cannot be worth having – which is precisely the conclusion which (as we saw in the preceding chapter) many sociologists and psychologists have adopted in the mistaken belief that only thereby can they maintain the scientific character of their discipline. But the true scientific spirit consists of trying to obtain the nearest approximation to truth which is possible under the circumstances, and it is puerile to demand either perfect exactitude or nothing. Those who refuse to deal with important and interesting problems simply because the relevant factors cannot be measured, condemn the social sciences to sterility, because we cannot get very far with the study of measurable variables if these depend on, and are closely interwoven with, immensurable factors of whose nature and operation we know nothing. A weakness of this kind diminishes the usefulness of economic theory: notwithstanding the great sophistication of statistical techniques and mathematical models, it remains incapable of predicting such a *par excellence* economic phenomenon as inflation, because it excludes from its universe of discourse immensurable but causally crucial factors (such as the balance of political power), abandoning them to the step-motherly care of sociology or political science (with which most economists want nothing to do), or simply relegating them to the category of those things which are treated as 'being equal'.

The mention of corruption in the preceding chapter brings us to an irrefutable argument against the view that an exact science of society (and especially of politics) can ever be constructed; because, like all other social phenomena involving deliberate secrecy, corruption is immensurable intrinsically rather than merely owing to the insufficient development of the techniques of quantification. We can make more or less informed guesses about whether the absolute or relative amount of wealth passing through this channel is larger in Jersey City than in Lagos, but it is inconceivable that a method of collecting exact statistical data on this matter could ever be devised, just as it is impossible to know how many murders are committed which pass completely unnoticed. If people were ready to answer questions about their embezzlements and bribes it would mean that these practices had acquired the character of legitimate tribute-levying and had ceased to be corrupt – which notion connotes the prohibited and shameful nature of the act. In other words, the phenomenon would have to disappear to become measurable.

To substantiate their claims, the advocates of an exclusive concentration on quantification ought to demonstrate either that corruption can be measured, or that it is a factor of no significance. The first, as we saw, cannot be done, while to maintain that corrupt practices play no important part in social causation one must be either a hypocrite or a starry-eyed dreamer. Actually (as can be seen in my books, *Parasitism and Subversion in Latin America* and *The African Predicament*) this factor more than any other accounts for the failure, or rather irrelevance, of the development plans prepared by the economists for the rescue of the poor countries.

Bribery, embezzlement and other variants of financial 'fiddling' do not exhaust the range of activities based on secrecy, which have always been, are, and (so long as human nature does not change out of all recognition) will remain an essential instrument for acquiring and holding power over others, as well as for escaping from their control. To bulldoze all the fences of privacy and confidentiality which impede an acquisition of complete and exact data about human behaviour would require power far greater in scope than Stalin and Hitler had; and as those who would have so much power would hardly wish to divulge their knowledge to all and sundry, secrets would continue to exist.

The slogan that knowledge means power, incidentally, has an unambiguous meaning when speaking about mankind's control over non-human nature; but becomes very ambiguous when applied to human relations, because then the question arises: who will be the knower and who the known? The social scientists often glibly claim that their studies hold the promise of giving us control over social processes without saying anything about who will constitute 'us'.

To come back to the question of quantification: if we look at the types of data utilized by the protagonists of the quantitative methods outside economics, we can easily see that the overwhelming majority consist of cumulations of responses to questionnaires – about the most superficial kind of information one can think of. It is as if somebody had tried to build a science of meteorology solely by making elaborate computations of the flutterings of flags. In fairly democratic countries votes provide a natural foothold for quantification, and analyses of results have yielded a number of quite interesting conclusions, but only a very naive or dishonest psephologist will claim that his craft gives an adequate account of politics. Only a thorough insensitivity to the logical use of words permits the affixing of the label 'political behaviour' solely to voting, as if backstage log-rolling, conspiracy, assassination, incarceration, revolution, bribery, war and a host of other unpleasant activities did not constitute equally, if not more, common ingredients of a political process. The same stricture, incidentally, can be levelled against the misleading title of one of the best recent books on political sociology – S. M. Lipset's *Political Man* – which throws interesting light on politics based on fairly free and honest elections, without attending to the less civilized deeds of the Political Man such as imperialism, intrigue or terror.

It is possible that the common devotion to quantification may be due not only to purism but also to the desire to have an excuse for sweeping dangerous or unpleasant issues under the carpet. This can be surmised from the reluctance – inexplicable on strictly methodological grounds – to use the ready-made criterion of financial transactions, although the variations on the amounts of money controlled by different groups, classes, cliques and institutions provide the best numerical indices of the changes in their power and status. Yet entire books are written on stratification or politics without a mention of this sordid but crucial factor. Strangely enough, the only book I know which goes the right way about this deals with a country whose economic statistics do not rank among the best in the world: *Le Dévelopement du Capitalisme en Côte d'Ivoire*, by an Egyptian economist, Samir Amin. Some sovietologists or sinologists also make good use of material of this kind, such as they can get, whereas sociologists writing about their own society never stoop to such crude matters, and confine their attention to what people say about who ranks above or below whom. The earlier American sociologists like Ross and Giddings, or even the 'social darwinist' Sumner, did not mind speaking about wealth and poverty, or even exploitation, but since the manna from the foundations began to fall, only one book on economic inequality in the United States has appeared: *Wealth and Power in America*, written by a 'New Left' historian, Gabriel Kolko. The fact that academics are much readier to apply this kind of analysis to hostile or defunct systems than to the one under which they live suggests that an imputation of mundane motives is not entirely out of place.

Massive quantitative data can seldom be gathered about anything that neither the government nor the other large organizations wish to know or divulge. Furthermore, whereas no great difficulties arise about getting truthful answers to questionnaires about a preferred colour of wrapping paper or a motor-car, it is practically impossible to obtain any sincere inside information about anything that is punishable or deeply felt as shameful. There are no conceivable methods which would enable one to measure exactly the degree of popular support which a terroristic dictator enjoys, or the amount of tax evasion. Statistical information about sexual vagaries began to be available only when people ceased to feel deeply ashamed about them. It follows that anybody who advocates the methodological canons which would exclude non-quantifiable factors from consideration, throws his weight on the side of conventionality and the establishment's proclivity for whitewashing.

During his stay at the court of Catherine II of Russia, the great Swiss mathematician Euler got into an argument about the existence of God. To defeat the voltairians in the battle of wits, the great mathematician asked for a blackboard, on which he wrote:

'$(x + y)^2 = x^2 + 2xy + y^2$
therefore God exists.'

Unable to dispute the relevance of the formula which they did not understand, and unwilling to confess their ignorance, the literati accepted his argument. Owing to the continuing widespread ignorance of this subject, the utility of mathematical formulae for the purpose of blinding people with science, eliciting their respect and foisting upon them unwarranted propositions, has hardly diminished. As neither the literary nor the illiterate as well as non-numerate door-to-door sociologists can understand formulae, while the natural scientists cannot grasp the issues to which these are supposed to apply, and imagine that writings which look like their own must be more scientific than the ones which do not, juggling with mathematical formulae and words like 'input', 'output', 'entropy' and other importations from the natural sciences, no matter how misplaced, brings kudos for a social scientist. At its best it enables the practitioner to kill two birds with one stone: to avoid having to express his opinion on awkward or dangerous issues, and to score points in the game of academic status-seeking. One of the most successful efforts in this direction is the so-called topological psychology of Kurt Lewin which consists entirely of platitudes made vague and incomprehensible by being couched in a language full of geometric decorations. Other examples (including the so-called sociometry) are given in *The Uses of Comparative Sociology*, Chapter 1.

Although during the latter decades of the last century French and Belgian writers were modestly using this term to denote statistical measurement of social phenomena, its recent version aims higher. Its founder, Jacob Moreno, says in the preface to his main treatise called *Who Shall Survive?* that 'the origins of sociometry are like the origins of Godhead'. As his forerunners he claims Jesus and Socrates, whom he has undoubtedly surpassed not only in earning capacity but also in the ability to avoid bodily harm.

The absurdity of putting banal half-truths into mathematical shape is well illustrated in H. A. Simon's *Models of Man*, where he gives a formalized version of Homans' 'theory' of interaction. The latter has been acclaimed by some 'critics' as equivalent to the books of Euclid, which shows that they have no idea about what Euclid really did, and mistake a pompous formulation of a few unsophisticated half-truths for laying the foundations of a deductive system. Here are the 'principles' formulated by Homans in *The Human Group*:

... persons who interact frequently with one another tend to like one another.

If the frequency of interaction between two or more persons increases, the degree of their liking for one another will increase and vice versa.

If the interactions between the members of a group are frequent in the external system, sentiments of liking will grow up between them, and these sentiments will lead in turn to further interactions, over and above the interactions of the external system.

This is how Simon in his book *Models of Man* rephrases them, but without offering a solution to the question of how to quantify a vague concept like friendliness – without which his equations must remain pure decorations:

$$(1.1) \qquad I(t) = a_1 F(t) + a_2 A(t)$$

$$(1.2) \qquad \frac{dF(T)}{dt} = b[I(t) - bF(t)]$$

$$(1.3) \qquad \frac{dA(t)}{dt} = c_1[F(t) - yA(t)] + c^2[E(t) - A(t)]$$

Simon's effort shows that deploying mathematics (up to an engineering degree standard) will not help you to make discoveries if you are insensitive to the meaning of words and unaware of the complexities of social life. The mere fact that in a number of western countries the largest number of murders are committed against near relatives suffices to show that the frequency of interaction as such, far from always producing a liking, may generate a most atrocious hatred. The frequency of interaction between a sadistic guard and a prisoner, a cruel drill-sergeant and an awkward recruit, or a school playground bully and his favourite bookish victim may generate some of the deepest hatreds known to man; while every child-psychologist knows that often more squabbling and teasing goes on between siblings than between children who do not live together. Only when it is purely voluntary on both sides can interaction be interpreted as a pointer that mutual attraction may exist; although even in such cases there are many exceptions due to deception, as when a confidence trickster is cultivating his prospective prey. It requires an extraordinary obtuseness to imagine that you can understand human behaviour by forgetting about the nature of the contacts, and looking only at their frequency. It is even below the level of the Kinsey reports where (not to speak of the absurdity of equating 'human' with 'American') the relations between men and women are reduced to the frequency of orgasm.

Wading through the massive array of formulae, the reader of *Models of Man* will not learn about a single case of real social setting (to use the expression which appears in the title) which corroborates or is explained by or (to reduce our demands to a loosest minimum) might be better understood with their aid – not even the chapter on Election Predictions, which is one of the rare fields of political science where there are abundant and relatively precise quantitative data. The only concrete example mentioned in the entire book is James Joyce's *Ulysses*.

To give a physical analogy of what passes for mathematical sociology, we would have to put into a mathematical formula statements like 'if you bang them hard enough, most things crack up'. Actually this is being charitable to Simon because the last statement, though exceedingly vague, is at least true. A better physical equivalent to Simon's formalization of Homans' theories would be a sentence like 'the wind bloweth where it listeth'; which could also be written in the mathematical symbolism of vector calculus: $v_b = v_L$

Most of the applications of mathematics to the social sciences outside economics are in the nature of ritual invocations which have created their own brand of magician. The recipe for authorship in this line of business is as simple as it is rewarding:

5

just get hold of a textbook of mathematics, copy the less complicated parts, put in some references to the literature in one or two branches of the social studies without worrying unduly about whether the formulae which you wrote down have any bearing on the real human actions, and give your product a good-sounding title, which suggests that you have found a key to an exact science of collective behaviour.

Most large corporations have diagrams which depict the organizational skeleton by a tree-like structure of lines and points, and which supply a preliminary orientation about whom to approach on a particular question. Such drawings have been acclaimed as providing a foothold for an application of various branches of mathematics such as set, graph and lattice theory, which would help if it were true that interaction between human beings (or even animals) could be represented by a line with two end points. Unfortunately (or fortunately) next to nothing can be inferred about what people do from seeing their names joined by a line; and consequently, an elaborate theorizing based on such a far-fetched assumption boils down to status-seeking prattle.

The above mentioned foibles are rooted in a rather simple-minded reification. As Max Müller abundantly showed a century ago, all abstract words have originated from concrete through metaphoric use. Thus to describe what people do to one another we employ words like 'form', 'structure', or 'relation' (taken from the crafts of pottery, masonry and basketry) because we have nothing better, but we should beware of imagining that social phenomena offer anything but the vaguest analogy to the things or physical operations for which these words were first coined. To take another example: when we talk about status being higher or lower, we are entitled to use the latter words only in a purely metaphoric sense; and should beware of making a gratuitous assumption that the multifarious behaviour which we label as the relations of status is in fact amenable to a univocal linear ordering within which every individual must have a precise location. The assumption about the linearity of status seldom holds even for a pecking order of a few hens; because even there we often find such a situation that A pecks B, B pecks C, and C pecks A, not to speak of even more convoluted permutations.

The basic point is that you cannot convert vague and dubious approximations (not to speak of nonsense and half-truths) into a mathematical science simply by transcribing them into the symbolism of mathematics. Not even the most powerful theorems of to-day's mathematics could be of any help in an attempt to make aristotelian physics into an exact science. The principle that 'nature abhors a vacuum' was a valuable idea at the time – even useful for practical purposes such as making pumps – but no amount of juggling with symbols could convert it into a proposition of mathematical physics. Galileo's mathematics was quite simple, and his achievement did not consist of applying it to the physics which he found, but of creating new concepts capable of yielding genuinely new kinds of information when manipulated with the aid of mathematics.

Whatever criticism might be levelled at the irrelevance of the formulae propounded by Simon and other exponents of the same line of thought, including many economists, their equations are at least genuine mathematics, whereas the signs employed by Lévi-Strauss in his latest volumes merely look like mathematics, while being sheer substitutes for ordinary words. (This, however, is not the case in the mathematical appendix to *The Elementary Structures of Kinship*, written by André Weill.) Thus, Lévi-Strauss puts the conventional sign for 'to minus one power' where the word 'opposition' or 'contrast' is appropriate. For instance: since many cosmologies treat fire and water as opposites, he writes 'fire $=$ water $(^{-1})$' – a strange and meaningless scribble which is neither an equation nor a sentence. When in a myth an ant-eater figures as the opponent of a jaguar, Lévi-Strauss 'analyses' this by writing 'Jaguar $=$ ant-eater $(^{-1})$'. If we took the sign (-1) at its face value we would come to the phantasmagoric conclusion that a jaguar equals one divided by an ant-eater.

When one myth looks like a modified version of another, Lévi-Strauss labels them by algebraic-looking letters such as M_z and M_x; depicts the connection between them with the aid of the symbol $(\vec{F})$, which in mathematical texts often stands for a functional relationship between two variables, and writes

$M_z \rightarrow M_x$. This, of course, is an utter travesty of mathematics,
(f)

because a myth is a definite and highly differentiated historic individuum – not an algebraic variable – and a mathematical function is a relationship which determines how changes in one variable are related to the changes in the other, and therefore cannot hold between individua.

When we have three myths, and the third appears to be derived from the second in a way somewhat similar to the derivation of the second from the first (and I deliberately say 'appear' because the volumes of *Les Mythologiques* are full of conjectural assertions of this kind without any kind of supporting evidence or even arguments in their favour, not to speak of anything that might conceivably be acceptable as a proof) he affixes to this vague analogy a mathematical sounding label 'isomorphism', symbolized by $\approx$, and writes the following formula:

$$[M_z \rightarrow M_x] \approx [M_x \rightarrow M_y]$$
(f)$$(f)

(Le Cru et le Cuit, p. 205*)*

Far from having the meaning which we associate with this sign in mathematics, the brackets merely signify that there is a connection between the included items. Elsewhere in the same book the brackets mean that a connection between two traits or items holds within one and the same myth. Presence or absence of a theme or item is denoted by $+$ and $-$ respectively, which again looks like mathematics. Thus on p. 201 of the same book we are told about the theme of extinguishing fire with urine – apparently common in the myths of one Amazonian tribe – and depicted by Lévi-Strauss by [urine $\rightarrow$ fire (-1)], which in his parlance says that urine is transformed into a negation of fire. This is accompanied by an assertion that this theme has been 'transformed' into (which in a sane language might mean that it has evoked through some process of suggestion by analogy) the idea, expressed in a myth of another tribe in the same region, that manioc originated from woman's milk dropped on the soil. This explanation is transcribed by Lévi-Strauss as follows: [Milk $\rightarrow$ plants $(+)$]

and can be translated into his jargon as 'milk is transformed into positive plants'. As usual we are offered no evidence in support of the view that the latter explanation of the origin of manioc in fact originated as a 'transformation' of the idea of extinguishing fire with urine present in a myth of a different tribe. Instead of arguments to this point, we are expected to be convinced by the following mathematical-looking symbolization of this psychedelic supposition:

[Urine → fire (−)] → [milk → plants (+)]

As is well known, in many cosmogonic myths the relationship between heaven and earth is conceived as resembling the relationship between the sexes, and all kinds of things are viewed as engendered by their union. Employing the sign : : to signify resemblance (or, as he prefers to call it more prestigiously, homology) he depicts this loose set of notions by the following pseudo-mathematical formulation:

heaven : earth : : sex_x : sex_y

Whichever of his later books we take, we find constant repetition of completely misplaced terms taken from mathematics or linguistics. Crazy formulae, like those just mentioned, are called canonical, a thread in a story is called a syntagmatic sequence, and any kind of assemblage of words written inside a square is dignified with the mathematical label of a matrix. Although in *Le Cru et le Cuit* we have many pictures of animals, as in children's books, no story is given a name which would help us to remember what it is about, but only a number; and (with hundreds of them) this is a good method of numbing the reader's critical faculties.

To give another example, on p. 260 of *The Savage Mind* we find (with the inevitable pseudo-mathematical decorations) the following explication of the obvious point that historiography cannot describe everything that has happened in the past, and that gaps in our knowledge will always remain:

Given that the general code consists not in dates which can be ordered as a linear series but in classes of dates each furnishing an autonomous system of reference, the discontinuous and classificatory nature of historical knowledge emerges clearly. It operates by means of a rectangular matrix:

. . . .
. . . .
. . . .
. . . .
. . . .
. . . .

where each line represents classes of dates, which may be called hourly, daily, annual, secular, millennial for the purposes of schematization and which together make up a discontinuous set.[1]

On the next page we get the following piece of mystification (with intimidating terms, indiscriminately drawn from all kinds of sciences, displayed regardless of their meaning) which refers to the simple distinction between various levels of generality in historiography and the degrees of stress on anecdotal narrative at one end of the spectrum, and institutional analysis and theoretical explanation at the other:

Each domain of history is circumscribed in relation to that immediately below it, inscribed in relation to that above it. So each low-powered history of an inscribed domain is complementary to the powerful history of this same domain (in so far as it is itself an inscribed domain). Each history is thus accompanied by an indeterminate number of anti-histories, each complementary to the others: to a history of grade 1, there corresponds an anti-history of grade 2, etc. The progress of knowledge and the creation of new sciences take place through the generation of anti-histories which show that a certain order which is possible only on one plane ceases to be so on another. The anti-history of the French Revolution envisaged by Gobineau is contradictory on the plane on which the Revolution had been thought of before him. It becomes logically conceivable (which does not mean that it is true) if one puts oneself on a new plane, which incidentally Gobineau chose clumsily; that is to say: if one passes from a history of 'annual' or 'secular' grade (which is also political, social and ideological) to a history of 'millennial' or 'multi-millennial' grade (which is also cultural and anthropological), a procedure not invented by Gobineau which might be called: Boulainvilliers' 'transformation'. Consequently,

1. Claude Lévi-Strauss, *The Savage Mind (La Pensée Sauvage)* Weidenfeld & Nicolson, 1962.

depending on the level on which he places himself, the historian loses in information what he gains in comprehension or vice versa, as if the logic of the concrete wished to remind us of its logical nature by modelling a confused outline of Godel's theorem in the clay of 'becoming'.

The impressively erudite citation of Gödel is completely beside the point, as his discovery has nothing to do with the philosophy of history. The title of his famous paper is *On Formally Undecidable Propositions of Principia Mathematica and Related Systems*, and it contains a demonstration that it is impossible to give an absolute proof of the consistency of such a system with the aid of its postulates alone.

No doubt the chief reason why Lévi-Strauss's inconsequential musings about applications of mathematics to the study of culture have found such a wide acclaim is that they affect many people as hallucinogenic incantations, inducing fantasies that the mind has been expanded to computer-like dimensions through constant invocation of the sacred word 'binary' – to which the non-numerate literati attribute occult powers far beyond the prosaic fact that it simply refers to a special way of writing numbers to make them suitable for calculation by computers.

While dazzled by flashes of mathematical symbolism, the reader can titillate himself with morsels of surrealist pornography or coprology, presumably dug out of the subconscious of the benighted savages, of which the following is a fair sample:

If excrements are interchangeable but not the eyes, it follows that an interchange of the eyes (in contrast to an exchange of excrements) cannot consist of the change of the owner, with parts of the body remaining identical, but of a change of the parts of the body, the owner remaining identical . . . (*Le Cru et le Cuit*, p. 198 – translation is mine).

Among the innumerable even juicier titbits for the psychedelic generation, the following passage from the third volume of *Mythologiques* has been conveniently translated by Edmund Leach in his little book on Lévi-Strauss:

(there is) an analogy between honey and menstrual blood. Both are transformed (*elaborée*) substances resulting from a sort of *infracuisine*, vegetal in one case . . . animal in the other. Moreover honey may be either healthy or toxic, just as a woman in her normal condition is 'a honey', but secretes a poison when she is indisposed. Finally we have seen that, in native thought, the search for honey presents a sort of return to Nature, in the guise of erotic attraction transposed from the sexual register to that of the sense of taste, which undermines the very foundation of Culture if it is indulged in for too long. In the same way the *honey*-moon will be a menace to public order if the bridal pair are allowed to extend their private game indefinitely and to neglect their duties to society. (O.M.: 340.) (Edmund Leach, *Lévi-Strauss*, Fontana/Collins, 1970, p. 70.)

One of the great attractions of this kind of poetry masquerading as science is that it would be very difficult to invent a topic more remote from everything that matters in social life, and better fitted for a non-committal conversation among pseudo-intellectual international bureaucrats of most divergent outlooks and loyalties.

The reverence with which vain invocations of mathematics are treated among trendy intellectuals is not so very different from the superstitiousness of illiterate peasants, to judge by the experience of a friend of my parents who used to be a bank director in Kharkov, and after the revolution fled to Poland, having become what the Russians call an ex-person. With the remnants of his capital he bought a cottage in a region where people had had no contact with the Russians. Having some knowledge of first-aid he tried to be helpful, and to his surprise soon acquired a reputation as a great healer because, while putting on bandages, he used to mutter to himself absentmindedly in Russian, which many peasants interpreted as powerful magic.

To avoid misunderstandings, I must repeat once again that I fully appreciate the usefulness of quantification whenever it can be done in an honest and sensible way. What I am arguing against is the soul-destroying taboo against touching anything that cannot be quantified, and a superstitious reverence for every scribbling which looks like mathematics. These attitudes have already deprived psychology of most of its relevance to life; with the consequence that if you want to understand your own actions or other people's behaviour towards you, or why they believe or cherish or hate what they do, you may get some enlightenment by reading novels, but the last person to be able to help you is an academic psychologist of the dominant cybernetic-behaviourist persuasion. The obsession with quantification – promoted mainly by the desire to claim the status of an exact science – has led an increasingly large proportion of psychologists to abandon all the higher forms of human conduct and thought and to concentrate on the simplest forms of behaviour of rats, or even lower animals – seldom doing justice to the mental powers of even these creatures, as everything that cannot be transcribed into quantified terms of stimulus and response (or to use the latest jargon, input and output) is left out.

True, the application of experimental methodology (recently aided by cybernetics) has led to a certain number of discoveries but (apart from the older studies of perception) they belong mostly to neurology or endocrinology rather than psychology – if we use the latter term in its etymologically justified sense of having something to do with the human psyche. It hardly needs saying that neurology and physiology are highly meritorious disciplines, and anyone interested in them has a perfect right to concentrate on his subject; but he should have the honesty to give up the label 'psychology' – particularly if he believes that there is nothing to which the word psyche could legitimately be applied – so as to leave some room in the academia for people who wish to study those aspects of the human mind which cannot be reduced to physiology.

There is no point in consulting the quantophrenics (as Sorokin calls them) in the hope that they might say something interesting about such matters as the conflict between the generations, or the conditions of matrimonial harmony. If you want to understand the role of religion, you will do better to read Nietzsche than the current journals of psychology; while if you are interested in cliques you will get more enlightenment from Schopenhauer than from all the volumes on group dynamics, despite that writer's paranoiac exaggerations. Many fundamental insights into real life situations can be obtained from Freud, Adler and even Jung, as well as from their more sensible and critical followers; but none of these

5*

thinkers – not even the great Freud – had a sense of proportion, while many of their devotees are plainly mad. So we are left in the void between quantified trivialities and fascinating but entirely undisciplined flights of fancy.

Though not mentally ill, Freud fits rather well the common anti-intellectual notion that genius borders on madness – not because of his style, which is perfectly clear and unemotional, but because of his habit of writing down his thoughts wherever they might lead him, without much weighing or doubting; which habit, no doubt (coupled with an extraordinarily powerful intelligence and fertile imagination) enabled him to make his epoch-making discoveries. The price of this un-bridled creativity, however, is the plenitude of ridiculously far-fetched assertions which surround insights of the greatest originality of which the human mind is capable. To give an example of a childish misconception: the explanation of totemism and the taboo offered in *Totem and Taboo* is on the level of primitive myth-making, whereby a widespread custom is explained by an *ad hoc* invented story, and is methodo-logically on the same level as the story of Cain and Abel as an explanation of human aggressiveness and war.

Freud's pan-sexualism bears all the hallmarks of a neurotic obsession, no doubt instilled by his early upbringing, while the invention of a death instinct (which would make any species unviable) must have been a rationalization (in his own sense) of his own concern about approaching death. Nonetheless, he was one of the most creative minds that humanity has pro-duced; and perhaps a greater concern for consistency and evidence would have prevented him from discovering the mad logic of unconscious tendencies. Since psychoanalysis has become a religion, its more dogmatic devotees have been push-ing the master's errors to ever new heights of absurdity; but no matter how crazy their ideas, they cannot be accused of either banality or irrelevance to the real problems of human life, characteristic of the behaviourist school.

As in so many other branches of the study of man in society, we witness in recent psychology a flight from the middle ground of good sense which used to be cultivated by people like William MacDougal or J. C. Fluegel, notwithstanding their mistakes. Thus we get on one side irrelevancies and trivialities produced with the aid of ultra-sophisticated statistical methods (usually employed with a sad deficiency of philosophical acumen and an even sadder unconcern for what words mean), while on the other, we have dogmas emanating from flights of disordered imagination. The latter are rammed down the throats of the gullible public as recipes for living by prestigious specialists whose every word is taken as gospel, although on closer acquaintance neither they nor their wives (and least of all their children) strike one as examples of happiness and health.

The case of the British psychiatrist Ronald Laing offers a good example of the common phenomenon of how one can become the centre of a cult by holding views which correspond to what a large number of people want to hear. Laing has made a few serious contributions to the understanding of schizophrenia by offering interesting and plausible interpretations of the postures and movements of the sufferers; but his popularity among the trendy crowds is due to the message (which is the only conclusion that clearly emerges from his tenebrous disquisitions) to all the youthful (and not so youthful) freaks that no matter what they do they are entitled to blame it on other people, especially their mothers.

At the other end of the spectrum, quantophrenic psychology gratifies the bureaucrats, big business, and the advertisers, by telling them what they want to hear. For it would make the job easier for the bureaucrat or any other kind of manipulator if everybody (except himself) resembled a push-button automaton, with perfectly predictable outputs following known inputs. The insidious educational bureaucrats also like to take the view that the material they are handling have minds like a *tabula rasa* (to use Locke's expression) whose content and character can be determined wholly by circulars about methods of 'processing'. The input-output conception of human nature appeals to the advertisers too; and I doubt whether it was accidental that the founder of behaviourism, J. B. Watson, became an advertising executive. To reduce wayward human beings to the condition of dependable automata has always been every drill-sergeant's and every tyrant's dream; while the creator of 'scientific' management and time and motion study, Frederick Winslow Taylor, unabashedly tells us in his book how he searched for workers characterized by cupidity, stupidity and docility. It is, I believe, the harmony between such wishes and the reductionist view of the human mind propagated by quantitative behaviourist psychology that accounts for the preference it enjoys among the controllers of funds on either side of the Iron Curtain.

The popularity of psychoanalytic follies is in many ways the reverse side of the same coin; because the increasingly standardized, bureaucratized and cyberneticized world frustrates so many basic needs of human nature, that moderation, a sense of proportion and balanced judgment become increasingly difficult to sustain, as more and more people seek solace in psychedelic drugs or irrational (if not anti-rational) beliefs – which creates happy hunting grounds for all kinds of quacks.

Money provides a ready-made quantified criterion, and so economics has been able to develop much further than the other social sciences. Nor, unlike psychology, can it be accused of having abandoned its proper objectives for the sake of quantification. Nevertheless, even here we can see the harmful effects of confusing the availability of 'figures' with an attainment of true exactitude, aggravated by the fact that the introduction of mathematical formulae into economic theory has produced amongst economists a tendency towards splendid isolation, based on the belief that their discipline dealt with autonomous and measurable variables. This belief, however, appeared plausible only because the sociological assumptions of economic theory were more or less modelled on the dominant characteristics of the societies in the midst of which this theory grew, and to which it was most commonly applied. The evolution towards diffuse pluralistic collectivism, involving growing inter-penetration of government, pressure groups and the organs of economic control, has considerably enlarged the discrepancy between current reality and the tacit sociological assumptions of economic theory (which applies even to such recent additions to it as the Keynesian models): but the arbitrary nature of these assumptions has been fully revealed only when conclusions about the affairs of underdeveloped countries, drawn on the basis of conventional economic theory, have proved to be manifestly false. The perplexity engendered by the failures of their predictions has given rise to an extensive literature supplying modifications of economic theories designed to fit them for dealing with pre-industrial economic structures. So far, however, only *ad hoc* qualifications have been proposed, without attempting to treat the fundamental problem of institutional limits to the validity of various parts of economic theory.

The sophisticated mathematical models, which one finds in books on economics, might mislead an unwary reader into believing that he is facing something equivalent to the theories of physics. The truth, however, is that – whereas the formulae which figure in textbooks of physics have been directly or indirectly confirmed by countless experiments and constant industrial practice – none of the more complex models of economic theory has been corroborated by unambiguous statistical evidence. While a debate is still raging between Milton Friedman and his critics about one of the simplest theorems of economics, and one of the earliest to be put into an algebraic form – namely, the quantity theory of money – ever new and more sophisticated models succeed one another on the pages of the learned journals. It must be said in their defence that, unlike the cybernetic models in political science discussed in Chapter 14, these models are genuinely clever, plausible and usually testable in principle – that is to say, one can specify what kind of empirical data (were it possible to collect these) would corroborate or invalidate them. Nonetheless, there is a big difference between theoretical testability and having been tested; and if we look for the latter quality we are reduced to the simplest and oldest parts of economic theory such as the laws of supply and demand or the quantity theory of money, taken as rough approximations.

Actually, even the shapes of the demand and supply curves for most goods are surmised rather than reliably ascertained by econometric methods, while in the input-output models, simplifications about transformation ratios and their relationships (such as representing by linear functions relationships known to be in reality non-linear or even discontinuous) are made for the sake of making calculations manageable. Even in their simplified forms, realistic input-output models of even the smallest national economy are overwhelmingly complex; and it is not my intention to denigrate people who are trying to make some sense out of such a welter of data. My only objections are directed against those who equate the mathematical form of a theory with the exactitude and reliability of its empirical relevance. Such people are usually found among the lesser lights, while Keynes, for instance, was very explicit about the dangers of this kind of confusion. The founder of the input-output method, Wassily Leontieff, also says in one of his essays that only simple mathematics is of any use in empirical matters, while the very sophisticated models are sheer exercises in virtuosity, inapplicable to reality.

Notwithstanding its inability to explain adequately the matters which fall within its province (owing above all to their dependence on the non-economic aspects of social reality) it can at least be said in favour of economic theory that, though insufficient, it is nevertheless indispensable for understanding how the economic system works. Even more: whereas no dire practical results would follow from a sudden disappearance of all the psychologists, sociologists and political scientists, a similar vanishing of economists would, I am sure, make the management of economic affairs even more defective than it is. Without, for instance, the knowledge imparted to us by Keynes we could easily find ourselves in a situation like that of the thirties. Nevertheless, it is important to bear in mind that even in the branch which has opportunities for measurement unrivalled in the other social sciences, an infatuation with numbers and formulae can lead to empirical irrelevance and fraudulent postures of expertise.

The most pernicious manifestations of the last-named tendency (abetted by the natural proclivity of every occupation to extol its wares) have been the claims of numerous economists to act as arbiters on matters of planning, on the assumption (whose efficacy depends on its being tacitly made rather than explicitly recognized) that the factors which can be measured must serve as the basis for decision. In truth there is no reason whatsoever to presume that amenability to measurement must correspond to importance; and the assumption in question has often led economists to aid and abet the depredations of a soul-destroying and world-polluting commercialism and bureaucratic expansionism, by silencing the defenders of aesthetic and humane values with the trumpets of one-sided statistics.

Chapter 11

Promiscuous Crypto-Conservatism

Many of the most important insights into the nature of human society came from speculations and discussions about how it might be improved. Plato and Aristotle formulated the first known propositions of sociological theory while expounding their recipes for a perfect society; the first relying chiefly on imagination and speculation, while the second laid the foundations of comparative method by making a survey of over a hundred constitutions of Greek cities. Voltaire, Adam Smith, Saint-Simon, Auguste Comte, Marx – to name but a few – wrote their treatises in order to tell people what they ought to do to bring about a better social order. Keynes – to move over to the most recent times – devised his General Theory with the aim of finding a cure for unemployment. Broadly speaking, the social sciences have developed as an offshoot of reformist strivings in step with the growing realization that the knowledge of causal relations is a prerequisite of effective action. No less fruitful than the reformist and revolutionary angles have been the conservative or even reactionary criticisms of the shortcomings of the utopias and plans of reform. Malthus, for instance, began his epoch-making work in order to demonstrate the impossibility of James Mill's plans for a perfect society. Auguste Comte's system, despite its hostility to the existing order, can be viewed as a reaction against what he regarded as the lack of realism in the ideas of the French socialists, including his former master, Henri de Saint-Simon. The most outstanding works of the late nineteenth and early twentieth century emerged from arguments against Marx, as in the case of Mosca's theory about the ideologies and élites, and Michels' Iron Law of Oligarchy. Pareto's conservative politics stemmed from (or, if you like, were justified by) a theoretical system which amounted to a dismembered marxism: the inevitability and ubiquity of class struggles, the epiphenomenal character of ideologies and laws were all there, but the messianic expectation that it will all come to an end one day was replaced by a vision of an eternal cycle of circulation of élites. Max Weber's studies were clearly inspired by the desire to provide a corrective to Marx's thesis of the primacy of the economic factors, while his political views were anything but sanguine in respect of the chances of improving the social order. Herbert Spencer as well as de Tocqueville must also be classed as conservatives in virtue of their scant faith in the efficacy of reforms, and their lack of enthusiasm about the trends which prevailed during their later years. So it can hardly be claimed that a conservative stance on the issues of the day incapacitates one from making contributions to the social sciences.

As a matter of historical fact, the understanding of social processes has advanced only during eras of heated controversy between the reformists and the prophets of revolution on one side, castigating the vices of the existing order and propounding peaceful or violent remedies, and on the other, the conservatives, stressing the virtues of the status quo in comparison with what might happen in consequence of rash tampering. Such debates have not only prompted factual inquiries into social circumstances which would not otherwise have attracted attention, but have also raised the question of causes and effects, and thus provided a stimulus for fruitful theorizing.

Although conservative political views often went together with new ideas on the nature of society, all the creative thinkers of this persuasion were ready to admit the shortcomings of the social order which commanded their allegiance, and which they defended, not by denying its defects, but by arguing that it was better than the most likely alternatives. Pareto's acceptance of fascism, for instance, stemmed not from a rosy view of the character of that movement but from a profound pessimism about the possibility of eliminating force and fraud from politics. In an article written shortly after Mussolini's rise to power, Pareto freely admits that the chief characteristics of fascism are readiness to use violence and success in propagating myths, and then proceeds to defend it on the grounds that it is inevitable owing to the disintegration of the liberal order. (The severity of Herbert Spencer's criticisms of the institutions of his day can be seen in the articles reprinted in *Herbert Spencer: Structure, Function and Evolution.*)

The approach which has emerged in America after the Second World War, and has since blighted sociology and political science throughout the non-communist world, differs radically from conservatism honestly rooted in pessimism by its unspoken determination to gloss over all the unpleasant facts, to cover up all the explosive issues, and to exude an aura of optimism reminiscent of a public relations man's office. Its chief message is that all is for the best in the best of all possible worlds and that (as in a Hollywood film) everything will turn out right in the end. Apart from the newer fans of cybernetics, the main school of this great movement is known as structural-functionalism, whose chief apostles are as frequently cited and quoted as they are influential in allocating funds and deciding upon appointments and promotions.

Structural-functionalism has many times been accused (notably by Wright Mills in *Sociological Imagination*) of smuggling in a conservative ideology under the cover of devotion to the ideals of science. Though perfectly justified, this judgment does not do justice to the insidiousness of a doctrine capable of carrying its adherents far beyond ordinary and honest conservatism, which entails a loyalty to some definite order, accompanied by a deprecation of systems or doctrines opposed to it. The ideology of structural-functionalism, in contrast, bestows its blessing on every system which exists, so long as it exists; which means that it throws its weight on the side of the powers that be, whoever, wherever and whenever they might be. To distinguish it from decent conservatism, openly committed to the principles of a definite social order, I propose to call the doctrine characterized above 'promiscuous crypto-conservatism'. And why 'crypto'? Because, rather than propagate this attitude openly (which would be less effective), its partisans insinuate it surreptitiously (and often, no doubt, unconsciously) through ostensibly scientific value-free propositions and definitions. In the next chapter I shall try to substantiate these accusations by analysing the salient concepts, but in the meantime let us look more closely at the distinguishing features of promiscuous crypto-conservatism from the view-point of the sociology of the social sciences.

Blind adherence to everything that is 'done' usually goes either with a low intelligence or with a neurotic fear of using one's brain. In the first case it is a perfectly rational attitude because, if the reasons for extant arrangements are beyond one's comprehension, then the sensible course is to follow the mass rather than tamper with things one does not understand. It makes little difference in this respect whether the lack of understanding stems from a small brain power or the exiguity of the existing knowledge. Thus the conservatism of a tribesman need not amount to an irrational 'resistance to change' but may be a perfectly reasonable reluctance to plunge into the unknown. Readiness to experiment becomes reasonable only when our knowledge allows us to make predictions which give us a better chance of success than mere guessing. The elemental or primordial conservatism of this kind – for which the early Italian criminologist Cesare Lombroso has proposed the term 'misoneism' – is something quite different from a political conservatism which, in the last resort, normally boils down to a defence of privilege, and is often combined with a readiness to welcome innovations which bolster up this privilege or at least do not threaten it. After all, 'conservative' businessmen have wrought the most revolutionary changes in the conditions of living.

The rise of the social sciences was closely connected with the decline of misoneism concerning social arrangements, which in its primordial forms amounted to the inability to conceive that the existing way of life could be changed. But this rise was not, to repeat, more intimately linked with the critiques of the existing order than with the arguments of political conservatives in its defence. Indeed, the earliest flickers of sociological or politological theorizing appeared in writings purporting to convey advice to the rulers, such as the works of Shang Yang and Han Fei Tsu, Macchiavelli, the philosophers of the Enlightenment, and the eighteenth-century German specialists in bureaucratic efficiency known as 'cameralists'. It might even be argued that, insofar as science presupposes rational inference from the available experience, the conservatives have been on the whole more 'scientific' (and consequently more effective) than the utopians and the revolutionaries; although it is only fair to remember that without the latter there would have been no discussion at all and therefore no progress in understanding.

It may be worth remarking on the margin that the old quip about the English being less 'logical' than the French has never been justified as far as politics and society were concerned because, in the absence of any tested theory from which reliable predictions could be drawn, the most logical thing to do was to muddle through by piecemeal adjustments rather than attempt to implement a comprehensive blue-print for a new society. But let us go back to the main theme.

Despite the inherently subversive nature of cerebration, the awareness of the fragility of civilization and the fear of the mob have led many outstanding minds to a kind of resigned conservatism, which caused them to opt for the devil they knew in preference to what they regarded as a *fata morgana*. True, there have been many apologists and propagandists who did their best to conceal the more brutal facts of social life under the effusions of 'idealistic' social and political philosophy or economic theory – like the economists and the Hegelians rightly criticized on this score by Marx and Engels. None of the writers, however, who have made enduring contributions to our understanding of man and society has sinned in this way. If we look at the pronouncements on current affairs by Herbert Spencer, Max Weber or Gaetano Mosca – whom the marxists automatically classify as conservatives or reactionaries – we find that they are full of criticisms of the establishment of the day, made in a tone which no noted American sociologist, economist or political scientist since Veblen has dared to adopt, with the sole exception of C. Wright Mills. The latter's originality consisted simply in not participating in his colleagues' recidivist evasion of important issues, and in dealing with the kind of problems that preoccupied the founders. Not even his model Thorstein Veblen was of the same intellectual stature as his great European contemporaries, while Mills himself certainly fell far short of greatness and can in no way be credited with having created a New Sociology – as claimed by the adulators who began to surround him as soon as he allied himself with the communists. Nonetheless, despite the latter lapse (which, I believe he came to regret shortly before his death) he deserves our respect for his determination to uphold the tradition of courageous critique of society in the midst of a very corrupted environment.

The discrepancy between professed ideals and social reality has always been so great that mealy-mouthed apologetics and diplomatic pussy-footing have never been compatible with serious inquiry into the facts of life, or even a minimally realistic speculation about the nature of society. Honest conservatism can only be based on the judgment that the system under which one is living is on balance less imperfect than its likely substitutes. Entailing a commitment to a definite way of life and its ideology, a non-promiscuous conservatism exposes its adherents to an enmity, not only from the reformers and revolutionaries from inside, but also from the conservatives who belong to other systems based on opposed principles. You cannot oppose radical reforms in Britain with the same arguments you might have to use if you wanted to defend the military dictatorship in Brazil. If you are a Russian conservative who opposes any watering down of central planning, you cannot give your blessing to the German *Wirtschaftswunder*. You cannot use the same arguments to prove that what Mao is doing in China is just right, and to demonstrate the perfection of the American way of life. If you sincerely take up any of these causes you might be mistaken, or even downright foolish, but you cannot be legitimately accused of failing to commit yourself and of attempting to appear to be on everybody's side. To achieve the latter result you must make vague pronouncements which refer to nothing that really happens, so that nobody can pin you down. The supreme feat in this genre is to bestow a blessing on every existing structure of power without specifying any concrete traits thereof – a blessing which must be surreptitious, yet perceptible enough to make the potentates feel flattered and reassured that it would be good for their subjects to absorb such a message. In their day Hegel and his disciples did not do too badly in their adulation of the bureaucratic state, but changing semantic fashions call for new versions couched in a new phraseology.

Although Max Weber's centenary has brought forth many celebrations, it is significant that none of the volumes published on that occasion contains a single example of an attempt to follow the most essential point of Weber's approach: namely, the use of widely ranging comparative analysis for the purpose of unravelling causal chains and establishing inductive generalizations. Therefore, notwithstanding Max Weber's greatness as a thinker, one may wonder whether this is the only reason for 'the cult of personality' which is growing around him. Marx, to take the most obvious example, has come to occupy the place of God, not by virtue of his great contributions to economics and sociology, but because of the messianic myths and vitriolic curses in which his cognitive insights were enveloped; and because (unlike the other prophets of socialism) he has never drawn any concrete plans, and confined himself to asserting that the future society would be very, very good, thus giving a blank cheque to those who claim to be his followers. Could it be that the vogue for invoking Weber's name has something to do with his relatively favourable attitude to capitalism and bureaucracy, and with the fact that of all the founders of sociology (with the exception of Durkheim) he was the least given to muck-raking, and has said little that throws a bad light on issues such as fraud and violence in politics or monopolistic exploitation? The heaviness of his style, moreover, lends itself to a 'processing' through which sociological sedatives can be distilled which provide a blessing for the status quo whatever it might be, and can therefore be expounded with equal ease in Dallas, Moscow, the Vatican, Jakarta and Pretoria. Perhaps for these reasons even people whose work reveals no trace of Weber's influence feel under an obligation to pay homage to his memory.

Not that he could be justly accused of timorous evasiveness or surreptitious apologetics. On the contrary, he was a man of great courage and saturnine temper, and he took a resolute stand on many current issues, but these were specific to the Germany of his day, and have little relevance to the wider problems of our times. Moreover, his extant major empirical studies were focused on ancient and exotic civilizations (as he died before getting down to more recent times) and so they contain little that anyone would strongly wish to conceal today. Thus, though by no means an ancestor of this breed personally, Weber lends himself better than the other great figures of sociological thought (with the possible exception of Durkheim) to be cast in the role of the promiscuous crypto-conformists' totem.

It was not accidental that the most perfect form of promiscuous crypto-conservatism came into existence in the United States during the last two or three decades; because under a bureaucratic oligarchy like the old Prussian, or under a unitary capitalist ruling class as in England before the Second World War, only an unambiguous subservience to the ruling class and its coherent ideology could offer good prospects of a career to an intellectual without the talent needed for making a mark as an iconoclast. The present American power élite, on the other hand, is less homogeneous in ethnic and class origins, religion and occupation; and consequently a verbal concoction capable of pleasing all of its sectors must be much vaguer – not to speak of the necessity to flatter the masses as well. In other words, a more pluralistic power structure gives an advantage to a more promiscuous and more surreptitious brand of conservative formulae. On top of this, there is the international stage of UNO, UNESCO and similar bodies, where it is even more difficult to say anything concrete that would offend nobody, let alone please everybody, and where extreme vagueness constitutes an essential protective colouring.

Every writer likes or would like to be widely read, cited, quoted, translated and praised; and in every branch of learning thousands are striving and competing for fame. So, if someone becomes very famous – let alone the most famous in his field – there must be an explanation. It may be sheer intellectual merit or a gift for self-advertisement and manoeuvring in the corridors of power. Sometimes the popularity of writings derives exclusively from the position of their authors, as in the case of Stalin's works or Eisenhower's memoirs, to mention two out of many possible examples. Or the book may appeal to common and commonly unsatisfied aggressive and sexual impulses. There is no mystery about the success of a book like *The Naked Ape* by Desmond Morris whose pseudo-science provides an uneducated public and semi-literate scientists with an excuse for titillating themselves with rather childish pornography. Nor is it very difficult to understand why the neurotic rhapsodies about violence by assorted pseudo-revolutionaries appeal to the soft-living intellectuals and organization men who have to grin all the time at people whom they would love to murder. But how can we explain Talcott Parsons' rise to the position of the most famous sociologist of today?

Nobody can become the most renowned writer in his field without possessing some special quality . . . by sheer accident. And it does require a genius of a peculiar kind to be able to establish a new language, which may not be very helpful in furthering our understanding but which cannot be said to lack originality or fascination for many minds. The next chapter analyses in some detail the latently (and unintentionally) propagandist content in the pronouncement by Parsons and like-minded authors, which add up to a most potent love-for-all-the-establishments potion ever invented. Here I should only like to point out that, even apart from the hidden ingredients of promiscuously conservative ideology, the nebulous verbosity also reinforces the status quo in a simpler way, namely by throwing a spanner into the brain works. Once somebody succumbs to this kind of cloudy scholasticism, he becomes like a white mouse in a treadmill and expends all his energies on getting nowhere as far as knowledge of the real world goes; which ensures that he will never say anything that might cast unwanted light on something that really takes place. Every bureaucrat, politician or ruler – whether capitalist, communist, clericalist, monarchist or fascist – will find a disembrained social scientist of this persuasion a safe man who will give him no trouble. The hordes of devotees, whose lack of brains would have debarred them from intellectual occupations in more civilized times, naturally adore the apostle who has enabled them to make an easy living by posing as scientists, and their resounding chorus helps to drown the scattered voices of the opposition.

That the chief attraction of this school lies in its promiscuously crypto-conservative message can be inferred not only from an analysis of their publications, but also from the welcome extended to them by governments wedded to contradictory ideologies and intolerant of all deviations. Not surprisingly, as far as I know, no dictator has yet banned the books of the archpriest of euphemistic sociology, although in most communist countries even Keynes is forbidden. In Spain, where being a mild liberal, or not pious enough, suffices to disqualify a candidate for a post in sociology or political science – the road to which normally leads through an apprenticeship in the Ministry of Information – translations of Parsons are published and sold without restrictions. The Polish communist bosses of 'culture', who have been busy purging the ranks of intellectuals or deviationists (recently under the pretext of fighting zionism), have not only allowed his books to be translated but have even organized a reception for him. He is equally welcomed in Moscow. The publication of the translation into Polish was delayed not because the censor objected to anything that Parsons said, but because a leading official exponent of marxism who wrote the introduction had been purged for his connections with zionism and had become an unmentionable non-person whose name must under no circumstances appear in print. In South Africa, where even simple fact finding enquiries are often forbidden, the course in sociology in the Fort Hare University for the Bantus is based on Parsons' works, the main textbook being *Sosiologie*, by S. O. Celliers and D. Joubert, which is an exposition in Afrikaans (rather than a formal translation) of the Parsonian doctrine.

More than once I have heard the argument that such a universal acceptability, far from giving grounds for suspicion, proves the objective and scientific character of Parsons' works. Perverse logic! Given that these regimes inculcate ideologies containing blatant falsehoods which, to boot, are mutually contradictory, it follows that only a theory which contradicts none of these falsehoods will be tolerated by them all. And only a string of completely vacuous statements can be compatible with a set of mutually contradictory falsehoods concerning the same matter.

To forestall a misunderstanding, I must stress that I do not accuse (or even suspect) Talcott Parsons of deliberately concocting a stunt, although I do suspect that there are some brazen charlatans among his acolytes. I am sure that, like all the effective sorcerers, the Grand Master sincerely believes what he says. I am told by a good friend of mine who knows him personally that he is an honourable man who takes no part in the intrigues and machinations rampant among the academic jet-set, and that for this reason he has been cold-shouldered by the common run of manipulators since his retirement, despite his great fame. I regret, therefore, to have to make such caustic remarks, but the future of the social sciences is at stake; for, notwithstanding his dedication to scholarships and considerable erudition, Parsons' influence on their development has been disastrous, as error may be corrected and lead to further knowledge, whereas confusion constitutes an absolute dead end.

Chapter 12

Ideology Underneath Terminology

Most of the terminological quarrels in the social sciences drag on endlessly because, far from being purely intellectual debates about the heuristic value of various usages, they boil down to disputes about the right to the exclusive use of certain approval- or disapproval-eliciting signals for labelling whatever the speaker is for or against. The interminable debates about what is democracy have little to do with the difficulty (formidable enough) of finding a scientifically satisfactory classification of political systems. The real bone of contention is the exclusive right to use this approval-eliciting sound to induce a favourable attitude in the listeners towards the regime or policy of one's choice. Consequently, if we look for a common denominator of all the connotations with which it is being used, we find that it has simply replaced the old-fashioned word, 'good', so that we could justifiably speak of democratic soups and steaks. With 'reactionary' it is the other way round: and if we hear somebody call another person 'reactionary', all we can conclude is that he does not like him, but can infer nothing about the views of the person thus labelled without knowing the political stance of the speaker. In the debates about what fascism is, the most usual aim of the participants is to tamper with the meaning of the term so as to fit it for their enemies and divert it from their friends.

Sometimes the mixture of a propagandist and cognitive intent is more difficult to disentangle. 'Totalitarianism', for example, was invented in order to designate a political regime whereby the government controls the totality of social life. Complications stem from the fact that, although some governments have come near the mark in this, no government has ever controlled every action of every citizen, and therefore we must decide at which point of extension of governmental control we are prepared to classify a regime as totalitarian. It might be argued, for instance, that the Fascist regime in Italy was not really totalitarian as it never seriously interfered with the activities of the Church. Another difficulty stems from divergencies of directions in which control is extended. Thus, for instance, the control over British economy exercised by the Labour Government from 1946 to 1950 was more extensive, and a great deal more effective, than that of Peron over the economic life of Argentina, notwithstanding his suppression of civil liberties. Suppression of political opposition has always been a common phenomenon to be found in many states which accommodated themselves to the independent power of the Church, and even supported the doctrine of *laissez-faire* in economic matters: as was the case of the Second Empire in France, to mention one of many possible examples.

It is clear then that autocracy does not imply totalitarianism, but does totalitarianism imply autocracy and tyranny? Up till now all totalitarian states have been despotic, but we cannot exclude the possibility that the Soviet regime might evolve into a form of totalitarianism which will be oligarchic and fairly law-abiding, as has already happened in comparison with the Stalin era. To allow for such a possibility it is preferable to define totalitarianism as a regime where a government recognizes no limits to its interference, controls in considerable measure all aspects of the lives of its subjects, and permits no independent organizations. This definition covers Nazi Germany and all present day Communist states excepting Poland. Gomulka's Poland and Mussolini's Italy fall into the category of semi-totalitarianism because of the independent power of the Church within their territories.

Even from a purely heuristic standpoint then, there exists a genuine problem of how to define totalitarianism most usefully. But the doubt surrounding this question allows the meaning to be stretched in all kinds of ways to suit the purpose of the speaker. The New Leftists, among others, reject it altogether because of the implication that there are important similarities between the nazi and the communist systems, which they deny, as this automatically discredits the latter in view of the fact that the nazis have few admirers since they lost the war.

Even concepts which refer to phenomena seemingly remote from today's issues can become subjects of a crypto-propagandist tug-of-war, as can be seen from the next example. The term 'feudal' began to be used in the eighteenth century to describe the general condition of European society during the Middle Ages. Soon afterwards, European travellers, struck by the resemblances between what they read about the history of their countries and what they saw in the East, began to apply this term to the institutional arrangements of non-European countries. When Saint-Simon, Auguste Comte and Marx put forth their evolutionary schemes, they included feudalism as one of the necessary stages through which humanity must pass. This gave rise to a long drawn out debate on whether feudalism was something peculiar to Europe, or whether it was a phenomenon of a more generic nature. Historiographers (owing, no doubt, to their love of detail and dislike of generalities) favoured, on the whole, the former view. The tendency was to restrict the denotation of the term to Western Europe. Even Poland and Sweden were considered as not having passed through feudalism, because in Poland the nobles held the land as hereditary property (i.e., the tenure was allodial – not feudal), and in Sweden the nobles never acquired judicial authority over the peasants. On the other hand, in historical sociology, and above all in political debates, the meaning of feudalism was becoming very wide. The marxists were and are always determined to call feudal every society which is neither capitalist nor socialist nor tribal. As is well known, Marx envisaged social evolution as going through the stages of tribalism, slave-owning, feudalism and capitalism in order to arrive at the ultimate goal of socialism. The vested interest which the marxists have in finding feudalism everywhere stems from the fear that, if we admit the possibility that one of the intermediary stages is not really necessary, we may begin to doubt the inevitability of the final goal. Often 'feudalism' is used simply as a term of opprobrium, implying the evils of inequality, exploitation and traditionalism. The values of most discussions among historians, on the other hand, has been impaired by the neglect of three rather obvious truths: first, that denotation of any concept depends on its connotation;

second, that in the realm of social phenomena presence or absence of a feature is mostly a matter of degree; third, that in dealing with clusters of imperfectly correlated traits, we are faced with variations in the relative degrees in which the constituent features are present in different cases.[1]

A visitor from Mars, unacquainted with human nature but equipped with a terrestrial dictionary, might well wonder why, over a large part of the globe, anyone who tries to use the word 'class' not in accordance with the conception given to it by a writer who lived a century ago, soon finds himself in trouble. Neither etymology nor the canons of scientific method can account for such purism, which can, however, be easily explained if we look at the word in question as a disapproval-eliciting signal which can be used for influencing behaviour.

The Romans (from whose language 'class' comes) used its prototype to designate legally defined groups of citizens classified according to their wealth, the type of weapons they could afford for their military service, the weight of their votes in the popular assembly, and the order of precedence in various ceremonies. Thus the ranking in respect of wealth, power and prestige went together; so that there was in Rome at that time what modern sociologists call status consistency, or status crystallization.

The forerunners of the social sciences (from Plato to Adam Smith) often discussed the differences and conflicts between the rich and the poor, the magnates and the commonalty, the haughty and the humble; although the word class in its modern sense came into common use only after the French Revolution broke the legal barriers between 'estates'. The distinctions between 'class' and 'estate' or later 'caste', however, concerned mainly the degree of differentiation and solidarity of the groups, as well as the nature of the barriers between them and their relative impassability, while taking for granted that all these terms had to do with the inequalities of wealth, power and prestige.

Marx did not deviate from this line by taking the relationship

1. An examination of this concept from the standpoint of its value to comparative analysis can be found in *Uses of Comparative Sociology*, Chapter 10.

(of ownership) to the means of production as the essential criterion of class, because under the capitalism of his day this relationship did on the whole determine the differences in wealth, power and status. In England (where the most ad-advanced forms of capitalism were to be found in those days) the most important division of society lay between the owners of capital (whether landed or industrial) and those who lived by selling their labour. In addition to wealth and political power, the former had an exclusive access to higher education, the lucrative professions, sinecures and posts, and enjoyed deference from their poor and humble labourers. True, a large number of independent craftsmen, owner-cultivators and petty traders continued to exist, but with a remarkable perspicacity Marx rightly forecast their sinking into insignificance. Though not so ignorant as not to know about the existence of powerful, affluent and revered officers and officials in the continental monarchies, Marx regarded them as relics of waning feudalism, imagining that the progress of industry would make the agrarian states of Europe resemble the England of his day, where generals and bureaucrats played hardly any role at all.

When he was analysing a concrete situation, Marx clearly assigned the generals and the common soldiers to different classes, although in the eye of the law they stood in the same relationship to the tools of their trade, and the general had no better claim to owning the coach at his disposal than his coachman did. Marx drew no inferences from this obvious fact because he regarded control without ownership as a trait of the vanishing pre-capitalist formations – in which, of course, he was completely wrong; and it was precisely the proliferation of bureaucracies (private as well as public) that nullified his prophecies. Nowadays, when anyone can see the vast advan-tages of income, ease and prestige derived from high positions in bureaucratic bodies, ownership can be regarded as only one of the determinants of inequality; and the criterion of class proposed by Marx has lost its validity: partially under capital-ism and totally under communism.

Why then do the communists and their sympathizers cling to Marx's definition? The answer is that by replacing 'in-equality' by 'class' and then equating the division between classes with the differences in the relation of ownership of the means of production, they can assert that inequality has disappeared (or will do so) in consequence of the abolition of private ownership of the means of production. Thus, by ramming the out-of-date definition down everybody's throat, the communist preachers aim at making people docile under their dispensation while turbulent under capitalism.

A number of other useful fictions rest upon this definition, such as the notion that the affluent party potentates belong to the same class (namely the proletariat) as the undernourished drudges in the factories and on the farms, because none of them legally own the means of production. So we can see why the spokesmen of the communist establishments cling to such a convenient conception. It does not follow, however, that those who object do so solely out of a concern for methodological propriety; because there are no strictly scientific arguments against leaving to the marxists their beloved word and letting them do with it what they like. No: the only true justification for prosecuting the verbal battle is that their opponents do not want to let them get away with this kind of manipulation through definition. Through constant employment as a word of opprobrium, the word 'class' has acquired an indelible emotional loading and, consequently, a considerable utility as a hostility-evoking signal; and so it is elementary tactics to contest your opponent's monopoly on its use. Nonetheless, though laudable as an endeavour to combat propagandist juggling with words, the opposition to the marxist usage of 'class' stems from political rather than strictly cognitive preoccupations.

While the adulators of the Socialist Fatherland keep waving the old conjurer's wand, the self-appointed public relations men for the American Way of Life attempt to conceal the magnitude of the inequalities in their country by banishing the sinister-sounding 'class' from their vocabulary and replacing it by soothing 'strata' and 'status groups'. Faced with incipient or virulent warfare between the rich and the poor in Latin America, political scientists from the United States try to conjure the spectre away by substituting 'sector' for the evil-boding 'class' – in the same way as the peasants of old used to call the devil by all kinds of nicknames lest uttering his real name might make him come.

Improving on mere ritual avoidance, the arch-priest of sociological orthodoxy has produced a conception better able to exorcise the evil thoughts about exploitation, oppression and injustice by propounding a system of definitions which leave no room for such phenomena. A man's position in society, according to this cheering view, depends solely on the degree to which he lives up to the society's ideals. Outdistancing Voltaire's Monsieur Pangloss by a long stretch, Parsons expounds his viewpoint over pages and pages, of which the following extract represents a sample:

There is, in any given social system, an actual system of ranking in terms of moral evaluation. But this implies in some sense an integrated set of standards, according to which the evaluations are, or are supposed to be, made. Since a set of standards constitutes a normative pattern, the actual system of effective superiority and inferiority relationships, as far as moral sanction is claimed for it, will hence be called the system of social stratification. The normative pattern, on the other hand, will be called the scale of stratification.

Since the scale of stratification is a pattern characterised by moral authority which is integrated in terms of common moral sentiments, it is normally part of the institutional pattern of the social system.

(Talcott Parsons, *Essays in Sociological Theory*, Free Press, Glencoe, Illinois, 1949, pp. 166–167.)

So when a slave is making obeisance to his whip-cracking master he is manifesting his recognition of society's values. All kinds of more up-to-date examples to the point can be found in gaols, sweat-shops, forced labour gangs and other places where irresistible naked power calls forth abject, cringing and anxious propitiation.

Often (especially in today's climate of mass-media inspired sensationalism) instead of smooth public relations jugglery, we find word-twisting with an opposite aim: namely in order to startle or even to shock; which may even have been the case with Freud (though perhaps not by design). While fully recognizing his greatness as an explorer of the mind, I think that he might have avoided some of his grossest distortions, and

6

consequently been even greater as a thinker, though much less of a success as a founder of a cult, had he not given to certain words a special twist, as if designed to shock. His power to scandalize ordinary people (without which he would not have achieved such fame), and to attract fanatical (because partly insane) devotees, was due above all to his habit of using 'sexual' when 'sensual' would have been more correct. Had he said that the infant's thought and behaviour were guided by the quest for sensual gratifications instead of calling them sexual; had he refrained from calling the infant a 'polymorphous pervert', and found a more sober label for its propensity to find pleasure in sucking its mother's breast or its thumb, or in relieving the tension in its bladder or bowels, Freud would have formulated a more tenable theory, but one which would be less apt for the role of a surrogate religion.

Among the many words which have suffered this fate, 'ideology' has received more than its share of propagandist twisting, whether of a deliberate or a semi-conscious kind. Having been coined with pejorative intent at the beginning of the last century, it has continued to carry imputations of at least partial falsehood. Abstracting from ulterior motives, it is not too difficult to arrive at an ethically neutral conception of 'ideology', defining it as a set of beliefs about facts, causal relations and values in human affairs, which support one another either through logic or the affinity of the sentiments inspired by them, and at least some of which are either unverified, or unverifiable, or false in the light of reason. To me it is as certain as anything can be in the study of human conduct that every social system supports and is supported by an ideology in this sense – which may be benign or wicked, fairly honest or outrightly mendacious . . . but that is another issue. However, since few people will admit that their ideals might rest upon unproven or unprovable or even disproved assumptions, they will resist any definition of 'ideology' which would extend to their cherished beliefs the insinuations of untruth which the word carries. As, on the other hand, they are only too ready to regard what their opponents believe as a pack of vicious lies, they will welcome a definition of ideology which will cover the beliefs of their enemies while excluding their own. I could give an account of some debates which I have witnessed and which would illustrate the point, but I shall skip it because the matter is quite clear, and it is generally known that the word 'ideology' is commonly employed as an ideological weapon. So instead of wasting time on this, I now invite the reader to look with me at some words which have been specifically designed as scientific terms, free of emotional or value-laden connotations.

One can hardly remain in the company of a psychologist, sociologist, anthropologist, politologist or educationalist for more than a few minutes without hearing many times the word 'socialization'. Now, this relatively recent fashion does not result from the emergence of a new idea which 'socialization' connotes, because (apart from mental defectives and children) everybody knows that an individual's character is formed by the environment in which he lives, and which gives him his language, skills, tastes and morals. The word 'education' used to be employed in such a wide sense; and when Durkheim (to quote one of the innumerable available examples) wrote about 'l'éducation morale' he did not confine himself to formal lessons in schools. Military training manuals have always been full of counsels on how to maintain morale and to inculcate the soldierly virtues. Nor could the psychologists and sociologists be credited with having discovered the less conspicuous and formal determinants of character such as the influence of companions (now scientifically renamed 'peers'), because this has always been common knowledge among teachers and mothers concerned about the company their children keep. Illiterate peasants have many apt proverbs to illustrate this piece of folk wisdom. Nor has this process only recently become a subject for learned disquisitions, as Plato has a great deal to say about it.

Although 'socialization' conveys no heretofore unknown idea, it might be defended as a handy label for the totality of the processes through which the environment shapes the personality. Even this claim, however, cannot withstand a moment's scrutiny, because less ambiguous words were current in several languages including English. In Alfred Kroeber's *Anthropology* (first published in 1923) you can find a discussion of how a culture *moulds* an individual. Yet this perfectly serviceable word was abandoned in favour of 'socialization'. Why? Partly, no doubt, because the latter word has '-tion' at the end, and therefore sounds more scientific, while 'moulding' smacks of some common manual craft. A commendation at least equally weighty, however, stems from the very different evaluative undertones which the two words echo. Since it tells us nothing about the quality of the product (which may be monstrous just as well as beautiful), 'moulding' should be preferred by the upholders of the canon of non-valuation; particularly as it runs counter to the grain of semantic associations to say that socialization is a bad thing. Despite its users' protestations of neutrality, the latter word inevitably gives a surreptitious blessing to whatever a society, a group or an institution does to its new members – even if it teaches them to shove children into the gas chambers and like it – so that it fits much better with the panglossian proclivities of the social scientists. 'Forming' and 'moulding', in contrast, sound not only less cheering but decidedly ominous, as they hint at the helplessness and passivity of the individual in the face of the irresistible force of collectivity – which more or less exactly mirrors the usual state of affairs. Making unenthusiastic conscripts into obedient and battle-worthy soldiers normally involves so much brutality that the horse-trainer's expression 'breaking-in' fits it much better than 'socialization'.

True, we could employ 'socialization' in a way which would better merit the implicit praise which its sound inescapably bestows upon the process, by adhering to George Herbert Mead's conception of the initial development of a newly born organism into a social being by learning to communicate and to interact, thus acquiring, among other things, the concept of 'I' as well as the word for it. We could thus define 'socialization' as the process of imparting thoughts, sentiments, skills and habits without which no social life of any kind could go on. One cannot imagine an enduring society where no (or only a few) children would learn to speak, to obey the rules or to work. Conversely, we could make a list of the types of behaviour which would destroy any society in which they became the common pattern: such as a complete lack of foresight, or a total inability to control one's impulses or to interpret correctly other people's intentions. We find plenty of examples of this kind of behaviour among madmen, but asylums can only exist when sustained from outside.

We could also restrict further the meaning of 'socialization' to the process of moulding the individual by society in such a way that it ensures (or at least would ensure in the absence of exogenous catastrophes) not merely a continuation of social life under some form or other, but the perpetuation of the actual social structure. There is a big difference between the two types of moulding, but it is of such a kind that the first includes the second as a special variant: because ensuring the perpetuation of a given structure entails satisfying the necessary conditions of social life in general, but not the other way round. For example: a trading community may fail to ensure its perpetuation by letting the skill of book-keeping become extinct, although this would not prevent its members from continuing to live by adopting an agricultural way of life. On the other hand, were this community to fail to teach its children to do any kind of work or obey any kind of rules, it would make its members unfit for any kind of collective existence, and they would either die of starvation or kill one another, or be enslaved or exterminated by foreigners.

A reader who has read so far may ask himself: why all this hair-splitting? To which I would answer that it does a great deal of harm to have a blanket term which covers up crucially important distinctions and prevents us from investigating their origins and results. Because the crux of the matter is that there are no reasons for taking for granted that most of the habits, beliefs and sentiments (let alone all of them) which a collectivity instils into its members must constitute either the necessary or the sufficient conditions of its perpetuation; not to speak of the idea (which appears in all its naked absurdity as soon as it is explicitly stated) that all the beliefs and habits that are being inculcated in a given time and place must be indispensable for any kind of collective existence.

Since few people would welcome an extinction of our species, they must approve of arrangements which are necessary for social life and, consequently, value positively all the activities which can be construed as socialization in the basic sense. Now,

Definition of socialisation compared
to definition of totalianism.

by applying this word as a blanket term which confuses what is
necessary with what merely happens, its users surreptitiously
convey the message that whatever prevails is not only inevitable
but also good. Thus, under the guise of scientific terminology,
we get the lesson that all is for the best in the best of all possible
worlds – to which Voltaire added: 'if this is the best of all
possible worlds, then imagine what the second-best must be
like'.

It goes without saying that a panglossian view of the world
must induce complacency about our social order, and the
indiscriminate use of the term 'socialization' exorcises all
doubts about the long-term effects of our educational practices.
Indeed, it camouflages the very real possibility that the habits
and attitudes which the young are acquiring may be highly
injurious to the society in which this process is taking place,
and in the extreme case may be bound to destroy it. In reality,
groups and institutions do often destroy themselves by moulding their members in a manner that unfits them for essential
activities; which largely explains why armies suffer defeats,
states succumb to conquerors, firms go bankrupt, administra-
tions disintegrate, families break up, and governments collapse.
In many such cases the members simply cannot resist an overwhelming external force, but often the principal cause – or at
least an underlying condition – is the failure to pass on to the
next generation the attitudes and skills which in the past have
ensured the given collectivity's survival. Although the whole
story is much too complex to be adequately explained by moral
decadence alone, it cannot be doubted that at the time of the
decline of their empire the Romans no longer possessed the
martial virtues which gave them mastery over the Mediter-
ranean world. The Polish magnates who, in exchange for
bribes, put their signatures to the pact partitioning their
country, could not have been indoctrinated with the sentiments
needed for the survival of the state which they were governing.
The French nobility, to mention another example, were
unable to control the revolutionary forces because they had
lost the virtues and skills required for maintaining their
supremacy. Indeed, Pareto built his theory of the circulation of
élites around the well-founded supposition that the privileged

classes invariably tend to fail to instill into their young the virtues needed for successful governing. The cyclical phenomena of the rise and fall of families, described in folk wisdom by the stories of 'from clogs to clogs in three generations', also tacitly assumes the perennial tendency of the processes of moulding the new generations to fail to result in 'socialization'.

Once we realize and keep in view the indubitable fact that political education can be self-destructive, we can see the expression 'political socialization' as one of the most brazen tricks of promiscuous crypto-conservative panglossism. Whereas there might be, to repeat, some justification for calling 'socialization' a process whereby a child learns how to communicate and collaborate with people, it is absolutely preposterous to apply this surreptitiously laudatory term to the learning of duplicity, cruelty, conceit and a host of other vices which people only too often acquire through exposure to politics. When a Congolese politician gets into the habit of extorting bribes; or when an SS man gets hardened to having to shove children into gas chambers, or an American soldier in Vietnam becomes inured to burning defenceless villagers; or when a communist official becomes ready to calumniate his friends as soon as they fall out of favour; or when a secret agent learns the art of blackmail and assassination . . . to call all this socialization amounts to the grossest kind of moral turpitude, particularly as it cannot even be claimed that all such customs are always required for the prosperity or survival of the organization which inculcates them. Often, in fact, quite the contrary; as corruption or unbridled violence has brought down many governments and states; and even the nazis might have won the war had they not antagonized the conquered populations by 'socializing' their compatriots into wanton brutality. So there are absolutely no grounds for assuming that the way in which a political system moulds the individuals must ensure its own survival, let alone be good for mankind.[1] And since a perfectly adequate and basically more neutral (though unpalatably realistic) word, 'moulding', is at hand, the predilection for the approval-arousing 'socialization'

1. More to this point can be found in my forthcoming book on *Antisocialisation and Mental Pollution*.

can only stem from ulterior motives, such as the desire to raise one's status by pretentious terminology, and to court favours from all the powers-that-be by giving the blessing of 'science' to all that they do.

The career of the term, 'ascribed', as applied to 'status' in the current usage, provides an even cruder example of propaganda masquerading as science; although Ralph Linton was probably only trying to cut the figure of an original thinker when he started this fashion of substituting 'ascribed' for 'hereditary', which has the serious disadvantage that everybody knows what it means. Like other pseudo-scientific innovations, the substitution in question kills two birds with one stone: it ministers to the sociologist's or anthropologist's effort in the game of academic one-upmanship, and at the same time serves the cause of our old friend promiscuous crypto-conservatism. Everybody knows that inheriting means being able to enjoy (or having to put up with) what the father had. When, however, instead of saying that so-and-so has inherited his social position we state that his status is ascribed, we give a different colouring to the picture by tacitly suggesting that the person in question owes his privileges or burdens to a deed of ascription performed by some Great Being, which must either be God or Society. But who is Society? Us, of course; and so it is we who have ascribed to the privileged few in our midst their enjoyable positions; and having done so, we should not grumble, even if we are at the unlucky end of the ladder.

As the opposite of the 'ascribed' (that is 'inherited') status, we have the 'achieved', which has at least the merit of being self-explanatory, although it represents no new idea whatsoever, having simply replaced the word 'acquired', which was used in pre-parsonian times to describe status which was not inherited. Why this substitution? Partly, no doubt, because a purely verbal change provides a gratifying illusion of scientific progress without demanding any real mental effort. The main reason for the popularity of this substitution, however, seems to be that 'achievement' sounds much more laudable than 'acquisition', which has some rather sinister mental associations after centuries of anti-capitalist pamphleteering. True, all this would make little difference in strict logic, but in a properly scientific discourse there should be no room for purely verbal substitutions. On the other hand, the advertisers have amply demonstrated that you can influence people's attitudes much more effectively by playing on vague associations of images than by sober logical arguments. The futility of the latter as a method of swaying the masses had already been recognized by Aristotle in his *Rhetoric*.

A hefty tome could be written containing nothing but translations of circumlocutory euphemisms current in the social sciences into plain language, but I shall make only a few more dips into this jungle, leaving the reader to employ his own perspicacity on the rest of this proliferating fauna. Take, for instance, 'universalism'. Does it not sound nice? Imposing and sublime, as befits a word invented by theologians long ago, it was imported into sociology by the Grand Master to replace the nasty and common-place 'impersonality'. So you need not feel bad about being treated solely as a number in accordance with rigid rules in a hospital or a chain store or a bureaucratized school when you learn that, far from suffering from the effects of impersonality, you are enjoying the benefits of universalism. I by no means claim that it is always better to be treated according to your personal relation to your interlocutor, or that impersonality is always bad, as obviously it has good as well as bad sides. My sole point is that, since impersonality and universalism mean exactly the same, there is no good heuristic reason for replacing one by the other, and that (apart from the usual motive of pseudo-scientific one-upmanship) the substitute has come into vogue because of its emotive undertones, which tend to give a rose-tinted view of bureaucracy.

Here is another piece of surreptitious white-washing: it has been known for a very long time that every group, club, army unit or any other kind of collectivity is based on some arrangements which permit its members to be distinguished from outsiders; and that when membership offers some scarce advantage, a mechanism for excluding outsiders must be in operation. Exclusion and monopolization, however, remind us too much what the world is like, and so they have been replaced by 'boundary-maintenance', pleasantly reminiscent of 'fence-mending', which in the American usage means reconciliation.

6*

If you feel tempted to grumble about the taxes or conscription or the way public funds are spent, you must remember that it is all for the sake of 'goal-attainment' – which will help to keep you contented so long as you do not ask the impertinent question, whose are these goals which are being attained? If you insist on asking such profane questions, you are a 'deviant'.

The term 'deviance' contains some of the most pernicious insinuations in the spirit of promiscuous conformism. True, in principle we could use it in a non-hortatory, ethically neutral sense of a divergence from the behaviour usual in a given society, but when you look at how the sociologists or psychologists actually use this term you will notice that they apply it only to certain kinds of deviations from the standard. Since the possessors of great wealth, power and glory are few, they are deviants in the statistical sense, so that on strictly logical grounds we could affix this label to all the prime ministers, presidents, millionaires, film stars, astronauts, famous scientists and so on. It will be said, of course, that deviance refers not to any unusual attribute but only to transgression of ethical norms ... but, then, why is not 'transgression' used instead of 'deviance'. In any case, this explanation does not seem very convincing when we notice that big business and politics, as well as the minor corridors of power, are full of people who habitually resort to unethical practices which barely fail to come under the criminal code. Moving down the social ladder we also find an abundance of petty exploiters, bullies, liars, intriguers, breakers of promises, slanderers, hypocrites, sneaks and the like, who clearly do not live up to the ethical norms and yet get no mention in the discussions of deviance. One of the most common types of transgression against ethics nowadays is bureaucratic intrigue, which probably inflicts greater damage on society than all the petty thefts put together, although it is not supposed to happen at all under the rule of 'universalism', and is the last thing which specialists on deviation wish to write about. They may say that so many people are engaged in this activity that it cannot be regarded as deviant, but then they get rid of the criterion of an offence against the commandments of professed ethics, and fall back on the purely statistical criterion of divergence from the mean, a consistent use of which entails the affixing of the label 'deviant' to presidents and millionaires. An answer that intriguers are not included because their malfeasance entails no breach of law brings us back to where we started, as it raises the question of why use the word 'deviance' at all when all we mean is crime? Although nothing is ever perfectly clear in the study of human conduct, it is certainly easier to decide whether or not a law has been broken than whether a given type of behaviour falls under the inconsistently used concept of deviance. True, since the law is often changeable and arbitrary, the same kind of action may come to be (or cease to be) a crime overnight, while the motivation or causation remains the same; which is the reason why it was thought that a wider or subtler concept than that of crime was needed for etiological investigations.

Actually, the ordinary language has a number of words for the various types usually treated under the heading of deviance, such as eccentrics, heretics, drop-outs, rebels, scoundrels, thieves, and so on; and the very mention of these words, indicative as they are of great variety, arouses the doubt whether they have any common denominator at all. By using the term 'deviance' we blandly assume their similarity, although nobody has explicitly proved it or even advanced good arguments that this is the case. So we have here a term which does exactly the opposite of what the concepts of natural sciences do: instead of revealing an underlying and hitherto unsuspected unity among seemingly disparate phenomena, it merely papers over the disparities and inconsistencies, functioning as a blanket term which is less precise and meaningful than the words of literary language, and which has gained currency not for heuristic but for crypto-propagandist reasons.

Apart from the usual attractions of ambiguity and pseudo-scientific novelty, the term 'deviance' renders important service to the ideology of promiscuous conformism (or, to use the earlier expression, promiscuous crypto-conservatism as well as its mirror image: promiscuous rebelliousness) by stuffing into one pigeon-hole the heretics, the intellectual innovators, the critics and the reformers together with thieves, prostitutes, drug-addicts and the monsters who strangle little girls. So, like 'dysfunction', 'deviance' is a blanket term useful as camouflage for sniping at all non-conformists in the name of science, tarring Socrates or Spinoza with the same brush as Al Capone and Jack the Ripper. It might be apposite to mention that in an American book on social pathology (the particulars of which I have unfortunately lost) I have seen a chapter headed 'The Intellectuals'.

I hope that the foregoing arguments do not give readers an impression that I subscribe to the cult of dissent or non-conformity fashionable at the moment. I think it ought to be obvious to any thinking person that the value of such attitudes depends entirely on what it is that you are rebelling against or dissenting from, and what you are proposing to put in its place. Worship of dissent for its own sake is just as stupid as blind, indiscriminating conservatism, or the belief that everything new must be better than what has preceded it, or the use of 'reactionary' as a blanket word of opprobrium, regardless of what it is that the so-labelled person is reacting against. The most profound contrast lies between sober, independent and skilful use of reason on one side and sheepishness or the Gadarene swine mentality on the other. As a matter of fact (and especially in the United States) the religion of promiscuous conformism has prepared the ground in more ways than one for the nihilistic cult of rebellion for its own sake.

It might be fitting to close the present chapter with one of the choicest morsels of the genre in question: namely, Talcott Parsons' conception of power, as explained approvingly by S. M. Lipset who (having written one or two good books) should know better, but who has for a time become more susceptible to the siren song of promiscuous crypto-conservatism:

Parsons has suggested that power – in his terms, the ability to mobilize resources necessary for the operation of the system – should be viewed in value-neutral terms, as follows. Inherent in the structure of complex society, especially in the division of labor, is the existence of authority roles, holders of which are obligated to initiate acts that are socially necessary. Most of the things done by those at the summits of organizations or societies are necessary. (Seymour Martin Lipset, *Revolution and Counter Revolution*, pp. 147–148.)

Therefore, if you are a Czech, do not bewail what Mr Husak is doing to Mr Dubček and other traitors to the workers' cause; if a Brazilian, do not harbour evil thoughts about the Death Squadron; if a Russian, do not hold it against Comrade Adropov that he has locked up a few irresponsible writers in lunatic asylums; if a Black South African, do not complain about Mr Vorster's implementation of Apartheid; if a Haitian, do what your hereditary president Baby Doc tells you. Hearken unto the voice of Science and heed its definitions from which it clearly follows that (like all the rulers of the past, including Caligula and Hitler) these gentlemen are only doing what is necessary.

Chapter 13

Techno-Totemism and Creeping Crypto-Totalitarianism

In one of his essays on the sociology of culture (published in English recently though written in the twenties), Karl Mannheim shows that conservatives have usually emphasized the organic analogy, while revolutionaries and reformers have tended to think of society as a mechanism which can be altered at will, taken to pieces and put together in a radically different form. As with all other sociological propositions, this generalization is not watertight; the most notable exception being Pareto, whose mechanistic system of sociology was as if devised to prove the impossibility of progress. Nevertheless, by and large Mannheim was right, and the parallel with the subordination of the organs to the head was repeatedly used to bolster authority, with the entailed lesson that rash tampering with the organic structure invariably leads to its paralysis or death.

The advent of servomechanisms made Mannheim's distinction out of date, because now we had machines whose central computers regulated movements of other parts; and which offered thereby an analogy to the relations of subordination found in human hierarchies. Indeed, as a parable of subordination, cybernetics is even better than the nineteenth century organicism, because a tissue controlled by the central nervous system performs nonetheless certain autonomous functions of metabolism and cellular homeostasis, whereas a subordinate part of a servomechanism can execute no movements whatsoever which are not determined by the controlling computer. There is no talking back and circumventing orders in a cybernetic machine; and so, by stressing the resemblances between such machines and human society, we can condemn insubordination without actually saying so. Here again we encounter a method of influencing behaviour which has no counterpart in the sciences of nature and which consists of propounding *persuasive* descriptions: by foisting upon people a certain image of themselves we make them live up to it. In the case in hand, if we manage to convince people that they are nothing but cogs in a machine they might behave accordingly.

Is there anything that can be learned about society and politics by studying cybernetics? Yes: but only if we content ourselves with indirect profit. The concepts of system, function, equilibrium and teleological behaviour entered our intellectual armoury a long time ago, but the knowledge of some of the conditions of equilibrium or teleological behaviour is new. For example, it is by no means obvious to the unaided common sense that a system containing a large number of variables can attain equilibrium quickly only if the relations between the variables can be expressed by what the mathematicians call step functions; that is to say, only if the variables do not react to small variations of other variables. Likewise, a social scientist might gain something from knowing how permutations of negative and positive connections between factors (of stimulation or inhibition in physiological terms), or the order or relative magnitudes and time lags of reactions, can make equilibrium stable or unstable or impossible, cause oscillations, or produce vicious or virtuous circles known as positive feedbacks, and so on.

Owing to the impossibility of measuring many crucial factors, the equations of electronic engineering cannot be applied to sociology or political science. Even in economics, with its far greater scope for measurement, attempts to apply cybernetic models (whether symbolic or material) have proved interesting, but insufficient to permit reliable predictions about the actual behaviour of the economy. A cybernetic philosophy of causal relations can be illuminating, but only insofar as it can suggest discoveries of hitherto unknown relations between observable social phenomena. However, when we look at the publications purporting to explain or analyse social and political processes with the aid of cybernetics, we find platitudes or banal half-truths, or outright distortions dressed up in scientific-sounding words.

In a moment I shall try to show how these absurdities won acceptance owing to their serviceability for veiled propaganda;

and that it was no accident that cybernetic models were embraced with the greatest alacrity in the field of political science. Before attending to the question of motives, however, I should like to dwell for a few moments on a purely heuristic plane, and to say a few words about some fundamental errors inhering in the cybernetic models for political science, which can be clearly seen if we compare them with the use of the cybernetic notions in economic theory.

As mentioned earlier, serious limitations to the predictive power of the models in economic theory ensue from the irregular movements (or the stochastic nature, if you like) of the variables, their large number and shading of boundaries, and above all from the practice of leaving out non-economic factors which are often crucial. Nonetheless, these limitations on their relevance to the real world do not make such models absurd, because the economists operate with entities which can at least theoretically be treated as variables in equations, whereas cybernetic models in sociology and political science rest upon far-fetched analogies between social organisation and machines, where persons or their roles are equated with parts of servo-mechanisms.

In the economic models we find variables such as gross national product, general price level, rate of interest, acceleration ratios, propensity to consume, capital to output ratios, accumulation rate, time lags in price movements, and so on. These entities are of a statistical nature: they represent the results of actions whose vast number and cumulative nature entitle us to make an abstraction from their individual peculiarities, and to concentrate upon the aggregate effects. Though often not quantified and not easy to measure in practice, these factors are at least quantitative in principle; and can therefore be treated as variables which increase or decrease, like the variables in the physicist's or engineer's equations. When, after perusing *The Mechanism of Economic Systems* by Arnold Tustin (an electrical engineer who first applied servomechanism theory to the social sciences), or the relevant chapters in R. G. D. Allen's *Mathematical Economics*, we pass to their supposed equivalents in political science, no intelligent reader can fail to be struck by the catastrophic drop in acumen. Instead of networks of relationships between abstract and at least theoretically dimensional variables, we get crude analogies between simple mechanisms and complex and fluid collectivities – with human beings equated with bits of hardware.

To take an example without inquiring into its empirical validity: in Tustin's cybernetic interpretation of Keynes' theory, the propensity to consume and the marginal efficiency of capital jointly constitute an entity standing in a relation to income and employment which offers a reasonable analogy to that which in a steam engine obtains between the angle of the gadget known as the governor and the velocity of the pistons and the wheel. On the other hand, in the politological cybernetic models the aforementioned gadget is regarded as a homologue of a manager or some other kind of boss, although not even the most soulless bureaucrat can be envisaged as an object capable of moving only in one dimension: up and down, or forward and backward. We can see how far-fetched are such comparisons if we bear in mind that one single living cell performs a variety of exceedingly complex homeostatic actions which no computer devised or even envisaged up till now can imitate. To find constituents of living matter of a simplicity comparable to that of transducers or wires, we must go well below the cellular levels: at least to the molecular if not atomic – because a larger size need not entail an increase in complexity, and an enormous chunk of iron is far less complex than the smallest virus. The smallest mammal contains about 10^{16} giant molecules; and the difference in this respect between a mouse and an elephant is only marginal. A human brain contains about 10^{10} extremely complex cells, and historical changes are outcomes of interaction of all the brains functioning at given times with the traces left by those no longer alive. We can talk colloquially about somebody being a live wire, but to take such metaphors literally borders on insanity . . . or rather would do so, were it not such a good business to juggle with this kind of pseudo-science.

Seeing the crypto-ideological message of cybernetic models (or rather parables), we can easily understand not only why their devotees enjoy enthusiastic support from the academic managers, but also why they became particularly popular in political science – the branch of learning which concerns itself most directly with the problems of obedience and command. As these questions always count among the most explosive, playing with far-fetched models has the added advantage that it enables the practitioners to avoid having to make concrete (and therefore controversial) pronouncements on such matters. In other words, this tactic enables its devotees to assume the ego-inflating role of a pundit on politics while saying nothing about it: an ingenious method of studying politics by overlooking the subject matter.

One of the subtler tricks in this strategy consists of diverting attention from the conflicts which inevitably arise within any organization in connection with the question of the goals which it ought to, or in fact does, pursue. A cybernetic model of a polity as a mechanism with pre-set goals excludes, by definition, the view of politics as an arena on which groups and individuals fight about whose values, opinions and interests shall prevail, and on a more prosaic level about who gets what, when, and how. The cybernetic idealization, moreover, overlooks the possibility (which in real life is a rule rather than an exception) that an organization, set up to serve a certain purpose, ceases to do so, acquires a good measure of autonomy, and embarks upon a policy of self-aggrandizement at the expense of the persons or groups which have brought it into existence. No such perversion of the original goal can take place in a servomechanism; and by insisting on cybernetic analogies, the theorists help to camouflage the true nature of human organization, to bolster up the powers-that-be, and to indoctrinate the public with a mood of undiscriminating submission.

Some seemingly wanton verbal contortions appear as suitable instruments of veiled propaganda of this kind. Look, for instance, at the fashion of speaking about the *output* of the political system. On the face of it it looks like a mere fad or a trick of pseudo-scientific one-upmanship, as no new knowledge is imparted by substituting 'output' for 'activity' or 'activities'. Actually, to speak of activities of the state or the organs of government is unquestionably more honest, because 'output' suggests measurability, which in the case of most public institutions remains in the realm of fiction. Provided we bear in mind the roughness of the approximation, we can reasonably speak of the output of the postal services or an individual post office or even a hospital, because basically these agencies constitute units of economic production. But what is the output of the Foreign Office, or of the Soviet Navy, or of the C.I.A.? We can describe what these organizations do (that is, their activities), but output? Or how do we measure the output of a court of justice? By the number of cases it handles or of sentences it passes, regardless of the care it gives to each case? Or by the man-hours spent by its personnel inside the building? And how does the output of the U.S. Congress compare with that of the Supreme Soviet? Can we make the required measurements by counting the number of resolutions passed, laws approved, words pronounced, or pieces of paper used? Or how can we calculate the output of the police force together with that of the ministry of information? By adding the number of arrests to the number of leaflets?

It suffices to raise a few questions of this kind to see the absurdity of speaking about the output of a political system. As a rule it is only the cost of the public services that can be measured with a bearable degree of accuracy, while the benefits remain vague, and often dubious. We can find out (at least in principle) how much an army costs, but whether its services are worth it normally remains a matter of opinion. Furthermore, we must ask: services to whom? An army may be bestowing upon the entire nation an incalculable benefit if it prevents its extermination by a relentless enemy; but in another case it may function as a pure instrument of internal oppression incapable of defending the country against a danger from outside; in which case its 'services' to the exploited classes will be entirely detrimental.

The last point leads us to an explanation of the popularity of the verbal substitution in question. An activity may be good, useful, laudable, but also injurious, disastrous or criminal; whereas 'output' has a favourable ring, evoking construction rather than destruction, which helps to exorcise disquieting thoughts about strife or oppression – for it goes against the grain of the normal usage to speak of intimidation, extortion and torture as 'output'. If we look at David Easton's *Political Systems*, or any book or article by one of the numerous writers of the same persuasion, we see that the entire terminology (if we can dignify it by this name) entails a complete bowdlerization of the study of politics by translating it into a restricted language which makes it impossible to mention anything that is not nice. The essence of equilibrium in a political system, according to this school, is the exchange of satisfactions of demands for support between the rulers and the ruled – whom Easton (in the style of public relations phraseology) renames 'the political system' and 'the internal environment' respectively. The latter euphemistic contortion seems venial in comparison with the sinister tacit message conveyed through the bland assumption that the subjects always *support* their rulers in exchange for getting *their demands* satisfied. It would appear incredible were it not open to inspection by anyone who cares to look at any of these books, that four hundred years after Macchiavelli, three hundred after Hobbes, two hundred after Voltaire, and one hundred after Marx, anyone could swallow as the latest word of science a theory of politics which views relations between governments and their subjects as invariably based on an exchange of services.

No doubt the devotees can counter these strictures by accusing me of misinterpretation, and by saying that they are writing words like 'support' in a neutral sense. And it is perfectly true that we can employ 'support' in a neutral sense as when we say that a column supports a roof. Nor do we imply willingness when we refer to the supplying of needed goods in a phrase like 'the taxpayers support the student rebels'. Nonetheless, in any discussion of politics the words 'to support' and '*supporter*' connote willingness rather than a resentful or even merely passive acquiescence. Nobody would speak of the inmates of the concentration camps as 'supporting' Hitler or Stalin merely because they were forced to supply certain goods or services to these benefactors of mankind. Why then use this word to describe a universal element in the relations between the ruled and the rulers unless one wishes to bowdlerize the study of politics?

True, many polities exist, and have existed, where the

majority of the population support the government – or at least its form (that is, the system) if not the actual incumbents of high office. Throughout the history of the United States, for instance, most of the citizens (with the exception of the Negroes kept down by coercion) have felt a genuine loyalty to the constitution, and recognized the obligation to obey their elected rulers. They might have hated the individual office holders, but only during the last few years have there emerged large sections which denounce the basic principles of the constitution. It is not only the democratic regimes, however, that can benefit from the loyalty of their subjects: many despotic kings and princes could rely on a doglike devotion from their underlings; and even usurpers and dictators often enjoyed massive support among the populace. Between his victory over France and the first defeats in Russia, an overwhelming majority of the Germans enthusiastically supported Hitler. Karl Jaspers estimates that only about one million persisted in inward hostility throughout the nazi period; while the number of those who did something about it was less than 1% of that number. But on the other hand we have innumerable examples of domination through sheer terror and fear in the face of an almost unanimous hatred for the rulers. One of the most important tasks of descriptive politology is to ascertain the nature and the measure of support given to rulers and regimes, while the question of what determines the variations in this respect constitutes one of the central problems of its theoretical branch. By surreptitiously expunging this issue through word-twisting tricks, the cybernetics fans in political science are enticing their followers into jettisoning the duty to enlighten for the sake of the more profitable occupation of pseudo-scientific public relations.

An even cruder piece of promiscuous crypto-conservatism is what they put on the other side of the equation: namely, 'demands' which a 'political system' (i.e., a political machine) must satisfy in order to obtain 'support' in return. The scheme unquestioningly assumes that it is the ruled (the 'internal environment' as they are euphemistically called) who make demands . . . not the other way round. Such a view may not be entirely false where the aspirants to supreme office have to

win free and honest elections with a wide franchise, although
even here the parties can frustrate almost universally held
wishes by a collusion to limit the electoral competition.
Furthermore, through various tricks of propaganda the
politicians can lead the public to believe that their wishes are
being met while it may not at all be the case – not to speak of
thinly disguised defaulting on electoral promises, the bribing
of deputies, intimidation of voters, fraudulent counting and
other tricks commonly employed throughout the world. Even
in fairly democratic countries, the cost of political action, as
well as the power of the self-appointed co-opting oligarchies
known as political parties, severely restricts the electorate's
freedom of choice – in addition to the inherently anti-demo-
cratic impact of the mass media controlled by a handful of
men. When we come to such worthy members of the United
Nations as Somoza's Nicaragua or Mobutu's Congo, or look
at Gomulka's rule in Poland or Husak's in Czechoslovakia,
only a public relations man inured to mendacity or a half-
baked student completely ignorant of the facts of life, could
maintain that these regimes continued to exist because they
satisfy the demands made by their subjects. Or imagine the
Russian peasants making demands on Stalin, or the Roman
slaves on the emperor Diocletian.

According to the scheme proposed by Gabriel Almond,
the output of the political system consists of: rule-making,
rule-application and rule-adjudication. That the organs of the
state engage in such activities we can find in Plato and Confucius who, however, were neither so foolish nor so hypocritical
as to claim that this is all that such bodies ever do; being fully
aware that the breaking and the circumventing of rules has
always been a common activity.

As if all these crypto-propagandist contortions did not
suffice, yet another denizen of the wealthiest university in the
world, Karl Deutsch, has revived an old trick of authoritarian
ideologies: the collective consciousness. This concept was emphatically assigned to the limbo of purely imaginary existence
a century ago by Herbert Spencer who introduced expressions
like 'the nerves of government' (which Deutsch has taken as
the title of his *magnum opus*) but explicitly recognized their

metaphoric nature. When it first came into circulation in the nineteenth century this concept (despite its usefulness to nationalist propaganda) had the merit of making people aware of how much their thinking was shaped by collective processes, which was unrecognized by the unrealistically individualist psychology of the day. By now, however, we no longer need to be reminded that an organism can become fully human only through interaction with other individuals, and by absorbing a culture produced by countless ancestors.

Since no group can exist without individuals, while no *human* individual can exist without a group, so-called methodological individualism can be accepted only as a programme to study collective actions by analysing them into their individual components, which need not involve us in the sterile ontological debate about whether it is the groups or the individuals that 'really' exist. Notwithstanding the vast quantity of ink and paper used up in debating it, this question does not appear to be 'real' unless we define the word 'to exist' in some very restricted sense. If (resorting to a definition in use) we say that an entity can be said to exist if an attribute can be predicated of it which can not be predicated of any other entity – including any of its constituent parts as well as any larger whole to which the said entity may belong – then it is clear that, not only groups and organisms, but any assemblage of objects exists just as 'really' as its constituents. Thus a heap of stones partakes of the attribute of existence in equal measure as the single stones because we can make true statements about the heap (such as about its height) which are not true about the separate stones. Every empirically observable entity is more than the sum of its parts because to be observable an entity must consist of parts standing in certain relationships to one another; and 'the sum' is a concept which abstracts from these relationships. To assert that whatever can be analysed into its components does not exist would entail the conclusion that nothing exists except atomic particles, so long as these cannot be shown to consist of smaller entities. As every aggregate consists of at least two elements and the relations between them, an ontological (as opposed to a merely methodological) individualism would pre-suppose that relations do not exist; and since the atomic particles can be known only through their relationships to directly perceptible physical occurrences, we would have to conclude that they do not exist either, and further that nothing exists. And if nothing exists, then 'the sentence that nothing exists' cannot exist either . . . which is a *reductio ad absurdum* of ontological 'individualism' or reductionism.

So we see that even a heap of stones is more than the sum of its parts, although we can call it a mechanic aggregate because its disappearance entails no change in the attributes of the individual stones other than their *relative* positions. In contrast, the essence of the organic aggregation is that the severance of a part's relationships to other parts entails a change in the individual characteristics of that part – a change so important that it may entail a disintegration of the part in question. A stone taken out of the heap retains all its attributes, while a hair pulled out is no longer the thing it was when it had its root. The same is true about a person and his group.

To appreciate the reality of the collective processes, we need not postulate that their modes of existence are equivalent to individual human consciousness, which we know through introspection. To attribute 'consciousness' to collectivities (especially the state), as Karl Deutsch does, is to revive the old war horse of authoritarian nationalism, according to which the inferior parts (like you and me) which cannot claim to be the seat of this collective consciousness, are expendable for the benefit of the controlling centres, which in concrete terms mean top people.

In the old debate about whether the individual is more important than the group, or the other way round, the issues have been obscured by the constant use of the expression 'the individual'; because, strictly speaking, there is no such thing as 'the individual' but only many individuals. An equally careless hypostatization underlies the frequently repeated cliché about man being able to control his future, often phrased as a rhetorical question. For as soon as we ask, 'Who is man?', we see that he does not exist, and there are only men and women with varied and largely incompatible sentiments, dispositions and aims. No doubt they could control many things if they would only agree, but they do not. Therefore, to speak of man deciding or controlling is nonsense. Once we get rid of this linguistic mirage, we can see that the liberal philosophical individualists were true collectivists in the sense of defending the interests of many individuals, as opposed to the prerogative of the powerful few; whereas the protagonists of collectivist ideologies (whether nation or class oriented) were busy justifying the right of a few potentates to sacrifice for their own ends (defined as the collective good) vast numbers of powerless people. That it was so with such great stalwarts of collective interest as Hitler and Mussolini need not be argued; but it may be worth pointing out that whereas in Britain (the home of philosophical individualism with Bentham's ethical ideal of the greatest good of the greatest number) not a single town has been named after an individual, the collectivist rulers of eastern Europe have named innumerable towns, streets and buildings after themselves and their dead or living friends. Actually, even the word 'marxism' contains an implicit negation of Marx's basic tenet that individuals are unimportant; from which it follows that, having been individuals, Marx and Lenin are unimportant – and therefore those who accept the collectivist view of social causation should forget about them instead of manufacturing their portraits and effigies in numbers, not to speak of dimensions, which by now must have exceeded those of the Catholic saints, making pilgrimages to the one who died late enough to be embalmed, and ceaselessly invoking their names.

To come back to pseudo-cybernetics: its veiled promiscuously conservative ideological message has endeared it to the bosses throughout the world (no matter whether capitalist, communist, clericalist, militarist, racialist or what not) and enabled its devotees to obtain control over funds which, of course, brought them applause from the academic multitudes. Profiting from the awe which any mathematical-sounding terms inspire among the non-numerate practitioners of the social sciences, as well as from the mathematically competent scientists' naivety about social and political problems, the pushers of pseudo-cybernetics have been able to achieve fame as experts on politics without ever having said anything relevant.

If he wishes to spare himself the tedium of having to plough through mounds of paper, the reader can obtain a bird's-eye view of this kind of theorizing from two moderately sized and priced summaries – H. V. Wiseman's *Political Systems*, 1966, and W. J. M. Mackenzie's Pelican, *Politics and Social Science*. Perhaps because they have had the benefit of a better secondary education, the British summarizers, despite sympathetic – if not enthusiastic – treatment, have done their American masters a gross disservice by putting their stuffed tomes into a more literate and concise form, as they have thereby made the sterility of this approach more apparent. Incomprehensibility and forbidding bulk deter critics who, unable to endure reading right through, do not dare to voice their objections; although they could very well take advice from old Dr Johnson, who said that 'you do not have to eat the whole ox to find out that the meat is tough'. If you follow Mackenzie's indefatigable explorations of this desert, you can admire his 'sitzfleisch' (to use the apt German expression), but you will find nothing which would enable you to understand better a single concrete political situation.

Chapter 14

The Law of Lighter Weights Rising to the Top

The proliferation of apparatus of physical research which has taken place during the last quarter of a century has not led, I am told by my physicist friends, to any fundamental discoveries which could be compared in originality to the contributions which Rutherford, Planck, Bohr or Heisenberg made with much smaller resources – not to speak of Einstein, who produced his relativity theory in his spare time and without access to a laboratory, while working for the Swiss patent office, after having been turned down as a candidate for a higher degree. There is nothing inexplicable in this, because organization involves subordination and dependence not only on the seniors but on the peers and even juniors as well, while the entire history of science abundantly demonstrates that really original ideas have nearly always met with obstinate resistance from the majority of the specialists. If this is the case even in the 'hard' sciences, where most of the assertions can be submitted to conclusive tests, then it is not surprising that in the controversial sciences large scale organization of research acts as a powerful brake on new ideas – which does not preclude an enthusiastic welcome being extended to verbal fads consisting of new labels for old and often worn-out notions.

Like many other things, the laudable ideal of combining education and research has its seamy side, in that graduate teaching offers an opportunity to recruit cheap (and in a way forced) labour for the captains of the research industry. Despite the lowering of standards connected with a massive increase in numbers, the fiction has been maintained that, in order to obtain a doctorate, the candidate must make a contribution to knowledge which, instead of an old-fashioned individual thesis, has more often than not come to mean a piece of work as somebody else's research assistant. In the United States, employment as a research assistant provides about 95% of the opportunities of obtaining funds for doctoral study in the social sciences, with only 5% remaining in the form of individual scholarships not tied to a big 'project'.

As the work of a research assistant is usually soul-destroying, this mode of financing graduate education adversely affects the quality of entrants into the profession, as many bright young men and women, prevented from really using their brains, and faced with the necessity of furnishing routine labour, prefer to do it for good money and gravitate towards advertising and market research. What is equally grave, moreover, the more intelligent students see through the sham of the whole enterprise and become either rebellious or cynical, or decide not to think too much and end by becoming timid and credulous conformists.

While repelling the clever and the upright, the social research industry attracts dullards, for whom indeed it offers the only entry into the ranks of 'scientists', because no other form of 'scientific' research demands so little intelligence as door-to-door sociology or the lower forms of rat psychology. Rather than spanning the two cultures, as they ideally ought to, most of the social research industry's employees fall between two stools, being neither literate nor numerate beyond the memorization of a few half-understood statistical formulae. To illustrate how far ignorance can go, I must mention that once I shame-facedly witnessed a conversation between a physician and a professor of sociology at an American university renowned as a centre for quantitative methodology, about what is a theory, hypothesis, law and fact, in which they both persisted in making the elementary mistake of confusing the credibility of a proposition with the nature of its logical form – which might perhaps be excusable in an ordinary medical practitioner. When the professor (who presented himself as an expert in quantitative methodology) not only revealed that he did not know that to obtain the probability of a joint occurrence of independent events you must multiply the probabilities of each, but per-sisted obstinately in claiming that you must add them, the physician to my shame triumphantly concluded that sociology is bunk.

One of the things which have stuck in my memory in connection with the image of the sociologist is a caption on a glossy pornographic paperback which I saw in one of those obscenity shops which surround the New York public library. The picture showed a couple about to engage in copulation or flagellation in a room with a window in a corner through which an emaciated and pale man was peeping from outside. The caption underneath ran: 'Stewart was a social scientist, a professional peeping Tom, but he believed in going where the action was . . .'. Moving to a different genre of literature, I remember a sentence in a philosophical journal published in Scotland, where the reviewer was discussing the reprint of Adam Ferguson's *The Origin of Civil Society*. Unworthy of attention, except for the light it sheds on the not entirely undeserved image of the sociologist among the more traditional philosophers, the phrase was: 'Ferguson was not a thinker but a sociologist...'. C. Wright Mills, who for a good many years was a neighbour of one of the biggest social research factories, well describes its human products in his *The Sociological Imagination* pp. 104–6.

To be sure, a great deal of routine data collecting is not only desirable but absolutely indispensable in a modern society. Obviously no planning, no rational administration, is possible without statistical data of all kinds. Public opinion polls, too, shed a valuable light on what goes on in a country. The deleterious effects of these activities stem from the fact that the necessary scale of operations gives a few individuals control over vast funds, and therefore power to dominate the entire field, and to stamp out the ideas and approaches which differ from their own.

An old-fashioned professor with tyrannical inclinations might (particularly if he were German) bully his assistants and students, but the number of his victims would be small; and as his likewise inclined colleagues would be indoctrinating their underlings with their own (and usually very different) idiosyncrasies, no one had much chance of acquiring enough power to impose his views upon many institutions. In contrast, a social research entrepreneur can expand his empire indefinitely, limited only by the supply of money; and the process of concentration of control and of destruction of independent craftsmen parallels the trends in other industries.

Apart from providing the instruments for imposing an orthodoxy, the concentration of control over research alters the mechanisms of selection for positions of influence. This happens because power and big money attract a special kind of man, seldom distinguished by a passion for the pursuit of truth. Even in physics and mathematics, where the threshold of acceptability demands real knowledge and intelligence, the increase in the scale of research has given prominence to the operator at the expense of the thinker – if we accept the view of the famous creator of cybernetics, Norbert Wiener who can hardly be suspected of sour grapes:

I am lucky to have been born and to have grown up before the First World War, at a period at which the vigor and *élan* of international scholarship had not yet been swamped by forty years of catastrophes. I am particularly lucky that it has not been necessary for me to remain for any considerable period a cog in a modern scientific factory, doing what I was told, accepting the problems given me by my superiors, and holding my own brain only *in commendam* as a medieval vassal held his fiefs. If I had been born into this latter-day feudal system of the intellect, it is my opinion that I would have amounted to little. From the bottom of my heart I pity the present generation of scientists, many of whom, whether they wish it or not, are doomed by the 'spirit of the age' to be intellectual lackeys and clock punchers.

There is no doubt that the present age, particularly in America, is one in which more men and women are devoting themselves to a formally scientific career than ever before in history. This does not mean that the intellectual environment of science has received a proportionate increment. Many of today's American scientists are working in government laboratories, where secrecy is the order of the day, and it is protected by the deliberate subdivision of problems to the extent that no man can be fully aware of the bearing of his own work. These laboratories, as well as the great industrial laboratories, are so aware of the importance of the scientist that he is forced to punch the time clock and to give an accounting of the last minute of his research. Vacations are cut down to a dead minimum, but consultations and reports and visits to other plants are encouraged without limit, so that the scientist, and the young scientist in particular, has not the leisure to ripen his own ideas.

Science is better paid than at any time in the past. The results of this pay have been to attract into science many of those for whom the pay is the first consideration, and who scorn to sacrifice immediate profit for the freedom of development of their own concepts. Moreover, this inner development, important and indispensable as it may be to the world of science in the future, generally does not have the tendency to put a single cent into the pockets of their employers.

Perhaps business has learned to take long risks, but they must be calculable risks, and no risk, by its very nature, is less calculable than the risk of profit from new ideas.

This is an age in which the profit motive is exalted, often, indeed, to the exclusion of all other motives. The value of ideas to the community is estimated in terms of dollars and cents, yet dollars and cents are fugitive currency compared with that of new ideas. A discovery which may take fifty years before it leads to new practice has only a minimal chance of rebounding to the advantage of those who have paid for the work leading up to it, yet if these discoveries are not made, and we continue depending on those which already exist, we are selling out our future and the futures of our children and grandchildren.

Like a tradition of scholarship, a grove of sequoias may exist for thousands of years, and the present crop of wood represents the investment of sun and rain many centuries ago. The returns of this investment are here, but how much money and how many securities remain in the same hands, even for one century? Thus, if we are to measure the long-time life of a sequoia grove in terms of the short-time value of money, we cannot afford to treat it as an agricultural enterprise. In a profit-bound world, we must exploit it as a mine and leave a wasteland behind us for the future.

Of course, the large laboratory can make out a limited case for itself. However, it is perfectly possible for the mass attack by workers of all levels, from the highest to the lowest, to go beyond the point of optimum performance, and to lose many really good results it might obtain in the unreadable ruck of fifth-rate reports. This is a real observable defect of large-scale science at the present time. If a new Einstein theory were to come into being as a government report in one of our super-laboratories, there would be a really great chance that nobody would have the patience to go through the mass published under the same auspices and discover it.

The great laboratory may do many important things, at its best, but at its worst it is a morass which engulfs the abilities of the leaders as much as those of the followers.

... There are many administrators of science and a large component of the general population who believe that mass attacks can do anything, and even that ideas are obsolete.

Behind this drive to the mass attack there are a number of strong psychological motives. Neither the public nor the big administrator has too good an understanding of the inner continuity of science, but they both have seen its world-shaking consequences, and they are afraid of it. Both of them wish to decerebrate the scientist, as the Byzantine State emasculated its civil servants. Moreover, the great administrator who is not sure of his own intellectual level can aggrandise himself only by cutting his scientific employees down to size.

(Norbert Wiener, *I am a Mathematician*, Gollancz, 1956, pp. 359–365.)

In the subjects concerned with human behaviour, where well-founded standards of excellence hardly exist, nothing debars selection for positions of power without the slightest regard for intellectual quality. Where the prizes are appetizing but the rules of the game are so vague that honest play can hardly be distinguished from cheating, it is not very likely that the idealists and the impractical seekers after truth will get to the top; and the larger the sums which come into question, the more ruthless is the scramble and the greater the chances that anti-intellectual manipulators will win it.

Concentration of control affects the dissemination of ideas through its effects upon the relative chances in the contest for fame; because power bestows status not only upon its possessors but upon their works too. Who, for instance, would have paid 200,000 dollars for Hitler's paintings (as has happened at a recent auction) on their artistic merit? Likewise, the copious citations and quotations which many contemporary academics enjoy are due to their positions in the corridors of power, and especially to their influence in the distribution of money, jobs and invitations. Somebody could make an interesting statistical study of how laudatory reviews written by European academics seem to be preceded or followed by their authors' profitable visiting professorships at the American institutions wherein the addressees of their adulation dwell. Those who would like to do field work in the sociology of the social sciences should go to conferences to observe how academic callboys solicit the favours of the foundation moguls, and to listen to the discussions in the dining halls and vestibules, which are single-mindedly focused on who can get what, and how.

The ability to raise funds provides a short cut to literary fame without the necessity of tedious study, by opening opportunities to publish books of awesome bulk under one's own name but written, in fact, by a host of research assistants, and polished up by consultants. Almost needless to say, this form of production has reached the highest state of development in the United States.

Looking through various fat books from under the pen of renowned American writers, I had often wondered how a professional scholar could put in so many repetitions, self-contradictions, words used in a wrong sense and even errors of grammar – not to speak of the quality of style. My suspicions that many of these books must have been written by several authors, despite having only one name on the cover, were fully confirmed when I had an opportunity to see what goes on inside the research factories, where (mindful of their career prospects) few of the forced ghost writers dare to complain.

One of the manifestations (unimportant in itself but very revealing) of the timorous but disingenuous humility characteristic of a burrowing apparatchik is the taboo on the word 'I'. 'One still shudders at the arrogance of the author in his repetitive use of the first singular concerning complex issues' – says a reviewer of one of my books, who for all I know may be the only creature in whom this obscene word can induce actual shudders, although by saying 'one' instead of 'I' he implies that most of his readers suffer from this allergy.

I doubt whether the reviewer in question favours the majestic first plural normal among the older French writers, and still common among their successors, but which in England is reserved for the Queen. Presumably he prefers the anonymous 'it'; and likes to see an expression like 'I think that . . . ' replaced by 'it is hypothesized . . . ', which (apart from expurgating the dirty word 'to think') ministers to the bureaucratic underling's predilection for submissive anonymity combined with oracular authority. I do not see why declaring that I – a mortal and fallible man but entitled to express his opinions – hold this or that view should be deemed more arrogant than pretending to be the Voice of Science.

To see the situation in the correct light, we must bear in mind that the adulation of the controllers of research funds is not entirely disingenuous because (as the old moralists from La Bruyère to Adam Smith have vividly described) people always admire wealth and power, and attribute to their holders superior virtues which they do not possess. What merits underlining, however, is that (apart from the destruction of enthusiasm and of the free play of ideas, so necessary for truly creative work) the regimentation of social research produces a mental deterioration in the bosses, whose powers of self-criticism atrophy in consequence of being surrounded by docile drudges and sycophants. So in addition to the initial negative selection of the lighter weights for the top positions in the social research industry, we have a secondary process at work which makes them ever lighter the longer they stay at the top. But there is even more to it than that.

In consequence of the endemic bureaucratic disease which Northcote Parkinson calls enjelitis, the more mediocre the boss, the more eagerly he tries to reduce everybody in the field to the status of a research robot. Apart from sheer envy, this tendency stems from the fear that, by demonstrating that equally or more significant results can be attained through cheap individual work, an intellectual craftsman weakens the case for spending vast sums on the social research empires.

When people, lacking either the ability or the desire for original thinking, judge what must or must not be studied, they invariably favour routine research rather than anything that might lead to a genuine discovery. Apart from personal inclination, common prudence requires a research boss to plump for safe mediocrity in preference to unpredictable originality, because his establishment needs money, controlled by bureaucrats and financiers who want to see 'the output', the quality of which they are unable to judge, and who lack the imagination to conceive what they might miss by not supporting more speculative lines of inquiry.

Even in the natural sciences, the fear of incurring their sponsors' displeasure at getting no results for their subsidies must have closed many potentially fruitful lines of inquiry, but the radical difference in social research is that here producing nothing calls forth less fury than a genuine discovery which offends the interests or prejudices. Can you imagine a medical or social research council subsidizing Freud's studies in 1900? But, you may say, that was in the bad old days: we are more enlightened now. The truth, unfortunately, is that, although we may be more tolerant about the prejudices of the past, there is no evidence that we are equally broad-minded about the current preconceptions.

The history of all the sciences amply demonstrates that the more original the idea, the greater the resistance it has met. We all know about Copernicus' fear of the stake, the tribulations of Galileo, the vituperations against Darwin, the horror which greeted Harvey's deviation from Galen's medical bible, and the attempts to oust Pasteur from the medical profession. Many other examples could be added: Einstein's having been turned down as a candidate for graduate studies, or the failure of Newton's early attempts to secure a fellowship in Cambridge, of Lobatchevsky being taken for a lunatic after he announced his discovery of non-Euclidean geometry. There are even more extreme cases: of the great mathematician, Abel, starving throughout almost his entire life and dying prematurely in consequence; of Gallois failing (twice, if I remember rightly) an entrance examination to a university in mathematics, a subject in which he had already laid the foundations for an entirely new branch now known as the theory of groups.

The laying of the foundations of the social sciences was made possible by cases of fortuitous confluence of talent, interest and unearned income: be it in the form of inheritance as with de Tocqueville, T. H. Buckle or Herbert Spencer, or quickly-made money as with Ricardo, or kind friends as with Marx and Auguste Comte, or sinecure as with Hobbes and John Stuart Mill. The disappearance of the leisured class has closed this loophole for cultivating cranky and unpopular views, which bodes ill for the future progress of knowledge.

What kind of practical lessons can be drawn from this? My advice to the statesmen who have to decide how to spend public money might be welcomed by them, though extremely unpalatable to the vast majority of my colleagues: namely, do not be too generous. A degree of shortage of funds for social research might make the researchers think about other things than money. There are many other worthy causes, such as old age pensions or adequate pay for elementary school teachers. In physics or technology there are urgent problems which cannot be tackled without a vast outlay on expensive machinery, but there are no such thresholds in the social sciences, apart from the collection of demographic and economic statistics which requires a large organization. In other branches of the study of man in society we not only have the law of diminishing returns, but even a law of negative returns, whereby (by virtue of the circumstances outlined above) a larger expenditure may produce less knowledge than a smaller one.

Barring outright censorship, nothing can prevent progress more than centralized 'co-ordination' of research in a controversial subject. Consequently, if the overriding concern were the desire to promote advancement of knowledge rather than furtherance of the vested interests of bureaucratic cliques, social science research councils would be disbanded, or at least explicitly confined to subserving the needs of the administration, and the remaining funds distributed to as many independent organizations as possible. There ought to be many small centres dispensing driblets, with interlocking directorates banned so as to forestall control by a single clique, as has happened to a large extent to the existing foundations. Even this would not prevent wing-clipping by the unimaginative mediocrities who commonly gravitate towards the sources of money, but at least it might favour a little variety, and make the imposition of a single orthodoxy slightly more difficult.

Seeing that it is usually the case that the larger the expenditure on a 'project' the more trifling its results, I often think it might be better if, instead of setting up mammoth foundations, the millionaires would maintain salons and dole out money personally, straight out of their pockets, as the old-fashioned patrons of writers and artists used to do. Because, to be welcomed in a duke's or banker's entourage, a scholar had to be witty and constantly able to tell people something interesting – the kind of gifts which Voltaire had in abundance and which induced kings to keep him at their courts despite his sharp tongue and dangerous views. If he had gone on and on droning about the same thing over and over again in the usual professorial manner, he would have been sent away the day he arrived. Though incapable of ensuring scientific reliability or true originality of thought, wit and conversational brilliance guarantee nonetheless a high intelligence and a wide range of knowledge; whereas persistence in filling in inane application forms for research grants must normally go together with a low intelligence because (as industrial psychologists have found out long ago) more intelligent people endure less readily dull and repetitive tasks.

What further tilts the balance so that research funds are allocated to those least capable of putting them to good use is the fact that, in contrast to the aristocratic and plutocratic patrons of old, whose status and self-esteem were based on criteria other than the intellectual, and who consequently did not worry about being surpassed in this respect by their protegés, the foundation and research council bureaucrats most often come from the ranks of academics who have lacked either the talent or the will power to make the grade as scientists or scholars, and who therefore are prone to use the power of the purse to assuage their resentment, to get even with their more talented colleagues, and to indulge in lording over supplicants who either take good care that their brains are not showing or have none to show.

Chapter 15

Gresham's and Parkinson's Laws Combined

Every modern society grants to its scientists many enviable privileges. Though much less wealthy than successful business-men, they earn a great deal more than the vast majority of the workers, and enjoy freedom, prestige and security far beyond the reach of the much better remunerated executives. So naturally many people would like to join their ranks; but, unfortunately, the natural sciences require a mathematical ability which only a small minority of the population possess, and demand a long and hard apprenticeship.

At this point of the present book the reader should need no convincing that the study of human affairs presents far more formidable difficulties than any which a student of nature may encounter; and actually, the very fact that the social sciences have advanced so much less, in itself corroborates the magni-tude of the obstacles facing them. Consequently, a really competent social scientist has no reason to feel inferior to his colleagues in the natural sciences on the ground that his under-standing of society cannot rival their theories in precision and reliability. When a runner on a hard track gets further within a given time than a late starter who has to wade through a swampy thicket, this does not prove that the first is a better sportsman. Likewise, it would be gratuitous to assert that Laplace was more intelligent than de Tocqueville, that Max Planck's achievement was more remarkable than Max Weber's, that Rutherford was a greater man than Keynes, or that Einstein's contribution to knowledge was greater than Freud's. Unquestionably, as judged from hindsight, mistakes made by the giants of the natural sciences are utterly insignificant in comparison with the fundamental errors into which the great figures of social and economic studies have fallen, but the former started from a much firmer ground, free from the abysmal pitfalls which surround mankind's study of itself.

Therefore, if he is honest, intelligent and has a wide range of knowledge, a sociologist or political scientist need suffer from no feelings of inferiority in regard to his colleagues in the natural sciences: and if they sneer at the shakiness of his edifice he can always answer: all right, if you are so much cleverer, why don't you try to say something about my subject that is new and can be backed by good arguments. This kind of challenge need not be purely hypothetical, because a number of distinguished natural scientists have ventured into the field of sociology, politics and economics without being able to make any contributions to them and sometimes voicing utter inanities; although their jejune pronouncements often received undue attention in virtue of the halo effect of a fame well deserved in their own disciplines. Without going back as far as Newton's discourses on witches, we can draw at random from a large number of recent examples, such as that of a prominent crystallographer and author of a serious work on the history of science, J. D. Bernal, whose writings on politics exhibit the mentality of a marxist backwoodsman who refuses to use his common sense. Einstein's statements about politics consisted of pious platitudes, while P. W. Bridgman's were as ill-conceived as they were presumptuous. Robert J. Oppenheimer's pronouncements were in the nature of banal sermons. Manchester University made an interesting experiment in this matter when (at his own request) it converted Michael Polanyi's post in chemistry into a chair of social studies, expecting perhaps that he would replicate his discoveries in a new field . . . which, as you might guess, did not happen. However, unlike the eminent scientists just mentioned, he did produce (apart from a much more significant book on the philosophy of science) some perfectly respectable books and articles in his new subject, although there was nothing very new in them.

Many eminent men of science genuinely believed all kinds of absurd dogmas, and were ready to accept the infallibility of the Pope or the General Secretary or Der Fuehrer. But when we move from the discoverers to the run-of-the-mill scientists who uncritically memorize and then routinely apply the formulae, without thinking about their nature or realizing their limitations, we often find troglodyte boffins, full of narrow prejudices and irrational personal enmities, in comparison with whose views on politics, ethics or aesthetics an average grocer appears as a fount of enlightenment. I do not, of course, maintain that all (or even the majority) of scientists and technologists are like that: but I have the impression (based on many years' observation) that, much more than lawyers or businessmen, they are prone to fall either into a rigid conservative or a totalitarian frame of mind, whether of the communist or fascist variety.

There is nothing surprising about all this, because to acquire and maintain competence in any of the exact sciences demands so much effort that little time or energy remains for thinking about other matters; especially if they be of the kind that require the laborious gathering and evaluating of masses of information, usually chaotically dispersed and often deliberately concealed and distorted. Furthermore, accustomed to operating with hard and fast rules, most natural scientists find it difficult to reason on the shaky basis, consisting of a tremendous number of tentative and very approximate judgments, which are neither logically concatenated nor fully independent. Used, moreover, to concepts which (though open to revision and epistemological doubt) are for all practical purposes rigorously defined (even if only implicitly through the structure of the symbolism) and relatively few in number, the exact scientist often lacks the semantic sensitivity – the feeling for elusive shades of meaning and their relationships – which in dealing with the blurred contours of cultural phenomena is even more essential than the ability to perform the operations of mathematics or formal logic. Sometimes these shortcomings appear in startling extremes, as when we find experts in physics or chemistry who seem incapable of reasoning in words or of expressing a simple idea in writing – which disparity brings to mind the well-authenticated cases of the calculators of genius who are literally morons in every other respect.

The foregoing considerations go far towards explaining why (beginning with the ancient Greeks) no one has made important contributions to the study of nature as well as of society. Aristotle stands out as the only exception to this rule which, however, is in all likelihood apparent rather than genuine, because his works represent a compendium of the then existing knowledge rather than an account of his own discoveries; and, as the sources on which they were based have perished, we have no means of ascertaining what was Aristotle's own contribution. Anyway, to avoid misunderstanding, I must stress that I am talking about first-rate creative work: I do not deny that it is possible to acquire a good knowledge of the other side of the cultural fence (as Bertrand Russell did), or that it is easier to shift from high-powered mathematics to verbal analysis than the other way round. In the case of the chemist turned social scientist mentioned earlier it can be said that, though lacking in significant originality, his writings on sociology and politics are at least free from the inanities commonly repeated by the run-of-the-mill professionals. It must also be added that quite a number of exact scientists, who have turned to politics or administration when their creativity has dried up, have done quite well in these fields, and their political judgment does not appear to have been worse than that of most politicians.

There is an asymmetry between the expertise in the natural and in the social sciences. Someone unacquainted with an exact science is completely dumbfounded in any discussion about it; but, being reduced to silence, he is saved from any possible temptation to spout nonsense. On matters pertaining to the social sciences, on the other hand, the opposite is the case: everybody feels entitled to express strong views, and there are no solid signposts to warn against the pitfalls of ignorance, sophistry, or even folly; while the lack of knowledge regularly breeds a conviction that things are simple and require no deep study – which explains why so many exact scientists have been ready to make silly statements about politics.

The contrast between exactness and certitude (relative but sufficient for most practical purposes) on the one hand, and vagueness and tentativeness on the other, entails a further asymmetry between the natural and the social sciences. A mediocre natural scientist, albeit unable to think of anything

7*

new, or even to keep fully abreast of current progress, remains nonetheless a repository of useful (even if limited and perhaps superficial) knowledge, whereas a mediocre social scientist, unable to distinguish between worthwhile ideas and the half-truths and inanities which flourish in his controversial field, will be an easy victim of deluded mystics and charlatans and will act as an agent of mental pollution. This difference explains why the vast expansion of educational institutions has had beneficial effects on the level of technical skills while helping to turn the humanistic studies into a massive pollution of the mind.

Owing to the interwoven quality of the various strands of social life, no narrow specialist can offer advice on policy which merits attention. Thus somebody who spends all his time on studying race relations may not be the best person to make forecasts about them, because future situations will, in all likelihood, be equally influenced by factors outside his field of interests, such as transformations of family patterns, political re-alignments, or the position of the trade unions. True, some degree of specialization is inevitable, but the impossibility of finding truly isolated social or cultural systems exposes the investigator to the danger that, in consequence of specializing too narrowly, he may be unable to understand what he is specializing in. By concentrating exclusively on one time and place an anthropologist may not be able to distinguish between what is peculiar to it and what is universal or at least widely shared. The massive trivialization of sociology and politology goes hand in hand with the increasingly common ignorance of history and ethnography among the practitioners. Moreover, owing to the slippery nature of the concepts he cannot avoid using, a social scientist ought to possess a high level of skill in logic and philosophy, as well as some grounding in the natural sciences – which is a tall order. Although the emotional and pecuniary allurements of nebulous verbosity may be so great that nothing could outweigh them, the obfuscating jargon might not have spread quite so easily as it did had a training in logical analysis been enforced as a prerequisite for studying the social sciences. As it happened, philosophy was discarded from sociological and politological education by 'hard-headed' but soft-brained devotees of scientism – with the results shown in the previous chapters.

There is a curious parallel to this development in the communist world, where the rulers of Poland no longer allow undergraduates to study analytical philosophy – which in pre-war 'fascist' days was taught at a very high level to wider audiences than anywhere else in the world – having no doubt found that a training in logical analysis fosters a distaste for the official ideology.

While demanding at least as much work and ability for a proper understanding as the natural sciences, the social sciences (with the very partial exception of economics) differ from them by having no natural threshold of acceptability. A physicist or a chemist may hold cruder views on politics, aesthetics or ethics than a shop assistant, but this is not what he is paid for. His status and salary are justified by his knowledge of chemical reactions, of the structure of the atom or whatever his speciality may be . . . and in such matters there is little room for bluffing. No amount of plausible talking and posturing will make a bridge stand if it has been incompetently designed; while ignorant dabbling with chemicals will soon lead to a fatal explosion. In contrast, nothing will immediately blow up or fall down in consequence of a politologist's or economist's inanity; while the harm caused by his ignorance or dishonesty may not materialize until years later, and will in any case be debatable and difficult to blame on a particular man. Related to this is the fact that, as the criteria of excellence are so dubious, it is impossible for a layman seeking advice to find who the real experts are. Neither a degree, nor a university chair, nor membership of a famous society or institution constitutes a warranty that a given social scientist deserves being taken seriously, because in the competition for these honours knowledge and integrity often matter less than skill at intrigue and self-advertisement. It is not surprising, therefore, that – far from being particularly good in sociology or political science – the wealthiest American universities contain an unusually large proportion of phonies who bask in the collective glory deservedly won by their colleagues in the exact disciplines.

Not only the exact sciences but also some of the humanistic

studies (such as sinology) have built-in hurdles which deter the seekers of an easy way to make a living or achieve fame. Even the more accessible kinds of historiography – which in their conventional form of chauvinistic chronicles almost justified Ford's famous dictum that 'history is bunk' – demand from their practitioners a notable perseverance needed for memorizing a large stock of dates and other pieces of information, all the more difficult to remember for being disconnected and trivial. For this reason, the old-fashioned schools of historiography produced large cohorts of dry-as-dust and none-too-intelligent pedants with very narrow mental horizons, but few charlatans.

To repeat once again, social and political studies have opened the gates of academic pastures to a large number of aspirants to the status of a scientist who might have been perfectly useful citizens as post-office managers or hospital almoners, but who have been tempted into charlatanry by being faced with a subject utterly beyond their mental powers. In economics this is true to a lesser degree, because its mathematical requirements deter or debar a good proportion of the population; so that, despite their limited horizons, even its most mediocre practitioners can be of some use as accountants.

As pointed out earlier, owing to its narrow-minded disregard of non-economic factors, economic theory provides a very shaky basis for economic policy; but, unlike most of what goes under the name of sociology, it does at least carry us beyond the reach of mere common sense.

Traditional political science did not really claim to be Science: and consisted mainly of the examination of the views of great thinkers of the past on how states ought to be governed, on the respective rights and duties of citizens and office-holders, coupled with some jurisprudence, exegesis of constitutional texts and an exposition of the organization of public institutions. In this shape political science remained purely academic in the pejorative sense of having little relevance to the practice of politics, and it contained no basis for a cumulative development of empirical theory. Nonetheless, this discipline produced cultivated minds, able to think and express themselves clearly, and consequently well fitted to make administrative decisions so long as no specialist knowledge was called for. Lately, however, the siren songs of pseudo-science have led many (if not most) cultivators of political studies to throw overboard their limited but respectable traditions, with the results which we have seen in the earlier chapters.

On the whole anthropology has been much less plagued by triviality than sociology because, until the recent half-baked ventures into the study of industrial societies, it has made it its business to supply information which was exotic to the readers and could never boil down to a restatement of the obvious. On account of their strangeness, the cultures studied by the anthropologist demanded from him a mental effort needed for an understanding of a totally new language and way of behaving, not to speak of the discomfort (and often danger) involved in visiting outlying places – all of which acted as a deterrent to the most unimaginative stick-in-the-mud types. True, many anthropologists never succeeded in learning the language of the people studied, while others lacked the traits of character needed for winning the trust and friendship of total aliens, which shortcomings condemned their work to superficiality. Others, having done their stint in a remote place for a year or two, never bothered to revisit the area or even attempt to find out indirectly what was going on there; never read anything, and kept talking for twenty or forty years about what they saw in their youth. Even such lukewarm scholars, however, could pride themselves on knowing what nobody else knew – namely 'their' tribe – and so did not have to resort to bluff to justify their claims to academic respectability. Like that of the historians, the anthropologists' knowledge might be regarded by hard-headed practical men as only fit for a museum, but not as non-existent.

An old-fashioned sociologist was an erudite scholar, on whom our managerial academics like to pin the epithet 'armchair', although they use this domestic object just as much, only not for reading books but for writing superfluous memoranda and for interminable sessions of committees. Thinkers like Karl Marx, Herbert Spencer or Max Weber would be exceptional in any age; but, even if we take writers of the past two generations, well below the genius rank, like Marcel Mauss, L. T. Hobhouse, Pitirim Sorokin, Celestin Bouglé,

Rudolf Steinmetz, Stefan Czarnowski, Richard Thurnwald, Franz Oppenheimer, Stanislaw Ossowski, Werner Sombart, Alfred Weber, Ferdinand Toënnies, Morris Ginsberg or Karl Mannheim – we can see in their works a clear evidence that even the less original of them were men of vast learning (acquainted with history, jurisprudence, philosophy and economics) who did not have to resort to an obfuscating jargon to conceal their inability to tell their colleagues in other fields anything which these did not know.

When books were fewer, one could not aspire to the status of an intellectual without having read the standard classics, but the present flood of print makes it utterly impossible for anyone to read a substantial part of it (which in any case would be a waste of time) while the mechanization of conferences and congresses has almost eliminated real debates and consequently the opportunities to discover who is knowledgeable and who is not; thus permitting many half-hearted academics to get away with reading next to nothing, and attracting entrants looking for an easy living. When we look at the subdivisions of sociology and political science, it seems that the average level varies with the magnitude of the deterrent: it seems to be highest in area studies which require learning a difficult language, and lowest among people who specialise in such things as race relations or the family in their own society. Not that it is easy to say something new and significant on the latter topics; but it does not take much effort to learn enough for plausible pontification to ignorant audiences.

The extent of ignorance one encounters among the licensed specialists in the study of mankind exceeds the bounds of imagination; and to forestall the impression that only the Americans are given to such foibles let me mention three random examples from the British scene. Thus I have heard a research fellow in one of the better-known departments of anthropology in Britain attribute to the head of that department in all seriousness the discovery of the importance of conflict in human society. Another luminary of British anthropology has been credited in speech and in print with having discovered that when studying social structure one must take time into account. Another example which springs to my mind as rather amusing is a review I read recently of a book which competently describes some examples (mostly from India) of village power politics, and which the reviewer rated as better than Machiavelli. He could have added that the worthy author must also be a greater traveller than Vasco da Gama as he got to India and back much quicker.

The trend towards shoddiness, due to the absence of in-built deterrents, is further aggravated in some places by special circumstances. In Latin America, for instance, academics do not earn enough to feed a family; and are therefore compelled to take other jobs which do not leave them enough time for serious study, let alone writing. In the United States the universities pay enough for all the material comforts, but their 'publish or perish' principle goads many people (who would otherwise remain honest citizens and perhaps competent teachers) into pretending that they have discovered something worthy of world-wide dissemination. Many American colleges have elaborate procedures for measuring the merits of the candidates for appointments and promotions, with so many points awarded for an article, so many for a book, so many for editing a symposium – depending on the length as well as the rating of the publisher or the journal. A chairman of a sociology department at one of the big state universities – a serious, middle-aged man whose veracity I have no reason to doubt – told me that to choose candidates for promotion justly, their dean gets his secretary to weigh their publications . . . literally, on the scales.

The absence of minimal standards offers unlimited scope for numerical expansion, which in the exact sciences is constrained by the scarcity of talent. This is the chief reason why (like the arts) the social sciences have been allowed to expand so much, because educational bureaucracy has a vested interest in boundlessly increasing the number of the inmates of its establishments, regardless of whether they learn anything; and in fostering one of the grossest superstitions of our times (bolstered up by the golden calf of pseudo-quantification) which equates the progress of education with an increase in the number of individuals kept within the walls of educational institutions. In reality (and especially in the case of the United States) one could say that never have so many stayed in school so long to learn so little.

The tendency towards a lowering of standards has been aggravated, among other things, by the shift of the intellectual leadership from Europe to America, due much more to the decline in Europe than to progress in the United States – which trend has been most marked in sociology, while in economics the British have been able to maintain good standards within the conventional limits, despite having lost the leadership. Seeing German sociology in its present state of dull imitation of the American wares, nobody could guess that until thirty-five years ago Germany was the foremost centre of progress; and that to become competent in this subject one had to know German. The elimination of the Jews – the most creative group since the ancient Greeks, who supplied one-third of the German Nobel Prize winners, while constituting 1% of the population – the expulsion of the more upright non-Jewish intellectuals, and the compulsory mental prostitution of the rest have irretrievably broken the great cultural tradition.

Having lived only four years under a relatively mild form of nazi rule, France has suffered no comparable breach of cultural continuity, although she lost a number of distinguished scholars. Nonetheless, the great cartesian tradition of clear and logical thinking has withered and made room for a predilection for mystification. Inaugurated by Henri Bergson, this decline continued between the wars in the shade of the epigoni of the great tradition such as (in sociology) Bouglé and Mauss; but the general collapse of the cartesian tradition (in the broad sense) followed the German invasion in 1940 which shattered the Frenchmen's serene self-confidence, which neither post-war prosperity nor gaullist touchiness have been able to restore. It seems that in consequence of the loss of faith in their traditions – even though concealed from their own eyes by chauvinistic boasting – the French have become enamoured of the worst features of teutonic culture, as represented by such producers of philosophical fog as Heidegger, Jaspers and Husserl, as well as Hegel and Marx. The old-style German scholars, however, though addicted to nebulous and pompous verbosity, usually had the saving grace of a vast store of knowledge; but, like the Americans, the French imitators have adopted their pretentiousness and obscurity without their bent for hard work and their enormous erudition.

In Britain the best brains (as far as the social sciences were concerned) have customarily gravitated towards economics. An urbane and enlightened tradition also continued to be transmitted in political science; but it remained rather narrow and legalistic, and no outstanding innovators of the calibre of Gaetano Mosca or Robert Michels appeared in Britain after Bentham and John Stuart Mill – which fact had a great deal to do with the abomination in which the very word sociology was held by the academic establishment, who took a century to recover from the shock of the French revolution, which they ascribed to excessive reasoning about the sacred foundations of society. The only tolerated kind of sociology was the study of subordinate exotic societies, known as anthropology. Actually, Britain did produce two great thinkers who took up Comte's idea of a general science of society – Herbert Spencer and John Mackinnon Robertson – but it was no accident that they had neither a university nor even a public or grammar school education, let alone an academic appointment; and although Spencer became very famous, his thought has been developed in France rather than England, while Robertson remains unknown to this very day.

These peculiarities of British intellectual history can be sociologically explained. In the first place, it is not surprising that economic theory was able to attract an ample supply of first-rate minds in the foremost trading nation of the world. Furthermore, this theory was able to progress by abstracting from non-economic factors treated as constant, which appeared plausible only in a country where the latter had the character of steady underlying conditions which did not obtrude upon the orderly functioning of the market process – in other words, only in a country whose social and political institutions were adapted to the exigencies of the capitalist economic system, which was more nearly the case in Britain after 1800 than in any other country with the exception of the United States. In the latter country, however, the economy had fewer world-wide contacts; and its problems were, consequently, less stimulating intellectually, apart from a generally lower level of sophistication. The harmony between the economy and its institutional framework, which conduced British academics to study economic mechanisms, discouraged them from probing into the non-economic aspects of social order regarded as natural if not perfect – while in Germany the survivals of pre-industrial or even pre-commercial customs and institutions were so numerous and strong, despite a more rapid development of industry than has ever been the case in England, that the relations between economy and society occupied the central place in German thinking and stimulated the efflorescence of sociological theorizing. Though of greater significance than in England, in France this particular disharmony was only of secondary importance as a stimulant of sociological theorizing in comparison with the impact of the revolutions, which drew the attention of the French thinkers (from Saint-Simon down to Durkheim) to the question of the consensus, and how to ensure social cohesion in the face of the decay of religion.

Just as most people do not take much interest in the physiology of their organs until these begin to give them trouble, an interest in the foundations of the social order is normally aroused by the impact of its no longer deniable faults; whereas if you feel that you are living in a perfect society, which neither needs to be nor can be improved, you are unlikely to ponder about the fundamental questions of sociology. The same applies to the special field of political science; and here again the success of the British constitution in attaining an extraordinary measure of liberty and internal peace, has had a soporific effect upon political inquiry; which accounts for the absence of truly original departures, despite an impressive level of scholarship and sophistication exemplified in the writings of its best representatives, such as James Bryce. It may be symptomatic, however, that Bryce's best books deal not with Britain but with foreign countries, while the most original work on British politics was produced by a Russian Jew, Moise Ostrogorsky.

In addition to the aforementioned factors we must take into account the strong ingredient of ritualism in British collective behaviour, which has begun to wane only during the last decade, because it stands to reason that if customs and political institutions are hedged by taboos, any attempt to dissect them will encounter a strong resistance. So it is not surprising that the only customs and beliefs which the academic establishment permitted to be analysed were those of the colonial subjects, while anything smacking of sociological theory was shunned by respectable academics until very recently. The only studies of social problems that were pursued in home waters were inquiries into poverty, which refrained from touching upon any wide-ranging or theoretical questions. Despite their un-doubted political usefulness as an antidote to the perennial tendency of the affluent to avert their eyes from the plight of the poor, studies of this kind (continued nowadays by Richard Titmuss and his disciples) were not very high-powered in-tellectually, and were marked by rather parochial mental horizons, which have left their stamp on what passes for sociology in Britain today.

The vogue for sociology which sprang up suddenly in Britain in the sixties fits in well with the foregoing diagnosis, because it occurred at a time when the loss of international power and of the empire led to a collapse of the sense of national superiority and of the faith that the British had dis-covered the secret of political and social perfection. The withering of a sentiment so deeply rooted has caused public opinion to swing to the opposite extreme – a masochistic wallowing in guilt for the sins of colonialism, coupled with an inordinate desire to imitate the Americans. Small wonder then that the academic by-product of this decline has been born very sickly indeed, infested by a multitude of dull young men who might have become useful citizens had they not been given tasks beyond their capacity, and who will clutter up the sociological departments of many British universities for thirty or forty years, thus blocking the outlets for the next generation – especially for those who might outshine the incumbents. Their single-minded devotion to every last-but-one transatlantic fashion (stimulated by a strong appetite for crumbs off the better garnished American table) makes it most unlikely that anything could be done to remedy the sorry state of the subject in Britain without an American lead.

Although the United States have produced so far only one thinker in the broad field of the study of society who has an indisputable title to greatness, and who was in his domain better than the best Europeans of his day – namely Lewis Henry Morgan – the American universities extended an early welcome to the social sciences on a scale unimaginable in Europe, with the University of Chicago establishing the first professorship of sociology in the world. It might be worth noting on the margin that neither Morgan nor the only truly great American philosopher, Charles Saunders Pierce, held an academic post. What went under the name of sociology and political science, however, was more in the nature of 'civics' (that is, instruction in how to be a good citizen) rather than the kind of philosophizing that was favoured on the continent of Europe at the time. As the population consisted in large measure of immigrants who had to be fitted into American society, the question of adaptation occupied the focus of attention, while the nature of the social order itself, being regarded as natural and unquestionably good, did not call forth any great discussions. In the latter respect the American intellectual climate resembled the British rather than the continental European, where the proponents of revolutionary doctrines were incessantly casting doubts on the justice of the fundamental principles of the existing order, thus obliging the conservative intellectuals to think about these problems in order to find good arguments for defence.

The focus on the more manageable problems of adaptation of immigrants fostered in American sociology a practical and empirical bent, exemplified best in the Chicago School which was the pioneer of the practice of detailed as well as massive observation of social reality. Despite a certain narrowness, this was a valuable contribution which stimulated parallel efforts in political studies, and constituted the originality of the American social sciences. The process of degradation set in after the Second World War with the unprecedented influx of money and the rise of the academic entrepreneur.

The American cultural climate has certain features which make it unpropitious to the progress of social thought, among which the most important is deference for the band-waggon.

True, the fear of being left behind the latest fashion is common enough everywhere, but in pre-television days it used to be less overwhelming in Europe than in America. Almost every European observer (beginning with de Tocqueville) has noted this American peculiarity; some viewing it as benign, others as sinister. A proneness to uncritical enthusiasms may help rather than hinder in the types of endeavour where there are irremovable mechanisms which quickly reveal and punish mistakes, as happens with technical inventions. In such fields as technology or business methods you cannot go very far wrong by being over-eager to follow the latest thing, because experience will soon show you whether the new ideas are any good; while competition ensures that those gadgets or methods which work will prevail. Thus in practical activities the American love for novelty and their lack of circumspection has led to great achievements which are too well known to call for enumeration. In contrast, dire results have ensued from the operation of the same bias in domains where there are no immanent mechanisms for eliminating error: where correctness and falsehood are normally a matter of degree, and truth can be only partially gleaned by a laborious crawl over dangerous ground between attractively camouflaged traps, and where every step calls for a suspicious examination and often a suspended judgment; and to top it all, where excessive incredulity can be just as misleading as gullibility. No wonder then that in the social sciences the Americans have tended to throw themselves with a tremendous energy into one silly craze after another, hailing every pretentious gimmick as an epoch-making 'break-through', and then employing their power and wealth to foist their manias upon the rest of the world. Even the new mood of disillusion with the status quo constitutes no exception to this rule, as it amounts to a swing from a gullible admiration to an equally uncritical denigration.

Amongst the vast population engaged in intellectual pursuits in the United States there are, of course, many men and women of remarkable knowledge and ability, but the sheer size of the mass ensures that the average level is low, while the egalitarian creed tends to push the minimal requirements lower and lower; with the consequence that in a field lacking a natural threshold (in the sense explained earlier) utterly ignorant and barely literate individuals find it quite easy to become researchers and professors. The proliferation of practitioners does little harm in the 'hard' fields with inherent and clear criteria of achievement, as there the mediocrities are forced into proper modesty and obliged to follow the best minds. In contrast, in a field where the rules of the game are arbitrary and vague to the point of non-existence, gimmicks bring more kudos than true intellectual merit. The mass of academic employees who have no real curiosity and are unaccustomed to a serious mental effort will readily acclaim only products which do not disturb their slumbers while offering a façade of ultra-scientific weightiness.

Equally harmful to the development of the social sciences has been another trait, which used to be commoner among the Americans than elsewhere: namely, the crassly utilitarian outlook which demands quick practical results and which probably accounts for the fact that, even in the exact sciences, the United States have produced so far only one great theoretician – Willard Gibbs, the creator of statistical mechanics – while bringing forth a plethora of practical inventors, including the most prolific of them all, Thomas Alva Edison. Although a desire for gain was certainly not their chief motivation, their work nevertheless conformed to the general respect for whatever is profitable – which, to repeat, has always been common outside tribal communities but which in America used to meet even less resistance than elsewhere and which the hippies are the first large segment of American society to disown. Again, in technical and business activities where it is profitable to know the truth, this cast of mind has prompted great feats of efficiency; whereas we have seen on the preceding pages what has been happening in the fields where it pays better to mislead or conceal than to reveal. Magnified by the impact of the mass-media (with their natural tendency to bring down everything to the lowest common denominator) the American predominance in the social sciences has helped to shunt them into the blind alley of pseudo-science.

Chapter 16

Ivory Towers or Bureaucratic Treadmills

As the research establishments have proved totally unsuitable as an environment for critical and creative thinking, and as in no country today is there an intellectually minded leisured class, only the universities remain as havens for thinkers. Unfortunately, however, they are gravely handicapped in performing this role by several deep-rooted weaknesses, both old and new. Among the former I must mention in the first place the often noted fact that teaching is bad for the brain – because, speaking habitually to a captive audience of one's mental inferiors, one easily falls into the habit of perorating rather than thinking and examining critically one's opinions. The other old weakness is the perennial drift towards parasitism in an occupation where the value of the work cannot be measured, and where the ill effects of a misguided approach or negligence will only afflict future generations.

It is agreeable to be in an occupation where the hours are short, the vacations long and the security of tenure so entrenched that neither laziness nor decrepitude will make you lose your job. If you are a chemist or an engineer you may be barred from the laboratory if people can see that you have become so deranged that you might cause a serious accident; but in the arts or social sciences you can carry on even when you are blind, deaf, half paralysed, and have forgotten almost everything you knew. If you go mad in a not too obvious way and are still able to emit recognizable sounds, you have a good chance of being acclaimed as a discoverer of unfathomable truths. As a matter of fact, one American writer has meteorically risen to world-wide fame on the strength of the books written shortly before he had to undergo an operation for a brain tumour. When asked afterwards by a newspaper reporter whether he still believed what he had written his answer (as reported) was not clearly affirmative.

In his remarkable *Histoire des Sciences et des Savants,* published in 1875, Adolphe de Candolle presents some statistics which suggest that fewer great scientists were born in university towns than one might expect; and he adds in the way of an explanation that 'the spectacle of the pettiness of the professors and of the laziness of the students is unlikely to inspire a child with the high ideal of the pursuit of truth'. So we can see that things have not changed all that much.

A lazy academic can get away with very little work – especially in the better universities which give more time for individual use. Nevertheless, though regrettable, this kind of waste has to be tolerated because any attempt to prevent it by imposing a system of controls would make things worse. You can compel people to sit in their offices, and you can check on their work if it is of a routine type; but if their task is to think creatively, it is difficult to find out whether what they are doing has any value or indeed whether they are doing anything at all. Furthermore, who is to judge whether the judges know better than the judged? Particularly as, owing to the tendency described earlier as the Law of Lighter Weights, the judges would in all likelihood be self-selected from among the less creative. What is equally important, the operation of controls (such as progress reports, clocking, etc.) dampen the enthusiasm of the creative minority, whose work often compensates society many times over for the expense of maintaining a number of pedants and sluggards. Only a feeling of moral obligation to do something for the communal good, in exchange for the sustenance one receives, can counter the temptation of sloth without destroying the environment needed for creativity or even for a really good higher education. In any case, hedonistic idleness among university teachers constitutes a trifling burden upon the community in comparison with bureaucratic parasitism which keeps people busy with useless paper work. A leisured parasite costs the community only what he consumes, whereas to evaluate the cost of a superfluous bureaucrat we must add to the money spent on him, the pay of the other paper shufflers needed to keep him busy, and the loss of production and enjoyment caused by inflicting time-consuming and soul-destroying paper work on people who could make better use of their energy. As they excite less envy than those who enjoy leisure, the superfluous bureaucrats proliferate with fewer obstacles, and consequently can become much more burdensome. In the communist countries they constitute a much greater burden on the truly productive population than did all the idle coupon-clippers and landowners of old.

Parkinson's laws have a particularly free scope in education because of the lack of a yardstick to assess efficiency, which makes it difficult to make rational decisions about the allocation of funds to various levels and kinds of institutions, or about the merits of varying methods and systems. What is equally grave, the lack of a valid yardstick makes it impossible to base selection for posts of authority on real merit, in the sense of proven capacity to do the job well. In consequence the road to becoming an educational administrator lies less through teaching well – or even organizing it so that it is done well – than through good showmanship in attending to trivial paraphernalia, or skill in politicking. In the institutions dedicated not only to the transmission of knowledge but to its augmentation, the problems of management present even greater difficulties because, firstly, the search for significant new truths cannot really be planned since no one can foresee in advance where they will be found; and secondly, because of the ineradicable incompatibility between intellectual creativity and routine administration. Apart from the obvious point that if you invest more time and energy in one of these activities you have less for the other, there is a deep divergence between the outlook of an administrator concerned with keeping order and tying everything down, and that of an intellectual explorer attracted to the unknown and the unpredictable.

All institutions devoted to the pursuit of knowedge face an inescapable dilemma: if authority is vested in professional administrators we get a situation in which the blind are telling the seers where to go, whereas if scientists and scholars have to undertake the tasks of management, they often turn into sterile neuters who can neither administer efficiently nor discover anything worthwhile. The universities which have the best record as centres of creativity have during that time succeeded in maintaining a delicate balance between the respective burdens and powers of the two breeds of men, with the aid of such devices as rotation in office, or the employment in supreme administrative posts of men well past the peak of creativity but whose record shows that they know from personal experience what intellectual creation involves and demands. Such compromises between very different types of ability and mentality, however, remain feasible only in fairly small institutions; and growth to a mammoth size inevitably entails a thorough bureaucratization.

On the Continent, control over the universities is vested not even in the internal administration but in the ministry of education, which vets examinations and textbooks – which is, I think, one of the main reasons why these countries have fallen behind Britain and America (where the universities are much freer) in scientific and even scholarly production. The shortcomings of the British way of running a university is that it tends to turn scientists and scholars into full time administrators as soon as they reach a professorship (which in Britain means a title distinction not given to every college teacher as in the United States), whereas the common American solution has been to give power to professional managers often drawn from business. This largely accounts for the alienation of the teachers, which aggravates that of the students.

I would venture a hypothesis that there is a significant negative correlation between the quality of a university (as measured by the contributions to knowledge by its staff and former students in proportion to their numbers) and the extent of the power wielded by professional managers. This relationship is obscured by the differences in size, which give people an illusion that the big centres are better because they contain a larger number of eminent scientists and scholars, although in relation to the total membership they may compare unfavourably with much smaller institutions. The same kind of error is often committed when comparing countries. It does not follow, for example, that either Russia or the United States is better than Finland in sport by virtue of having more Olympic champions, because to get a true picture we would have to take the size of the populations into account. Similarly, people get exaggerated ideas about the excellence of the

United States in science, which can be corrected by the following rough calculations. Among the Nobel Prize winners, seventy-nine were American and forty-six British, which gives a net superiority to Britain if calculated in relation to the population, even apart from the fact that a much larger part of the American winners were born and educated abroad. In relation to the money spent on higher education the British production of Nobel Prize winners is about twelve times greater.

Serious as it is, owing to its tendency to favour staleness and mediocrity, the internal bureaucratization of the universities pales into insignificance as an obstacle to the progress of the social sciences in comparison with the paramount importance of censorship. In an earlier chapter I have dealt at length with the more devious methods of restricting freedom of thought; and I do not need to go to great lengths to adduce evidence for the obvious truth that even without other forms of pressure, official censorship alone can suffocate science. What does call for some comment, however, is the seldom mentioned fact that intellectual freedom flourishes over a much smaller part of the globe today than in 1900, despite the vast increase in the numbers of the universities, learned associations and libraries.

At the beginning of the present century the social sciences were being fruitfully cultivated in all the European countries, with the exception of that corner of Europe which still belonged to the Turkish empire. True, few (if any) works which saw the light in the outer countries like Romania, Poland, Sweden or Spain constituted steps of epoch-making significance, but the best of them attained a very high level by any standards, while even the less remarkable constituted some contributions to knowledge, and a definite improvement on the earlier literature. Having a numerically larger pool of ability to draw upon, Russia produced a crop of outstanding thinkers in this field, such as Pavlov, Kondratiev, Kovalevsky, Klyuchevski, Tschuprov, Plekhanov, Barthold, Pavolv-Silvansky and Novikov, to mention only those who would rank among the best even in the most advanced countries, although it remains true that none of them could be put in the same rank as Herbert Spencer, de Tocqueville or Max Weber. Though obliged to exercise some caution, these scholars could pursue their work because, not being wedded to any definite doctrine, the tsarist censorship looked only for direct criticism of the regime or the Church and allowed people to write more or less what they liked about other matters, permitting even the works of Marx to be published. Lenin was allowed to write his biggest book, *The Development of Capitalism in Russia*, while in detention for revolutionary activity. Neither he nor his successors have ever given any of their prisoners a similar opportunity.

The Spanish intellectuals at the turn of the century were trying to catch up with the leading centres of European civilization; and although none of them has attained the level of originality of the best Russians, many were respectable scholars by any international standard, who contributed interesting insights into Spanish problems and were (not only in relation to the time but even in absolute terms) much better than the Information Ministry's creatures who occupy the chairs of sociology or political science in Spain today. In Portugal, and Greece too, there was more freedom of thought sixty years ago than there is today; and the same is true of Argentina and Brazil. The Hohenzollern and Habsburg empires contained the foremost centres of intellectual creativity in the world; so that nobody could keep up with the progress of knowledge without knowing German. It was the time when psycho-analysis was invented by Freud, the foundations of modern analytic philosophy laid by Mach, and sociology brought to the threshold of maturity by Max Weber; while marxism (which had not yet become the tool of an imperialist bureaucracy) still remained a spur to inquiry, and reached its apogee under the pens of Kautsky, Plekhanov, Hilferding and Loria.

Neither the First World War nor the crop of post-war dictatorships in the minor states of Europe led to any severe curtailment in the freedom to study society and politics, as even Mussolini's regime did not become very oppressive until the thirties, so that only Russia had to be written off as a source of contributions to the social sciences. The turning point was the rise of Hitler, who wrought a havoc upon European culture from which (in contrast to the economy) it has not been able to recover to this day. No scholar need nowadays learn German in order not to be left behind; and what we get in Germany in the social sciences is a pale imitation of America. It is important to bear in mind in this context that the supremacy of German literature in the social sciences outside economics before Hitler was not the work of ethnic Germans alone, but of all the eastern Europeans for whom German was the primary language of science. This was especially the case with the Jews, whose Yiddish language originated as a dialect of German, and who were the most effective spreaders of the Teutonic culture in the Slav lands.

Pre-fascist Italy harboured a number of pioneering thinkers in whom we can find many faults by hindsight, but who made a very significant contribution to the development of the social sciences: Mosca and Pareto in sociology and political science, Lombroso and Ferri in criminology, Niceforo and Colajanni in descriptive sociology, Barone, Pantaleoni and again Pareto in economic theory, Enriques in philosophy. In spite of Italy's remarkable economic progress, post World War Two literature contains nothing very original, and consists either of summaries of American textbooks or marxist hagiography. Nor has the admiration for things American (largely motivated by a desire for grants and invitations) led the Italian sociologists to imitate what is most valuable: namely the Chicago School tradition of field work – so that there are no recent descriptive studies of Italian society which are as interesting as the old works of Niceforo and Colajanni.

More than a quarter of a century after Mussolini, it does not seem plausible to attribute this sterility entirely to the breach in the continuity of intellectual tradition caused by twenty-two years of fascism, important as this must have been. The principal causes of the aridity of the Italian intellect of the present day seem to be: firstly, the bureaucratic stranglehold upon the universities, accompanied by unprincipled politicking within; and secondly, the disappearance of anti-clerical liberalism. The latter phenomenon is enmeshed with the domination of the Italian cultural scene, as well as of the political arena, by two blocs: a capitalist-led Christian Democracy which leans upon the Church as its ideological prop, opposed by the 'outs' who rely on marxist dogma and Soviet gold. As most of the academic and editorial appointments depend on political connections, a *de facto* dual censorship operates, which leaves few opportunities to a scholar who obeys neither the Catholic nor the communist doctrine.

Somewhat similar unofficial dual censorships operate in the few Latin American countries which are not under a dictatorship, as can be seen in greater detail in my *Parasitism and Subversion*, while in Africa (as shown in another book of mine, *The African Predicament*) the new native rulers fetter social thought much more thoroughly than the colonial governments did . . . at least in their last decades. The same applies to the post-colonial states in Asia. In Japan there is, of course, much more freedom of inquiry today than under the jingoist militocracy of the thirties; and possibly even more than at the turn of the century – which makes Japan one of the few parts of the world where during this span of time there has been no long term deterioration. Probably the only areas where there has been a net improvement in this respect are the culturally backward parts of the USA and Canada, where the rule of bigotry has abated. In eastern Europe, of course, the curtain is down.

Somebody has calculated that if the number of psychologists and sociologists continued to grow at the rate it did during the last decade, then it would overtake the total population of the globe within a few hundred years. Nevertheless, we need not be surprised that the world-wide mushrooming of the universities, the proliferation of political science, economics, psychology and sociology departments and institutes, and the ultra-rapid expansion of the corresponding national and international associations, have led to an equivalent increase in the production, and a dilution of the quality of printed matter, which conforms well enough to the catch phrase that 'more means worse'. Perhaps this is an inevitable result of foisting upon too many people a duty to be 'original'. Perhaps it would be better if they were allowed to confine themselves to transmitting to the young the ideas of a few great thinkers of the past, instead of being cast in the role of pioneers for which very few of them have either aptitude or inclination. Judged from this standpoint the recent revival of marxism among academics in the capitalist world may be regarded as a natural reaction to the loss of outlets in theology.

It seems that (like love or happiness) originality never comes to those who consciously pursue it, and is attainable only as a by-product of an activity motivated by a more specific desire. It does not appear that any of the great discoverers (or for that matter artists or novelists) deliberately tried to make their work original. As far as one can judge from biographies, they were simply interested in finding answers to questions which were preying upon their minds.

The swordsmen of old did not have to show their manliness by 'tough' talk of the kind that is so popular among the soft-living, passive telly viewers (or should we say voyeurs) of today; and, in the same way, people talk about creativity more and more as the real thing becomes rarer.

Chapter 17

The Barbarian Assault on the Corrupted Citadels of Learning

Like most social movements, the current wave of student unrest is a complex phenomenon, which manifests itself in varied forms according to the place (with corresponding differences in causes and effects); and which can best be understood if we think of it in terms of superimposing waves, each impelled by a different set of factors. In the United States, as everybody knows, student unrest is closely connected with the opposition to the illegal (because never declared) war in Vietnam, and with the Afroamericans' struggle for equality; while in Poland and Czechoslovakia the students, far from rebelling against the older generation as such, have simply tried to carry on the age-long resistance against foreign domination and the suppression of cherished native traditions. The heavy hand of the bureaucracy, which weighs upon the mass-production universities in France, Italy, Japan and (what few foreigners realize) the United States, produces a wide feeling of alienation among teachers and students alike, while the poor prospects of placement for the latter stimulate the mood of rebellion.

On top of this, the sensation-mongering television, radio and newspapers conjure up imitation waves which spread, regardless of the absence of local circumstances which might engender such behaviour unaided. Underlying all this is the vacuity of a civilization which frustrates the impulses of active sociability and of individual or collective adventure, and reduces its denizens to the condition of passive and dull telly gapers without other ideals than stultifying conformity to the norms of a consumer mentality; while society's power to contain the forces of discontent is being undermined by the ceaseless denigration of all moral ideals and of all forms of authority by advertisers and entertainers eager to make money by flattering the gullible young.

No amount of disingenuous fraternization can alter the fact that education consists of passing knowledge from those who know to those who do not; and of inculcating into hominid animals the habits and tastes which make a civilized human being. Up to a point this can be done by sheer coercion, but on a higher plane it requires a genuine respect of the pupil for the teacher; which in the educational institutions of today has been undermined, not only by the advertisers and propagandists, but also by the passing of the inner-directed, ruggedly idiosyncratic scholar (perhaps odd, querulous and vain, but unmercenary and passionately committed to ideas), and his replacement by the smooth other-directed, fund-raising and empire-building academic executive, who chooses his opinions, stances and morals as he does his friends: that is, in accordance with their usefulness to his career.

The mere cursory enumeration of some of the most general factors suffices to rule out the thought that the proliferation of the barbarians in institutions of higher learning might have been caused solely by the debasement of the social sciences which we have been discussing; notwithstanding the notorious prominence of their students among the wreckers. The latter fact can be explained by two factors: (1) that those who are dissatisfied with the existing order gravitate towards subjects which concern themselves with questioning it; (2) that studying such subjects makes people less inclined to take the existing conditions for granted or accept them as desirable. So even if their teachers and the textbooks were above reproach, the students of the social sciences would still furnish a larger contingent to the revolutionary ranks than the physicists or the medical students, whose exacting training and assured prospects divert their attention from politics.

Despite the foregoing exoneration, however, social scientists have much to answer for, and bear some responsibility for the inane nihilism of their pupils. The rebels could well be described as a sick product of a diseased society; and, although they are largely right about what they oppose, their programmes amount to an invitation to jump from the frying pan into the fire. But even in this respect, what may be more fatal than exposure to bad sociology or psychology is the present

8

overindulgence in passive viewing, and the consequent loss of will-power and mental discipline.

So long as the professor's position ensured the acquiescence of his pupils regardless of his capacity, and so long as the temper of youth followed the line of acquisitive conformity, any kind of donnish gibberish was duly absorbed – particularly when it absolved indolent and unintelligent youths from the need to think, and opened to them avenues of employment from which they would have been debarred in more demanding times. Unfortunately, however, this *dolce far niente* had some intrinsic weaknesses, one of them being that the abolition of standards of scholarship made everybody eligible for academic employment at any level, and converted the process of selection for appointment and promotion into a game of intrigue and luck; thus providing the 'outs' with a good justification for their natural grudge against the 'ins'. What is more, the ease with which the science of translating platitudes into jargon can be learned permits a slick second-year student to reach the level of a Harvard or Columbia professor, which nullifies the natural inequality between the teacher and the pupil, and removes the justification for an academic hierarchy, or even for the existence of educational institutions.

So long as the mood of acquisitive conformity lasted, the obfuscating operators had no trouble with buying deference and docility. But the new disregard for income and career among American students, whose family wealth can cushion them from the worst penalties of dabbling in revolution, has undermined the power of even the biggest academic manipulators, who have no idea how to deal with people to whom money does not talk. So one can see the pathetic sight of the internationally revered king-makers of the American academe, who control the flow of millions of dollars, and who at conferences and during visits abroad are surrounded by crowds of adulating scroungers, trembling before their students, sometimes not even daring to go out of their offices into the corridors lest their pupils button-hole them and subject them to questioning about their opinions and motives.

Once certain top professors came to be regarded as disingenuous windbags, the status of all their colleagues was automatically reduced, so that they lost the safety of authoritative expostulation and now have to enter into arguments and prevarications on every point, which makes nervous wrecks out of many of them, because it takes strong nerves and a quick wit to get the upper hand in every argument with a crowd of truculent and sometimes very clever youngsters, while one success in ridiculing a teacher may destroy his standing and self-assurance for ever. Now, since few teachers can meet such requirements, and in the social sciences they have hardly any core of indubitable knowledge to fall back upon, they often live in fear of their pupils and have in many cases abdicated their authority, submitting meekly to student politicians – which makes the teaching of these subjects even more grotesque than it has hitherto been.

Although some of the protesting students have potentially good minds, which enable them to see through the sham of conventional jargon, it would be a miracle if they could put their subjects on a correct footing without suitable preparation, particularly as exposure to a sloppy pseudo-science could hardly fail to have stultified their powers of logical reasoning. Moreover, once you jettison the canons of logic and clarity, you can believe any nonsense and you are perfectly free to choose your beliefs according to their emotional appeal. No wonder then that, nauseated by the boring meanderings of their jargon-ridden teachers, the more alert students fall under the spell of Marcuse's philosophizing which, though equally defective by any reasonable intellectual standards, at least contains on occasion a snappy phrase pinpointing some of the ills of our civilization, and which appeals to the idealism as well as to the vandalism of youth. And those who find Marcuse's brew not heady enough can take to the romantic and bellicose slogans of Che Guevara, or find a vicarious outlet for their sado-masochistic impulses in Franz Fanon's fierce belabouring of the white man.

Liberated by their teachers from the constraints of logic, the young rebels have no difficulty in reconciling the ascetic and disciplinarian collectivism of Mao with a compulsive eroticism inspired by a misreading of Freud, and a lipservice to the greatness of the 'workers' with a byronesque self-indulgent wilfulness, heedless of the feelings or the welfare of the common herd. It must be said in the defence of their adherents, however, that these concoctions are not much worse than many of the textbooks they are made to read; while if we compare the holy writs of orthodox communism with the products of the con- temporary 'classics' of the social sciences, or any of those massive, bureaucratically inspired symposia, we can see that not only Lenin and Trotsky, but even Stalin, were not only better writers but also better political scientists, sociologists and psychologists than the jet-set pundits, while Marx looms as truly superhuman.

Were we not accustomed to it as an everyday spectacle, it would strike us as absolutely mad that anyone should seek solutions to the predicaments of today's civilization in the works of a man who, though of undoubted genius, wrote when there were no motor cars, no aviation, no telephones, no computers, no statistics, no genetics – when it was not known that bacteria cause diseases or even that man descends from simian ancestors (about which Marx learnt halfway through his career as a writer). Yet the youthful rebels, who scorn the opinions of everyone over forty or thirty, or even twenty-five, eagerly lap up the adages of the septuagenarian chairman of the Chinese communist party, and take as gospel every word of the author of *Das Kapital*, who would be over 150 by now. This pre- dilection appears less surprising if we remember that everything is a matter of comparison with what you are used to. True, we know that, like every other thinker, no matter how great, Marx invented only a few items in his armoury, taking most of his ideas and materials from his predecessors and contemporaries. To imagine that everything in his writings is original is on the level of treating every formula in a textbook of physics as its author's own invention. Nonetheless, the works of Marx and Engels constituted a great intellectual feat at the time, and even today can supply interesting insights. They were erroneous on many points, even in the light of the knowledge available at the time of writing, let alone in the light of what we know today; but never did these authors fill their pages with meaning- less gibberish. The merit of a contribution must be judged in relation to the knowledge existing when it was made, but even if we disregard the dates, and focus on usefulness as a means of making sense out of the jumble of recent happenings, or for interpreting the present condition of our civilization, the works of either Marx or Engels alone have infinitely greater value than the total output of Parsons, Merton, Easton, Homans, Deutsch, Lazarsfeld, Skinner, Gurvitch, Lévi-Strauss and all their associates, disciples, followers and sympathizers put together. True, this contrast holds to a lesser extent for the epigoni of today than for Marx and Engels themselves; because, whereas even a very great thinker can make fundamental mistakes while groping for new insights, only a bigot will persist in treating the master as infallible when his errors have become perfectly clear.

Around the turn of the century there were among the marxists some genuinely creative thinkers like Karl Kautsky, Eduard Bernstein, Achille Loria and Ludwik Krzywicki; but this was when marxism was still a novel, plausible and evolving body of ideas, and had not yet become an ossified doctrine of bureaucratic establishments. Nevertheless, although they do not tower so high above the conventional social scientists of today, even the later marxists have contributed more to our understanding of social reality than the parsonians or the fans of misapplied cybernetics. If we compare Bukharin's exposition, *Historical Materialism*, written over half a century ago, with, for instance, *Introduction to Sociology* by a Harvard professor, Alex Inkeles (which is no worse than most) we can see at once that the first is a much more interesting and intelligent book. Perhaps it is not fair to compare examples of such unequal importance; but if, to equalize the chances, we match the products of two contemporary British dons of more or less equal standing in terms of reputation and influence and compare, say, Wiseman's *Political Systems* (mentioned in a previous chapter) with Ralph Milliband's *State in Capitalist Society*, the contrast in favour of the marxist appears equally striking. Small wonder, then, that – bored with the dreary mumbo-jumbo of their textbooks – many intelligent young men and women have fallen under the spell of an antiquated doctrine.

The enthusiasm for Marx among the students draws further nourishment from the studious avoidance on the part of conventional social scientists not only of his name – which is hardly (if at all) mentioned in some of the bulky histories of sociology, economics or political science – but also of the principal questions which he raised. Earlier American sociologists like Ross and Cooley (not to speak of the much more original Veblen) freely talked about exploitation, class conflict or the role of fraud and force in politics. But since the foundation-financed bonanza began, such topics have fallen under a taboo, with the consequence that students who read for the first time about them in Marx imagine, not only that nobody knew about these things before him, but that what he says represents the last word of science on these matters. So, by sweeping all the unpalatable aspects of social life under the carpet, the official pundits have endowed marxism with the appeal of a forbidden novelty; while, by removing from the minds of their pupils the constraints of clarity and logic, they have prepared the ground for vandalistic concoctions, in comparison with which orthodox marxism appears as a pure voice of reason.

Chapter 18

Conclusion: Ethics and the Advancement of Knowledge

Even if the diagnosis offered on the foregoing pages is only partially correct, we have no grounds for expecting any great leap forward in the study of society which would replicate the rapid advances of the natural sciences. True, it is quite easy to conceive remedies against many of the ills stemming from purely intellectual difficulties, which would work in a more perfect world. We could, for instance, insist that the economists should openly state the limitations and empirical reliability of their models, be prepared to take cultural (or, if you like, psychological and sociological) factors into account, and desist from proffering advice on the basis of one-sided and coarsely materialistic statistics. We could demand that the psychologists should acquire some general culture, and acquaint themselves with the subtler products of the human mind before setting themselves up as experts on human nature. We could compel the sociologists to learn about history and philosophy, and the historians about the social sciences. Above all, we need a kind of intellectual puritanism which would regard money as a clear (even though necessary) evil, and any manipulation of it as essentially polluting. Not that any great advantage would accrue if social scientists imitated monks and took vows of poverty; but, nonetheless, no steady advance will be possible without an ethical code which would forcefully condemn mercenary trimming as intellectual prostitution, and counter the natural human tendency not only to flatter and obey, but even genuinely to adore those who control money or wield coercive power. The snag is that it is difficult to visualize who could enforce such requirements, and how. The difficulty here is the same as with finding the best form of government: we can readily agree with Plato that the best system would be that where the wisest and kindest would rule, but nobody has so far been able to discover a practicable method for bringing about such a state of affairs.

Some years before the First World War, a Parisian periodical asked some of the most prominent French figures in the various branches of what we would now call social sciences, and which were known at that time in France as *les sciences morales*, about what they regarded as the most essential method in their field. While other respondents sent back learned methodological disquisitions, Georges Sorel replied in one word: honesty. This lapidary answer has lost none of its relevance; but it is difficult to find any reasons for hoping that we shall ever have a society where absolute frankness would be the best policy for self-advancement.

Despite these irremovable obstacles, my own view on the prospects for the social sciences might be described as a desperate optimism. I say desperate because I do not see how our civilization could survive without important advances in our understanding of man and society. Having invented so many wondrous gadgets which can be employed for its benefit only through the utmost use of reason, mankind has long ago passed the point of no return in this respect. No matter how valuable might be many ingredients of the old religious and moral traditions, the problem of how to reconcile human physical and spiritual needs with the environment created by technology, and how to assure mankind's very survival, will not be solved by going back to the good old ways or dogmas. Consequently, I have no doubt that if the social sciences fall into a total and irremediable decadence, this will be a part of a general collapse of civilization, likely to be followed by an extinction of our species. No matter therefore how heavy are the odds against us, we should persist in trying to do our best, because the alternative is resignation in the face of an imminent catastrophe.

Provided some freedom of expression remains, we have reason to hope that no branch of learning will come to a complete standstill even when its main trunk succumbs to decay; because, even during the ages of deepest ignorance and superstition, indomitable spirits with a natural bent for rational inquiry continued to crop up and add a brick or two to the edifice of knowledge. What made their cerebrations more effective in the long run than the efforts of the vastly more numerous priests and mystagogues was the fact that the products of rational thought are cumulative, whereas mystic visions, fads, stunts and phantasmagorias not only add up to nothing, but even cancel one another out and merely sway minds to and fro, hither and thither.

Though cultivated truly only on the fringes of various establishments and counter-establishments (if not by complete outsiders or even outcasts), while befouled in the centres of pomp and wealth, the social sciences will no doubt continue to progress if civilization survives at all. But rather than a resplendent 'take-off' the most we can legitimately hope for is a slow and intermittent cumulation of uncertain and often reversed steps forward: a process resembling the work of Sisiphus or the cleaning of the stables of Augeas rather than a triumphant *blitzkrieg*.

Even if you are mainly interested in such a practical and present day problem as the question of whether (and if so, how) a communal spirit could be created in cities, the following quotation from a work which towards the end of the last century was almost unanimously regarded as representing the summit of sociological theorizing will give you much food for thought; and if you begin to elaborate on it intelligently you could write a very interesting book:

The mere gathering of individuals into a group does not constitute them a society. A society, in the sociological sense, is formed only when, besides juxtaposition there is co-operation. So long as members of the group do not combine their energies to achieve some common end or ends, there is little to keep them together. They are prevented from separating only when the wants of each are better satisfied by uniting his efforts with those of others, than they would be if he acted alone.
Herbert Spencer, *Principles of Sociology*, (abridged edition, Macmillan, 1969, page 181).

Now, if you wish to rejoice at the general march of progress in this field – and hesitate to delectate yourself with yet another quotation from the most famous sociological theorist of today –

compare Spencer's statement with the following passage from a collective work by leading American luminaries:

Although sociology is now unable to specify the conditions required for sustaining universal laws it may, for exploratory reasons, simulate such laws by treating them as hypothetical generalizations. Thus, in the generalization, 'All delinquents are enculturated,' (All A's are B's), the term 'enculturated' may serve as a theoretical reconstruction of meaning elements common to writers in criminology. Insofar as delinquents are engaged in 'cultural conflict' (Sellin), or live in 'subculturally structured' environments (Cohen), or become 'rationalizers of deviance' (Sykes and Matza), and 'utilizers of illegitimate opportunities' (Cloward and Ohlin), their acts represent specialized interpretations of the abstract term, 'enculturated'. By asserting that if anyone has the characteristic of being delinquent he has also the characteristic of being enculturated, the generalization refers to abstract properties considered apart from their exemplification in particular individuals. Its ordinary English equivalents include such statements as 'Delinquents are enculturated' (A's are B's), 'Every delinquent is enculturated' (every A is B), 'Any delinquent is enculturated' (any A is B), 'No delinquent is not enculturated' (No A is not B), 'Delinquency implies enculturation' (A implies B), etc.

(*Sociological Theory: Inquiries and Paradigms*, Llewellyn Gross, Harper International Edition, Harper & Row and John Weatherhill, Inc., 1967).

As being 'enculturated' simply means that you share with people amongst whom you live certain habits, customs and beliefs, all this verbiage boils down to a platitude that delinquents tend to share with other delinquents a number of ideas and habits (such as breaking the law) which differ from those which are common among non-delinquents. In the first sentence quoted, on the other hand, the authors rashly generalize from their ignorance; as in fact hundreds of valid general propositions have been stated about social phenomena: no known case, for example, refutes Michels' Iron Law of Oligarchy or Engels' assertion that in all societies recorded by history larger than a tribe, a conflict between the rich and the poor was going on in some form.

Even during the brief span of two and a half years, which separates the writing of the first draft of this book from the present last retouchings before the typescript goes to the printer, several new fads have come to the surface. Visible breaches in the seemingly impregnable hegemony of the parsonians and the number maniacs have been made (though by the emotional onslaught of the New Left rather than rational criticism) with the consequence that the orthodoxy of the Harvard and Columbia pundits has in many seats of capitalist higher education been replaced by the older cult of Marx and Lenin (with Mao instead of Stalin nowadays completing the Trinity) mixed with an assortment of new voguish gimmicks.

Thus 'interactionism' has lately been acclaimed as a newly discovered approach which opens new vistas on human behaviour, although the only novelty resides in the use of the endings 'ism' and 'ist'; because, when stripped of the bombastic verbiage, the great idea boils down to a reaffirmation of the platitude that sociology and psychology are supposed to study interaction between people. A further embroidery on this scheme consists of the claim to have found the key to the secrets of social behaviour by interpreting it as 'symbolic interaction'. However, since all human activities (including solitary contemplation) involve the use of symbols, there is no difference between symbolic interaction and human interaction pure and simple; and the grandiloquent new approach amounts to pretentiously asserting what no sane person has ever doubted. If neither of these approaches satisfies our quest for profundity, we can adopt a 'situationalist' viewpoint which enjoins us to take into account the situation of whatever it is that we are dealing with.

Then we have 'phenomenology'. The first point to note is that, since everything we can perceive is a phenomenon, and since we can hardly study what we are not aware of, this label fits all possible branches of inquiry. The founder's (Husserl's) injunction to seek the essence of things boils down to the thoroughly banal advice that we should think about what we see, coupled with an utterly nonsensical notion that we can arrive at useful conclusions by sheer rumination about the essences, without bothering about what the empirical sciences have to tell us. Offering a considerable alleviation of mental effort, the latter absolution cannot fail to win many converts, particularly when coupled with 'critical sociology' the chief characteristic of which is the uncritical repetition of century-old doctrines and tireless invocations of the names of their apostles, which reminds me of those medieval Arab chronicles where every paragraph begins and ends with 'Allah is great, and Mahomet is his sole prophet'.

One of the latest additions to the array of impressive labels is 'ethnomethodology', invented, I believe, by an American called Harold Garfinkel. According to the definition by two of his followers – Stanford M. Lyman and Marvin B. Scott, authors of a book with a very 'turned on' title which could be made more descriptive of the contents by only a slight rearrangement of the words: *A Sociology of the Absurd* – this 'term refers to the study of the procedures (methodology) employed by everyday man (ethnics) in his effort to meaningfully cope with the world. Otherwise put, it seeks to give an organized account of the routine grounds for everyday action'.

In pre-scientific language this was called observing how people live – a pursuit not exactly unknown before the above-mentioned pioneers went into action.

As our authors say,

A new wave of thought is beginning to sweep over sociology. Aspects of the wave have been given an assortment of names – 'labelling theory,' 'ethnomethodology,' and 'neo-symbolic inter-actionism' – but these do not cover its entire range of critique and perspective. A new name must be found to cover a concept which presents not only a unique perspective on conventional sociology but is also a radical departure from the conventional.

We feel an appropriate name is the *Sociology of the Absurd*.
(Stanford M. Lyman & Marvin B. Scott, *A Sociology of the Absurd*, Appleton-Century-Crofts, 1970, p. 1.)

On page 3 another disguise of this new wave is exhibited. To explain its mystery our authors cite another initiate and write:

As Tiryakian has observed, existential phenomenology 'seeks to elucidate the existential nature of social structures by uncovering the surface institutional phenomena of the everyday, accepted world; by probing the subterranean, noninstitutional social depths concealed from public gaze, by interpreting the dialectic between the institutional and the non-institutional. . . .'

This is precisely what sociologists of the old Chicago School, like Park, Burgess and Thomas, were occupying themselves with in the early decades of the present century, when they were studying what used to be known as informal social relations. We can appreciate the magnitude of the progress accomplished since then when we realize that they did not even suspect that what they were doing was ethnomethodological existential phenomenology.

Apart from the consequences of almost everything becoming a part of the entertainment industry and being affected by the methods of high pressure salesmanship and advertising, another unexpected influence has begun to operate in the fields we are discussing. It seems that since they have become an established occupation, the social sciences have begun to attract the type of mind which in the olden days would have taken up dogmatic theology or preaching. This has been an unfortunate change, because the old theology and mysticism (regardless of which denomination) were linked to a moral code, whereas the new cults enjoin no firm rules of conduct, adherence to which was the price for an opportunity to satisfy a desire for the kind of admiration normally bestowed upon the licensed interpreters of the Holy Writ.

Instead of entertaining visions of a final victory of reason over magic and ignorance, we have to reconcile ourselves to the fact that the norms and ideals which permit the advancement of knowledge have to be defended in every generation against new enemies, who reappear like the heads of the Hydra as soon as others are decapitated, and who employ ever-new labels, catchwords and slogans to play on the perennial weaknesses of mankind. Whatever happens in the instrumental exact sciences, we can be sure that in matters where intellectual and moral considerations mesh, the struggle between the forces of light and the forces of darkness will never end.

The pioneers of rationalism inveighed against the traditional dogmas, ridiculed popular superstitions, campaigned against priests and sorcerers, and castigated them for fostering and preying upon the ignorance of the masses – hoping that a final victory of science would banish for ever the evils of unreason and organized deception. Little did they suspect that a Trojan Horse would appear in the camp of enlightenment, full of streamlined sorcerers clad in the latest paraphernalia of science.